PRAISE FOR *FINDING HER*

"*Finding Her*, Wulfensmith's wonderful memoir is filled with honesty and beauty, humor and poignancy and all and everything us humans go through in life. Her chapter about shame left me breathless, my heart pounding. Her writing is charming and visual and packs a solid punch. I hope this book finds its way into the hands and hearts of all young girls and young women and yes, women who need to stand in their truth, who need to own their truth, who need to know that they are not alone in the journey of discovering their true desires, finding a home within those desires and living life on their terms."

—Amy Ferris, screenwriter and playwright, author of *Marrying George Clooney* (Seal Press), *Shades of Blue* (Seal Press), co-editor of *Dancing at the Shame Prom* (Seal Press), and co-author with Rev Run *Old School Love* (HarperCollins)

"This is a memoir about one woman's journey from self-loathing to self-love in her search for the possibility that, in God's eyes, one can be both a Lesbian and a Christian. It's a hard-won struggle to stand against the hypocrisy of fundamentalism practiced by those who preach the love of Christ but hate Christians who love in a different way. I highly endorse this book for those who struggle to love God and themselves in search of peace, and for Christians who know not what they do."

—Carol E. Anderson, Winner 2019 Independent Press Award – LGBTQ, and author of *You Can't Buy Love Like That: Growing up Gay in the Sixties* (She Writes Press)

"In her engaging memoir, *Finding Her*, Wulfensmith takes the reader on a profoundly honest journey, wrestling God, the church, and herself in turn. She invites us to join her on a sometimes hair-raising ride as she navigates a call to ministry, her love/hate relationship with evangelical Christianity, and her sexuality. She reveals her own humanity as well as the humanity of the well-intentioned, at whose hands she suffered spiritual abuse. An insightful, well-told story worth every minute you spend with it."

—Connie Tuttle, pastor, feminist and author of *A Gracious Heresy: the Queer Calling of an Unlikely Prophet* (Wipf and Stock)

"Wulfensmith takes bodily risks that lead from one challenging experience to another, and her descriptions keep the reader riveted. I admire the author's capacity to move beyond outdated beliefs, to integrate seismic sexual-spiritual shifts, and to creatively express her story. Sensory prose invited me to pivot with her, accompanying Wulfensmith on a transformative journey much larger than personal. How do we know what we know? Find out in *Finding Her*."

—Judith Favor, minister, teacher, speaker, author of *The Beacons of Larkin Street* (Apocryphile Press), and *Silent Voices: A Family Memoir*

"There is no text that can capture the Infinity of God. But any book that demonstrates love and courage such as this certainly embodies Godliness. This book trains a lens on a tiny part of our culture, bringing us to a larger understanding of the Hope of seeing at some time—face to Face—the pure Spirit of Love, Joy, Peace, Forgiveness and Blessing in the world."

—Jane Engleman, author and designer of *FINIS* and *The Last Run* (Wordcraft)

FINDING HER

Memoir of a Christian Lesbian

Pat,

Life is a pathway that
we journey on for a
spell. Sometimes smooth,
sometimes hilly, or rocky.
But all the while a
treasure to travel.

Thanks for reading!

Sharon Wulfenson

FINDING HER
Memoir of a Christian Lesbian

By

Sharon Wulfensmith

Bookstand Publishing
www.bookstandpublishing.com

Published by
Bookstand Publishing
Morgan Hill, CA 95037
4786_2

ISBN 978-1-63498-948-0

Scripture quotations marked KJV are from the King James Version of the
Holy Bible, 1611, which is in the public domain.

Scripture quotations marked RSV are from the Revised Standard Version of
the Bible, copyright © 1946, 1952, and 1971 National Council of the
Churches of Christ in the United States of America. Used by permission.
All rights reserved worldwide.

Scripture quotations marked NIV are from THE HOLY BIBLE, NEW
INTERNATIONAL VERSION®, NIV® Copyright © 1973, 1978, 1984,
2011 by Biblica, Inc.™ Used by permission. All rights reserved worldwide.

Scripture quotations marked NLT are from the Holy Bible, New Living
Translation, copyright © 1996, 2004, 2007, 2013, 2015 by Tyndale House
Foundation. Used by permission of Tyndale House Publishers Inc., Carol
Stream, Illinois 60188. All rights reserved.

In every present moment
my past
is always present

DEDICATION

To Marcela Kanaama Aruho, smiling on me from above.

ACKNOWLEDGMENTS

Marcela Kanaama Aruho, my eldest. Thank you for letting me read aloud many chapters to you. I hoped that I could distract you a bit from the discomforts of chemo. You were one of my greatest champions and cheerleaders as I began writing my memoir. I wish you had stayed around long enough to see it published. (Marcela passed away on July 4, 2019 from AML leukemia.)

Micah Wulfensmith, my daughter. Thank you for your frank opinions and corrections to many of the seminal stories that wound up in this memoir.

Jane Engleman, my friend and co-conspirator in the Pasadena Writers' Group. Thank you for our many conversations about writing and publishing. You are a role model for me.

Thank you, members of our writing group that meets at All Saints Pasadena. You critiqued me, encouraged me, and kept pushing me in the right direction to become a published author. Bernice, Chad, Kres, Mike, Cheyenne, Keith, Marilyn, Edwina, Mary, and Alice.

Karen Vance, my faithful friend and beta reader. Thank you for challenging me to think deeply about my life's journeys to clarify my writing.

Brooke Warner, thank you for being my writing coach. You were the lighthouse that illumined my way to becoming a bona fide writer.

Krissa Lagos, my fastidious developmental editor. Thank you for your prowess in slicing out what needed to go while still maintaining my powerful writer's voice.

Roy Smith, my brother. Thank you for your artistic expertise on my cover design; and thank you for editing, proofreading and correcting millions of picky errors.

Shirley Turner, artist and photographer. Thank you for making me more beautiful.

Thank you to the many authors who inspired me as I wrote my memoir:

First and foremost, my mother, Bernell Warren Smith.

In addition to her, so many others: Amy Ferris, Linda Joy Myers, Connie Tuttle, Nancy Wilson, Jo Ivester, Austen Hartke, Chana Wilson, Dani Shapiro, Cheryl Strayed, Joshua Mohr, Carol E. Anderson, Terrence Moore, Rachel Held Evans, Colby Martin, Jeff Chu, Judith Favor, Barbara Brown Taylor, Amber Cantorna, Darlene Bogle, Barbara Smythe, Garrard Conley, Tena Clark, Michelle Obama, Paul Monette, Marilyn Ladd, Frank McCourt, Keele Burgin, Matt Kailey, and Max Wolf Valerio.

CONTENTS

CHAPTER 1

TRAIN RIDE

Beneath her shoulder-length soft black hair, her deep brown eyes peeked out at me, sucking me into her psyche. What could be going on inside that Barcelona-brain of hers? I yearned to be absorbed. Into her. We often held hands, but right now it hurt. Her vise-like grip pulled me close to her face, so we were practically nose to nose, and her voice was cold and insistent as she said, "Don't get off!"

At five-foot two, barely 110 pounds, eight years my senior, Montserrat could pack a mighty punch—but I was at least five inches taller and had some muscles on me.

Peeling away her thin fingers, I extricated my hand from her grasp and complained, "But we've been waiting here for almost an hour! Can't you see that this train isn't moving? I want to know why."

Those dark eyes glowered at me. "Never. Get. Off. A. Train." She huffed out a breath and shook her head.

Instead of inhaling her delicious *Maja* perfume (*Maja*— "beautiful," in Barcelona Spanish), I clenched my jaw, frowned, and huffed out an even bigger breath at her.

Who was she to tell me what to do? I was thirty years old, an impetuous redhead with a stubborn streak. I was going to do what I pleased. Regardless of what she said. I leapt from my seat, pushing open the miniscule doors of our glass cubicle, and slipped out into the thread of a hallway. Glad I was slender enough to squeeze by passengers hauling in their luggage, I found the doorway at the end of our car and escaped into the cool air and jumped down the few steps onto the platform.

The station name, printed in neat thick black lettering overhead, swayed from its metal rings. BERN. In smaller letters underneath, faded by wind and weather, I saw the word *Schweiz* (Switzerland).

Jubilant to be free for a fleeting moment, I smiled, looking over my shoulder as I meshed with the clamorous, pulsing throng. Montserrat had opened the window and must have been standing on tiptoe to spot me in the crowd. "Sharon!" her voice, a tightrope of sound, called out. "Get back on this train!"

Later, my Sweet One. My words teetered unsteadily inside my head. Giving her a cursory glance, I waved bye and then trotted along the length of the platform, watching for clues to what was holding up our train for so long. One, two, three... I counted down the line. Outside the last train car, wooden boxes of who-knows-what were stacked shoulder-high. Two men were hoisting the cargo into the dark doorway of the freight car. This must be the problem. Mystery solved.

I still wanted to stretch my legs a bit, so I wandered down the platform, confident that I had time. Just a little farther. And a little farther . . .

Passengers darted to and fro like ants building a home, stepping up into or down out of various train cars. Enormous train engines chugged and wheezed into their places. Children's voices called out as their parents tugged them along. Porters wheeled tall carts, wobbling with black and brown suitcases stacked up like club sandwiches. This platform looked very much like the others we'd seen the past few weeks during our travels through Europe.

I walked a bit more.

A shrill train whistle sliced into my thoughts, and I froze. *Oh no!* I thought. *I've walked quite a ways.*

I turned on my heels and started back the way I had come, quickening my pace. But I had to dart in between and around passengers and luggage because the platform had become quite congested.

Above the din, a familiar voice pierced my eardrums. "Shaaaron!"

Two cars down from where I was trotting, Montserrat looked like she was swatting a swarm of bees around her head. I noticed that she was on the last car of our train. But hadn't we been in a middle car before? *Did she change cars?* Then, like a bursting balloon, it struck me: she was on a moving train, and I was standing next to unmoving cars!

Panic sucked the breath out of my chest. I sprinted after the train, hurdling duffel bags and suitcases. Roadblocks yelled at me, saying, "*Achtung! Pass auf wo du hinläufst.*" I had no idea what they were saying, but it was probably something along the lines of, "Watch out, you stepped on my foot!"

My breath came out in ragged gasps, but I commanded my feet to keep moving, go faster. I recalled the time I'd caught a moving bus just a few months ago while I lived in Mexico City. I reasoned that if I could do that, then I should be able to catch this moving train! The handrail bars on the end of the car were . . . Just. Within. Reach. My arm telescoped out to grab a hold. I could almost touch it!

Standing behind the railing at the end of the train car, a man in a black uniform with an official-looking gold embroidered hat, bent down from his little perch. I just knew that he'd grab my hand and pull me up. He yelled a number at me—"Nine, nine!" I had no idea what that meant.

Running as fast as I could, I managed to touch the handrail bar with the tips of my fingers. I stretched out my arm to grasp his extended sturdy hand. A hairbreadth danced between our fingers. But just then he withdrew his hands, flapping them like wings of a baby bird and his deep voice shouted, "*Nein, nein!*"

His angry red face and dark eyes scolded me. Unintelligible words spewed from his quivering lips. I felt the spray of his spittle land on my upturned face.

Like a brick falling on my head, it hit me that he wasn't about to help me at all—and that without his help, there was no way I could haul myself up onto that little perch.

I abruptly halted, gulping in soot, dust and dread. My heaving lungs churned desperation up into my throat. Looking past him, I could see Montserrat, the love of my life, suspended halfway out the window. Her delicate frame grew smaller and smaller, as did the train cars. Could her upturned palms be a gesture of prayer?

That image of her disappearing from view as the train rounded a corner and faded out of sight would be forever chiseled into my memory.

Sure that a crowd of passengers was staring at this foolish American, I kept my eyes down and stared at my purple Nikes, the laces haplessly hanging on the platform's crusty surface. The dust tornadoes circling around me had calmed somewhat, but my inner tornadoes swirled ferociously.

An image of my wallet and passport resting on my now-unoccupied seat in our first-class cubicle pushed itself to the front of my mind.

She had warned me. I hadn't listened. It was all my fault.

Years later, I would wonder how my life would have turned out had I been able to stay on that train. That track. That path.

With that woman.

After enduring years of shame, guilt, pain, and wasted chapters of my own life, I eventually found my way back home like a lost puppy might—disoriented, bruised, and bleeding, but ready to heal.

CHAPTER 2
MONTSERRAT

I first met Montserrat Gregori three years before that train incident.

I was twenty-seven then, and the morning she showed up at my Baptist church in Columbus, Ohio—a crisp October Sunday morning in 1977—I didn't have a clue what she would do to me.

That day, Liam Feldon, a young man from another Baptist church, gave a slide presentation about a group in Mexico City called Spearhead. He explained that because Spanish was fairly easy to master, it might be a viable option for church members to consider joining the mission there for a summer, or even a whole year.

At the mention of Spanish being easy to learn, I thought back to my days in high school when I had almost failed my Spanish class. It certainly hadn't been easy for me then. My parents had many missionary friends, however, and I'd always imagined that it could be a wonderful experience to become a real missionary some day. Young, adventurous, and not yet aware of the impact that such an endeavor might have on me, I was eager to discover new worlds. I focused in carefully to the presentation, and by the end, thought it might be exciting to sign up for the following summer.

Liam concluded with a prayer, and I followed his while adding my own: "Lord, give me a sign if I should or shouldn't join this mission group. Amen."

After some announcements, our pastor invited people to share prayer requests.

"Lord, please give me a sign," I reminded God, in case he'd forgotten already. "Make me meet somebody who can help me learn Spanish."

5

I never dreamed that my prayer would be answered in the next sixty seconds.

On the other side of the sanctuary, a woman stood to give a prayer request. "This is my first Sunday at this church. I am a Baptist from Barcelona. Please pray that..."

I didn't hear her prayer request. The fact that she was actually Spanish, and spoke English with a thick accent, caught my attention.

Could she tutor me in Spanish? Could this be the sign I was looking for?

At the conclusion of the church service, I rushed across the room to meet this woman. We exchanged a few pleasantries and headed for the door.

"I've been working in Ohio for almost a year already, but hadn't found a church until this morning," she told me. Her small face danced with animation. "I prayed to God to show me a Baptist church and find some friends. And here you are." She smiled and gestured toward me. "Thank you, God." She quickly glanced upward.

I told her God had moved in my heart that morning, and that I thought I'd sign up for the Spearhead mission for next summer. "I've forgotten the Spanish I learned in high school and need some help," I said. "Do you think you could tutor me?"

By now we had walked out to the parking lot.

"Oh yes," she said, her eyes widening. "We could become friends. I would like that a lot."

We said our goodbyes and I walked toward my car.

As I got into my little red Toyota I noticed that she was still standing where I'd left her. Instead of driving away I circled around and stopped, rolling down my window. "Did you forget where you parked?"

She looked down. I hoped I hadn't embarrassed her.

"Actually, I'm planning on going to the bus stop. I haven't a car." Her voice was barely audible.

Reaching across the front seat of my car to pop up the door lock button I opened the door a crack, yelling, "Hop in. I'll be happy to drive you home."

Her smiling face filled the passenger door window. She got in and said, "*Hop in?* Hopping is done on one foot. Would it not be a challenge to enter your car that way?"

I didn't know if she was being serious or making a joke. But I burst out laughing, and so did she.

Ten minutes later, we sat in my car in front of her apartment building. Instead of getting out, we continued talking. I told her about my job as a music therapist working in a small school with profoundly developmentally challenged students. She shared that she'd graduated in social work in Barcelona, then did a practicum in London, where she learned English. Later, she wanted to travel. She came to the US with a group of social workers from Europe to learn our public social work system. The supervisor had assigned her to live in Columbus about a year ago. So far, she hadn't found a church, hadn't made many friends, and felt lost in a new culture.

"I enjoy talking with you, Sharon," she said, getting out of the car.

"The feeling is mutual," I offered, smiling. "See you again soon."

She poked her head into the car again. "Call me this evening and we can set up a tutoring schedule."

⁘

The first time Montserrat and I talked on the phone, we spoke for a whole hour, sharing stories of life, religion, education, culture, and dreams for the future. I was enchanted by her accent and curious British idioms.

A few days later, we met at my house for the first Spanish lesson.

"You don't have to pay me anything," she said when I asked her about payment. "I have very few expenses."

"Really? I can pay you by the hour," I insisted.

"*Por favor*, please no. I'd like to do it for free. We can be better friends that way. You can help me with my English in exchange. Alright?"

Our first tutoring session was to be only a half hour but ended up going for almost ninety minutes, and yet I didn't learn a single verb in Spanish. Instead, we talked about her job, her time in London, her family, her Baptist church in Barcelona, and more.

There was something fascinating about Montserrat. I wanted to be her friend, not just her student. I felt attracted to her but couldn't quite put my finger on why. I didn't know it then, but I wouldn't be able to put my finger on that kind of thing for a long time.

꧁ೋ꧂

A week later when we met again, she said, "No English allowed until you've studied Spanish for a full hour. *¿Vale?*" And then she launched in to teaching me a list of verbs and their conjugations. She was a tough teacher. I liked that.

Her Spanish accent sounded a little strange to me—for example, when she asked, "*¿Conothes Barthelona?*" (Are you familiar with Barcelona?). I wondered why, if she didn't have a lisp, she pronounced some words with "s" sounds with a "th" sound instead. I had no clue what Castilian Spanish sounded like, much less the Catalàn flavor from Catalonia.

Montserrat educated me about all this in addition to teaching me the language itself.

꧁ೋ꧂

Over the next six months, I found myself chanting verbs constantly and almost thinking in Spanish without even trying. I followed Montserrat's instructions and memorized hundreds of verbs, conjugating each of them in the seventeen verb forms indicated in the 501 Spanish Verbs textbook she told me to buy. I told myself that I was motivated because I wanted to become a good missionary, but I couldn't quite ignore the distant, tiny voices dancing in my head that told me that I was learning Spanish just to be near this captivating Catalàn woman. Instead of listening to them, I resolved to find ways to silence those annoying little elves.

By springtime, Montserrat was drilling me harder, quizzing me relentlessly, and refusing to speak any English with me at all. The more I learned, the more interesting our discussions became. Why hadn't my high school Spanish been this much fun? Only a few months remained before I would join Spearhead in Mexico City, and I felt mostly ready. Nonetheless, sometimes my Spanish would run out of gas and my *carro* would putter to a stop.

Once in a while we'd do something fun besides studying or chatting. My apartment in Columbus was near the Olentangy River, slow moving but not very deep. Bushes and flowering plants bordered the muddy bank. The adjacent woods shadowed the pathways wending to and from the river. Often I invited Montserrat to join me treasure hunting there. Feet sinking into the sucking goo, I would pull a unique find from the muck and hold it up for her to admire, the brown syrup dribbling from my hand and down off of my elbow.

"This brick was made in 1942. Look!" I swished muddy water over the brick to reveal the indented mold of the date.

Montserrat scooped up some mud. "*!Mira! Aquí hay tres más.*" (Look! Here are three more.)

Together, we lifted out the bricks, took them to my yard, and hosed them off, then pulled some discarded wood shelving from the dumpster, inspired to make shelves for her apartment. Just some cleaned up bricks, sandpaper, and varnish, and a bookcase would be born!

A couple of days later I went to her apartment to help her set it up.

I thought the bookshelf should be placed *here*; Montserrat thought it should go over *there*. After a few minutes of debate, we got into a little spat about it.

Throwing her hands in the air, she said, "*Yo me rindo.*" (I give up.) Her voice had a sharp edge.

I sat cross-legged on the floor, not too close, and studied my shoelaces. I was ashamed for being so bossy. I sputtered out, *"Lo siento mucho. No quiero hablar contigo así."* (I am so sorry. I don't want to talk to you like this.) Then I began to cry.

She motioned for me to come closer to her, took my head in her hands, and placed it on her lap. Her hand gently smoothed over my hair as my tears soaked into her jeans.

At that moment, something awakened inside of me.

Montserrat and I were much more than tutor and tutee. Much more than Christian Baptist sisters. Much more than just friends. We were . . .

I had no words to describe *that*.

I also had no place in my worldview for *that*.

That comforting moment with Montserrat scared the shit out of me. My inner spirit knew it was what I had longed for all of my life; but I also knew it wasn't something I could ever have.

After this profound moment (for me, anyway), we found more time for quiet conversations, more time to linger within the privacy of my little Toyota to touch hands, or fix a stray lock of hair behind an ear, or absorb the softness of a light kiss on the cheek.

Only two months remained before I had to move out of my rental house and go to Mexico. Montserrat's two-year stint with the social work program would end at the same time. Then what?

Our impending separation felt like a ticking time bomb; I dreaded leaving her. I had grown to love her. At twenty-eight years old, I had never experienced such intense feelings about another person before. I'd had a college boyfriend, but that was nothing compared to the connection I felt with Montserrat. Even though I cursed my body's pull toward her, I never wanted it to stop. Had I fallen in love?

I told myself that it would be best for us to go our separate ways. To avoid temptation, of course.

I was surprised when she came up with an adventurous idea.

Sharon Wulfensmith

CHAPTER 3
ROAD TRIP

"Since we both love being out in nature, let's go camping before we have to part ways." Those dark brown eyes of Montserrat's danced. "Let's go from Ohio all the way to California! I'd love to meet your parents in Santa Barbara."

The following week, in my living room, we started laying out some camping supplies that I had stored in my basement. "You got a sleeping bag?" I asked.

"I have a big one that someone gave me last year." Montserrat smiled as she sorted stuff and put things into cardboard boxes.

"Terrific! I have an old one I used in high school that's still good. It probably needs some airing out." I scuttled down the basement steps to look for my old sleeping bag. There it was, on a spidery shelf. Brushing it off with my hand, I recalled something about that old bag. It certainly did need some airing out. It had been packed away for thirteen years and was more than dusty and musty.

In it I had packed away all the shame and guilt I felt about the stories I had told my friend Vicky one Good Friday more than a decade earlier.

In 1965, my Lutheran church youth group from East Cleveland joined several other groups for a large Easter weekend retreat at a nearby Christian college. The girls slept in sleeping bags spread out over the floor of the gymnasium, and the boys stayed in the chapel auditorium. Vicky Volkova, from another high school, was my very best buddy that weekend. Both fifteen and in tenth grade, we had a lot of *boy talk* to discuss with the other girls.

I was beyond thrilled to flaunt the fact that I had a boyfriend that weekend: Charlie Bennett, also fifteen—and my very first one!

Another couple invited us to go out with them for *parking* on Friday night. I wasn't sure what *parking* was, but the undertone of the conversation suggested that it was very special. Vicky wasn't invited.

The driver chose a somewhat lonely spot to park in. Charlie and I both sat in the back seat with a space between us. The two heads in the front seat meshed into one. Faint slurping sounds slid into the back seat. *This must be what parking is about*, I realized. *This is what I've been waiting for!*

Charlie pulled me to his side, wrapped his hands around the back of my neck so he could guide my face to his, and started kissing it all over. I'd heard of necking before, but I was only getting a crick in my neck.

Finally, he relaxed enough to kiss me on the mouth, and he pressed his slobbery wet lips to mine until I thought I'd suffocate. *Eeew!* I thought. Each time he changed positions, I gasped in a breath. Lucky for me, I'd been a swimmer in high school and could hold my breath for a really long time. His eyes were closed during the whole ordeal, but mine were open wide, watching cars pass, wondering how long I'd have to endure this misery.

After what seemed like ten hours of *parking*, the driver guided the car back to the college campus. As soon as the car rolled to a stop, I opened the door, finally freeing myself from the prison-like capsule. I drank in the fresh night air as I scampered across a grassy area and slipped in through the back door of the gymnasium—which Vicky, as planned, had propped open for me with a stick. It was just minutes past midnight.

"Sharon, over here!" Vicky hissed through her giggles. She held open my orange sleeping bag and helped me snuggle down inside, then moved close to me. "Tell me everything," her shushed voice commanded.

"It was fantastic," I lied in a whisper, my lips tingling as they brushed against her ear. "His hands were all over me and his kisses were so warm . . ."

Vicky begged me to tell detail after detail. Each time I told her another jewel of invented information she scooted closer to me, stifling her snickering.

I nestled in closer to her face. Each time I inhaled the fragrance of her breath, I felt a pulse between my legs. I couldn't understand why my underwear felt so wet. It hadn't felt that way in the car when I was with Charlie.

The following morning, I awoke in a very bad mood. I realized that Sunday was Easter. That's what the Christian youth weekend was supposed to be about. Oh no! I must be an awful sinner to have committed all these sins on a holy day, Good Friday. Jesus must have died on the cross just because of me. My guilt grew inside like a smelly mushroom, pushing everything else out of its way.

⌒ℓℓ৴

I still stood in my Columbus, Ohio basement, staring at my rolled-up orange sleeping bag on the dusty shelf. My vision abruptly came to a stop. I wiped the spidery strands and dusty memories on my jeans and headed back upstairs, clutching the orange bundle. "Montserrat, I finally found it," I announced in a sing-song voice as I walked back into the living room. I hoped I hadn't spent too much time reminiscing in the basement.

I loved how she looked sitting cross-legged among the camping gear, glowing with sweat, her plaid shirt unbuttoned a little too far down. Gazing at her, my words bounced with happiness as I said, "Let's open it up and air it in the sun."

As we laid the orange nylon bag over a plump hedge in my backyard, my heart sizzled with the prospect of lying next to her in a pup tent for a few weeks. Would my sleeping bag again absorb similar secrets? Part of me wanted something special to happen, but a hidden part of me skittered away into shadow at the mere idea.

I had no idea what these conflicting, jumbled thoughts meant, so I whisked them away along with a few stray spider web strands still clinging to the fabric.

After packing two tons of stuff into my little car, Montserrat and I hauled my furniture a couple of houses up the street to a neighbor's; they'd told me I could store it all in their basement while I was away. I would pick it up next year, when I came back.

I had already resigned from my music therapy teaching position, telling my principal a white lie—that my mission in Mexico City began on May 15—to free myself up for three weeks to travel with Montserrat and also have a few days at my parents' house in Santa Barbara. The mission start date was actually June 10.

Walking away from my school a month before the end of second semester was hardly the responsible decision of a professional teacher, but I had only one thing on my mind: Montserrat.

The day of our departure, my little red Toyota's tires were pressed down with the weight of all we'd jammed inside: a tent, air mattresses, sleeping bags, food boxes, a Coleman stove, fuel, marshmallows, graham crackers, Hershey bars, and other camping essentials. Plus an old Singer sewing machine that I planned to return to my mom, and a lot of other items that I just couldn't part with. Sitting in the driver's seat, I realized that our cargo reached up to the ceiling. We'd have to use the side mirrors.

Westward ho! I looked forward to exploring the plains and farmlands of the central states, Mount Rushmore, Grand Tetons, Rocky Mountains, Bryce, Zion, Arches, Mojave Desert, and the West Coast. But mostly I looked forward to spending three whole weeks with my special friend.

Taking day hikes through some of the most beautiful landscapes our National Parks have to offer was spectacular. Sitting on a fallen log, cuddled together around the campfire on chilly evenings roasting s'mores, singing hymns together, holding hands while praying—we were two Christian sisters, close friends enjoying each other's company. Except . . .

In the pup tent, every night, I drank in Montserrat's tantalizing Maja perfume, our faces millimeters apart. To say goodnight, her lips would graze my cheek, then gently tug at my eyelashes, then slide down to my chin, avoiding direct contact with my lips.

It was all I could do to lie motionless. I wanted, more than anything, to lie naked with her in the same sleeping bag. Could she be feeling what I was feeling?

I didn't dare speak of any of this with her. I had learned by now not to mention such personal details—or, shall I say, *inclinations.*

I first learned, the hard way, not to speak of *such things* when I was nineteen.

In 1969, as a junior, I transferred out of a Christian college to attend a large secular state school. On Clubs Day the first week of classes, I signed up to join a Christian group.

The Navigators was an ultra-conservative evangelical campus ministry whose motto was, *The Bible says it. I believe it. That settles it.* Relationships with women were characterized by sisterly companionship and relationships with men could be friendly but not sinful (as in, feeling any sexual attraction whatsoever before marriage). I ended up bowing to their misogynist male leadership ideal, even though that wasn't what my parents had taught me growing up. The Navigators taught that God, in his wisdom, would choose the man I'd marry someday, even though I thought that idea rather preposterous. The deepest desire of my heart was to love and obey God in everything. So, I swallowed their teachings whole.

The Navigators convinced me that I should receive Discipleship Training and learn how to share the Gospel with anyone and everyone. As a result, I *witnessed* to anyone who had two legs, spoke English, and was unfortunate enough to be corralled by me to have to listen to the *Navigator Bridge Illustration of Salvation,* and pray the *Sinner's Prayer of Repentance.*

Sarah Szabo was, like me, a music major. We met in one of my music classes, and she fell easily into my evangelical Christian cultic clutches; she readily became *saved,* and began attending Navigator meetings with me.

Like Montserrat, Sarah had thick beautiful black hair, dark brown eyes, and a captivating smile. We became best friends. I loved her—as a sister, I told myself, but something inside of me called out for something more. I had no words to describe what that "something" was, only feelings of guilt that reached back to my tomboy days as a young girl. Whenever I was with Sarah, no matter how hard I tried, I couldn't extinguish the passionate feelings the simplest glance or touch from her ignited in me.

After a whole year of wrestling with my unwanted sexual pull, I had to speak up. Surely a brief conversation could clear the air, I reasoned.

"Let's go to the library and sit on the emergency steps at the very top," I suggested to Sarah one afternoon after classes.

"What for?" She scrunched up her pretty black eyebrows.

"Just a private place so we can talk." I fidgeted with my nails.

"Talk about what?"

I didn't respond.

She shrugged. "If you insist. Let's go."

We climbed up to the fifth floor instead of taking the elevator and sat side by side on the top step.

I picked at a cuticle. "I need to share... I can't control... Maybe God will heal..." I searched for the words, but they melted like ice on my tongue.

"You have a disease? Not cancer!" She scooted over and put her arm around me.

I put my face into my hands, hoping to mask my shame.

"You're trembling. Tell me what's going on." She squeezed my shoulder.

I found some words, unsure if they were the right ones. "This is really hard... I want to remain friends. I have this problem. I feel turned on by women, not by men. You turn me on, and... I just don't know what to do."

She leapt to her feet. "How can you say that?" she shrieked. "That's abominable! Don't you ever mention this to anyone! Don't ever touch me again!"

Sarah raced down all five flights of stairs and left me sitting there. Alone. Crying.

Why was I cursed with something that I had never chosen and couldn't seem to control?

Sarah and I continued to be friends for several years, but we lost something precious that day.

～ه‿ع～

Could I, would I, should I ever have that kind of conversation with Montserrat? We were already doing things that I had never dared with Sarah, but even so . . .

One cool afternoon, while we were at a rest stop along the highway in the Rocky Mountains of Wyoming, I dared to broach the forbidden subject. I feared that she would respond like Sarah had, but my feelings couldn't be quieted any longer, so I took the risk.

"Montserrat, I have to share something with you." I looked down. "I have some sexual inclinations towards you when we are together—especially at night, when we're lying so close."

Instead of the explosion that I feared might come, she just said, "It's okay to tell me what you're feeling."

She listened as I shared a bit more. When I was done, she said, "I think that it must be a phase with you. It'll pass soon enough. Just enjoy the friendship that we share, and everything will be fine. Remember, we are Christians, and God will lead us to his truth."

Her answer only frustrated me all the more. I was convinced that I was sinning, but at the same time I had no control over how my body was reacting to her, so how could I be sinning? Wasn't sin when you *chose* to do something you knew you weren't supposed to do? I felt trapped in a prison, unable to find the key to get out.

I resolved to just enjoy our trip and ignore my nighttime feelings.

Somewhere along a highway in southern Colorado, I found a pay phone to call my brother, Thomas. He was almost two years older than me and was also an evangelical Christian. I wanted to talk to him one last time before he headed to Germany for a year on a mission trip with the group he had been involved with in college, Inter-Varsity Christian Fellowship. He and his fiancé, Miriam, were visiting my parents in California, but they would have to leave before Montserrat and I arrived.

"I'm sorry I won't be able to see you before you go," I told Thomas when he got on the line. "I just wanted to say good-bye." My hand sheltered the phone receiver to shield it from the whish of the gusty wind.

"We're going to be driving opposite directions," he said. "Maybe we can meet up." He tried to tell me about the route they'd planned, but I couldn't hear him clearly.

Anyway, I didn't know how in the world how we'd find each other in the middle of Utah somewhere in a couple of days.

After we hung up, I climbed back into the car, where Montserrat was sitting and waiting for me.

"My brother thinks that we can find each other in the middle of nowhere," I said, laughing. "That's crazy. Let's forget about it and just keep going west through Arizona."

We continued driving for that day and the next, the temperature rising five degrees every minute. The following day, we drove on isolated, two-lane highways through rocky desert terrain, baking ourselves like two sugar cookies in my Toyota, which didn't have air conditioning. We threw water from a bucket over our heads, sang, laughed, and told each other stories in Spanish as we whiled away the long hours.

As we were wending our way along the curves of the Colorado River in Arizona, headed toward Lake Mead, a car whizzed past us, honking its horn. I stopped in the middle of the road, thinking that the person must need help. A man jumped out and began running toward us, his image distorted by the heat waves undulating from the hot pavement.

It was only when he was twenty feet away that I realized who he was.

"Thomas!" I shrieked.

"Sharon!" He grabbed me and twirled me around in a big hug. We laughed together, clutching each other at arm's length. "I prayed that God would lead us to find you," he said. "And here we are. It's a miracle."

Indeed it was.

Together, we came up with the makings of a perfunctory picnic: white bread slices, tuna fish, peanut butter and jelly, and warm water from a once-cold thermos. We located a shady spot alongside the highway, and with Thomas and Miriam perched together on a fallen log and Montserrat and me sitting on separate boulders, we recounted our travels of the last several days and marveled at the serendipity of running into each other in the middle of the nowhere in Arizona.

I watched Thomas talk about Miriam. He looked so animated, and Miriam's face seemed to glow with new love. He had found the woman he wanted to marry. And me? I had found the woman I wanted to . . .

I drew a blank.

I didn't know what to think or what to allow myself to feel. Would I ever find a man to marry? I didn't feel like I was good enough for that. On the inside, I didn't feel normal at all. On the outside, I had to maintain an appearance of what I thought *normal* looked like. I really hadn't the faintest idea. It took a lot of energy to keep up the charade.

⌒⟋⟍

After another day and a half of driving in our Toyota toaster oven, we arrived in Santa Barbara. We stopped first at Walgreens to drop off our rolls of film to be developed—and then, tired and sweaty, we headed to my parents' house.

After sticky hugs and smiley introductions, we took showers and changed into clean clothes.

I couldn't help but breathe in her scent as she walked past me.

Ahhh, she must have put on a fresh layer of that Maja perfume.

Was she trying to kill me?

⌒⟋⟍

The next morning we retrieved our slides from Walgreens. My father set up his slide projector and filled the carousel with our photos, and the show began in the living room.

Telling our camping adventures to my parents made me feel more comfortable around Montserrat. My mom and dad treated her like she was part of the family. I didn't even dare to imagine that maybe one day she might be. Could that even be possible? How?

⌒⟋⟍

We stayed with my parents a few days, sleeping on the lumpy pullout sofa, lying close but not daring to spoon. I didn't want to risk my father traipsing through, saying that he'd forgotten something in the living room, and catching us snuggled together.

Sometimes in the middle of the night we'd roll close, our bodies touching from head to toe, but I told myself each time that it must have been by accident.

On our last night together, however, a butterfly wing tickled my ear. "Sharon," Montserrat whispered, "I love you. I can't bear the thought of returning to Spain without you."

I felt my heart rip right down the middle. The blood oozed out onto the sheets.

I wanted to meld with her, melt into her, mold my body around hers. What was I supposed to say after she said, "I love you"?

As a good Christian, of course, I restrained my hands from embarking on the journey they yearned to take. Instead, I just sucked in her Maja scent and whispered, "I love you too."

Saying those words, I wondered what kind of love it was that we shared. My heartbeat throbbing down low, I felt my wetness, though I still couldn't admit to myself how sexually aroused I was lying so close to Montserrat. A wailing cry reverberated inside the hollowness of my chest, but I didn't dare let it escape.

"I have always wanted to see Mexico City," she whispered into my neck. "I can call a travel agent to change my flight. I want a few days to see Mexico City with you before you have to start your mission program."

"*Mi corazón*," I murmured back. "I would love for you to do that."

Her voice barely audible, she said, "Let's fly to Mexico on the same flight this Friday. Just a little more time together, *mi cariño*."

Our arms encircled each other, and her smooth fingers brushed away my tears as we fell asleep, arms and legs entwined.

Two days later, we flew to Mexico City.

Sharon Wulfensmith

CHAPTER 4

SPEARHEAD

In stark contrast to the silence of Bryce Canyon or the grandeur of Zion National Park, our time together in Mexico City was anything but relaxing or romantic. We stayed in a noisy rooming house near Palacio de Bellas Artes, where the Ballet Folklórico performed regularly. After a couple days of sightseeing, we took a taxi to the Zona Rosa, the touristy part of downtown, where I planned to meet up with the Spearhead Mission group. This was the first time I had traveled to another country.

The taxi ride itself was an adventure! Tires screeching, the driver careened into the melee of traffic. I caught a few Spanish words as he screamed out the window, "*¡Madre! ¡Pendejo! ¡Chinga!*" (Mother! Stupid! Fuck!)

I remembered that first word from tutoring, but Montserrat must have left out the other two. I'd have to look those up in my Spanish-English dictionary later. Lucky for me, I couldn't see the terrifying traffic anyway; my own enormous yellow suitcase pressed into my face, blocking my view from the back seat. It was too big to fit into the trunk.

The sidewalk in front of the mission office on Avenida Insurgentes was crammed with young Americans waiting to meet their Mexican host families. I clung to one of the straps on Montserrat's backpack, ensuring that we wouldn't be separated within the crush of bodies. With her black hair and diminutive size, she blended in. She almost looked like a host family mother waiting for her Spearhead volunteer. But she wasn't waiting for an American to take home with her—she was about to say goodbye to an American whose heart was breaking into a million pieces.

I glanced at her, pressing my quivering lips together. She quickly dropped her gaze. My tears spilled out and unabashed rivulets ran down my cheeks as I clutched her shoulders and pulled her to me.

"Adios," I said. *"Te amo mucho."* As I spoke into her Maja-fragrant neck, the breeze tossed a strand of her hair between my lips. I wanted to bite it off and swallow it, making a tiny portion of her a part of me.

She pried me away and held me at arm's length. "When will you come to see me in Barcelona?"

Our eyes locked. Dark brown to light blue. Catalàn to Ohioan. Woman to woman. Lover to . . .

No. I couldn't say that one.

Drowning in a sea of sadness, I squeaked out, "Soon."

At that, she whirled around and whisked away, clutching her small luggage tightly. My eyes drank in how her hips swayed ever so slightly as she moved down the sidewalk in her black pumps. I wondered if she was crying too.

My lump of sadness felt like a great glob of oatmeal stuck in my throat. Not enough milk. And no cinnamon and honey.

Two twenties-something, smiling young people greeted me on the crowded sidewalk—*"¿Eres Sharon Smith? Somos tu nueva familia."* (Are you Sharon Smith? We are your new family.) I was glad I could understand them.

Standing beside them was a young woman, perhaps in her late teens, with long, stringy hair that was plastered against her sweaty, pimply, pale forehead. Her blue eyes examined me through her black-rimmed thick glasses as she held out a wilted hand and said, "I'm Melody Miller. We're assigned as roommates for the Spearhead summer."

I shook the wet fish and lied, "Nice to meet you." Inwardly, I sighed with disappointment. They'd assigned me *this* girl to live with for the summer? Dread dragged me downward.

"*¿Listas?*" (Ready?) Genaro had already flagged down a taxi and was loading our suitcases into the trunk.

Again, my yellow suitcase wouldn't fit. I wedged it in front of me on my lap and stared out my window.

⁂

Another wild ride—this one fifty minutes long—took us to Colonia Viaducto Piedad, south of downtown. It was like a Disneyland ride but without the Disney fun. Fortunately, we arrived unscathed.

"*Hola Sharón! Hola Melodía!*" the red-lipsticked, flowery-dressed Señora Vazquez greeted us in front of her blue-and-turquoise painted house. "*Mi casa es su casa.*" (Make yourself at home.) She grabbed us both, kissed our cheeks, and gave us hugs. When she embraced me, I felt abundantly conscious of how the mound of her bountiful breasts pressed against my smaller ones.

Señora Vazquez showed us to our lovely bedroom as she babbled in Spanish. In vain, I tried to catch some of the verbs I'd memorized. She talked so fast.

⁂

That evening, after we put our things away, Melody and I chatted a while, lying on our double bed, elbows propping up our heads. After she told me where she was going to college as a freshman, I began to tell her about my friend from Barcelona and our camping trip, but I was still coming to grips with the fact that I would be spending tonight sharing a bed with this young college co-ed instead of Montserrat, and my words caught in my throat like a prickly artichoke leaf.

Melody encouraged me to continue, asking, "How did you like Mount Rushmore?"

I was mute. *South Dakota . . . I savored the smoky taste of the hot chocolate with marshmallows Montserrat and I had warmed over our campfire. Her small hand pulled me along as we walked, crunching crispy leaves, stopping in a clearing to gaze up at the starry sky. But we couldn't see the pinpoints of light, because a kaleidoscope of flashing light painted the heavens with swirls of rainbow colors, swooping turquoise, blues and greens, pinks and violets. The master-piece of some ethereal artist in action right before our eyes. Basking in the wonder of the Northern Lights, we stood in awe, arms draped over shoulders, until the show ended over an hour later. Silently, we retreated to our pup tent and spooned, drifting off into colorful dreams of tranquility.*

Melody interrupted my reverie. "Did something happen there?"

My vocal cords only could produce little squeaks.

Melody reached over and rubbed my back, and I recoiled as if she had burned me. "Nothing happened!" I croaked, rolling away from her touch.

I tried to muffle my sobs with my pillow as I cried myself to sleep.

The next morning my brain felt as wrinkled as the bed covers. Taking control of the moment, I asked Melody first, "How did you sleep?" and forced a smile.

Biting her lower lip, she said, "Last night you talked about your camping trip. Your Barcelona friend must have been very special to you, because the way you talked, and the way you cried... You sounded like someone who had said goodbye to a boyfriend or a fiancé." She scrunched up her face and turned away. "What is with you?" she called over her shoulder.

The sharp knife of her words sliced deep. I couldn't quite make sense of why her words lacerated me so deeply, but they cut me to the core.

CHAPTER 5

FOLLOWING THE CALL

Still licking my wounds, I thrust myself headlong into the ministry I felt God had called me to at that Columbus, Ohio Baptist church one year earlier. It was now the summer of 1978, and my mission activities and responsibilities postponed my sadness, allowing me to deflect what I couldn't bear to face.

Alongside fifty other young Spearhead summer recruits, I diligently studied Mexican culture, language, and religion. I adored Señora Vazquez and my Mexican host family. I formed positive relationships with the people in the Lutheran church I was assigned to serve in. They even invited me to preach from their pulpit after my first month there!

The mission had few rules. The most important one was, "Never say 'No' to an invitation." My type A personality ate this up. I eagerly accepted the invitation to speak.

That Sunday, my feet tentatively ascended the steps up into the enclosure of the church's carved wooden pulpit, which was not unlike the one my Lutheran pastor had preached from in East Cleveland, Ohio.

I began tentatively: *"Buenos días. Que Dios les bendiga."* (Good morning. God bless you). I was okay with simple phrases like that. People had told me that my pronunciation was pretty good, which was gratifying.

I went on to read the Gospel lesson from Matthew 13 about the Parable of the Sower and the Seed. Feeling more confident, I launched into the sermon I had painstakingly prepared the evening before, mostly reading from my notes. A couple of times I found myself able to extend my explanation of seeds—how they were planted, how they grew, and such. As I continued, my confidence grew. *I can do this!* I told myself. I held up an avocado seed, then an apricot seed, and then the smallest seed I'd been able to find—I think it was from a kiwi fruit.

Those poor parishioners, listening to me, a *gringa*, droning on in elementary Spanish, as if they didn't know how to plant, sow, and reap. For goodness' sake, many of them had their own fruit trees and vegetable gardens at home.

A glow of satisfaction shone from my face as I returned to my pew after the sermon and sat down next to Melody, who leaned in and hissed, "A whole hour, Sharon! I thought you'd never shut up!"

"Shhh!" I frowned and pressed my finger to my lips. *Why don't you shut up, smart-ass!* I thought, but I corked up my angry words. Oh, how she grated on my nerves.

I certainly did *not* experience any sexual pull toward this gal. I detested sharing a double bed with her. I clung to the far edge each night to make sure that not even my pinkie toe touched any part of her body.

Our summer program lasted only two months, after which that pimply-faced Melody went back to her kindergarten college in Kentucky, or wherever she was from. Good riddance! I didn't like her, but even more so, I was afraid she knew something about me that I did not yet want to know.

⌒⊸ℓℓ⊸⌐

During that first summer, I was thrilled to buy a hand-made Mexican guitar with a pearl-shell design embedded around the sound hole. I had borrowed guitars from my new Mexican friends the first few weeks and learned dozens of *coritos* in Spanish. Now, having my own guitar gave me independence and a sense of being a real missionary. I did street evangelism, singing my way along unpaved roads of cobbled-together houses with corrugated aluminum roofs and volcanic rock walls. I was a pied piper. Children followed me, quickly picking up the simple lyrics to the songs and belting them out with gusto as our line snaked up and down the pockmarked dirt pathways. Other Spearheaders did the same in nearby areas.

After winning the hearts of the children, we gave out tracts and free New Testaments to the kids, telling them to go home and invite their families to a neighborhood Bible study. For six weeks, we conducted a special mission outreach in the southern part of the capital, below the famous Coyoacán, the home of Frida Kahlo.

That fall, 1978, twelve of us stayed with Spearhead to participate in the yearlong program, doing similar evangelism projects with various churches. I had planned to stay only the summer, but at the last minute I decided to stay longer. I remained in Mexico City until January of 1979, when I left to work with more church contacts in the state of Morelos, training pastors in Puebla and Cuautla. It was peculiar that we—young *gringos* new to Latin American culture and language—were entrusted to train pastors twice our age and with much more experience, but the pastors had requested that our mission group send us there to help them recruit more members into their respective churches by blitzing their areas with tracts, Bibles, and personal invitations. White, struggling with Spanish, and singing *coritos* at the tops of our lungs wherever we went, we were an item in their neighborhoods. People would flock to their churches to see the *Americanos*, and after we moved on to another location, the pastors would continue their outreach to their new recruits.

⁓ 🙰 ⁓

In March we traveled to Guatemala City for a month, and after that to Tegucigalpa, Honduras for several months, doing more of the same, until the next summer rolled around.

During my second summer with Spearhead, I became a Team Leader. By now I had signed up to continue on for a total of three years plus a summer. I was efficient, proud of my Spanish fluency, and had high expectations for our success leading Latin Americans away from Catholicism and toward the evangelical churches we worked with. I believed that my leadership skills were helping to win many souls for Christ.

I made no time to feel sorry for myself. I made sure that there was no opportunity for lustful, same-sex thought patterns to creep in. I carefully ensconced my yearning to be with Montserrat in my heart, not acknowledging it to anyone, even myself. *If you hide it well enough, maybe it will eventually fade away*, I reasoned.

I was oblivious to how this deep, unfulfilled desire was sapping my inner energy, leaving me with an oozing sore. This was the beginning of a significant discontent in my inner spirit that would rear its ugly head from time to time in the future.

During the Central America tour I began in January of 1980, I took a risk and allowed myself to form a too-close friendship with one of the Spearhead volunteers. I wasn't vigilant enough to notice that danger might be lurking around the corner in the form of another young college co-ed.

Tamara McCann was a couple inches taller than me, very white, and had curly, bouncy blonde hair. I felt attracted to her bubbly personality. Frequently, on our long drives south through Guatemala to Honduras with the team, she and I would ride together in the back seat of the mission vehicle, a Volkswagen bus with no air conditioning. With ten of us crammed into the VW, our bodies melted like candies in the heat, our limbs entwined, our heads wedged between luggage and shoulders.

Sitting next to Tamara in these conditions, my cursed body blossomed again with those damned, dreaded, sweaty, sexual feelings. I didn't seek them out; they just happened. Why couldn't I just make it stop? I could sit next to the guys in the VW—snuggle up to them, enjoy their company—and not feel any sexual pull at all. What was going on with me?

To escape my attraction to Tamara, I'd grab a spot next to Kev Davis, one of the Spearhead volunteers from California. I enjoyed having theological discussions with him. He was taking a year off from getting his MA at Fuller Theological Seminary in Pasadena.

One insufferably hot afternoon, Kev explained, "I'm studying to become a Presbyterian pastor. My seminary is open-minded but evangelical. Even women can become pastors. You should look into it, Sharon. I think you have the gifts to become a great minister."

Even though I had been out of college for almost a decade, Kev's energy was infectious and planted a seed. Maybe someday I would try seminary. I couldn't believe that someone thought I would make a good pastor. My confidence soared. I imagined a mission like Spearhead spreading beyond Central America. Maybe I could be the missionary that would take Spearhead to another continent. Europe, perhaps?

In her letters, Montserrat often asked me when we would be able to see one another again. Shortly after we had parted ways on that crowded Mexican sidewalk, I received a small painted card with a poem written in her delicate cursive Spanish.

> *Goodbyes are happy*
> *when seen through the eyes of hope*
>
> *With a future in your heart*
> *and a flame of love in your spirit*
>
> *Goodbyes are happy*
> *when the people who leave don't really leave*
>
> *But stay inside you, talking and singing,*
> *reaching out a hand, giving a kiss*
>
> *We leave and come back to find each other once again*

Find each other once again. How I longed to hold her in my arms. Her words pulled my heartstrings toward Barcelona. I had to find a way to see her sooner than later.

I'd been in Latin America for about two years by now, and my friendship with Tamara was a stark reminder of how much I missed Montserrat. When my yearnings swelled for her, I'd reread that poem before bed, hoping she'd visit me in my dreams.

Finally, I couldn't take it anymore. I decided to come up with a plan to travel to Spain—and to do it without forfeiting my mission commitment.

A few days later I spoke with the Spearhead director, Gordon Everett.

"Has Spearhead ever considered Europe?" I asked him.

He shook his head. "In Latin America the people are warmer, more pliable."

"But I have contacts in Barcelona through a large Baptist church."

His face serious, his fingers drumming on his desk, he said, "Sharon, if you can present me with a feasible goal by the end of the month, I'll take it to the mission board and we'll see."

Hope sprouted within me like one of those seeds I had preached about. I could almost see the green shoots poking up from the ground. That evening, I thought, prayed, dreamed, and scribbled a plan on notebook paper. Having no typewriter, I revised it by hand, printing clearly on plain paper. I devised a detailed strategy for outreach, evangelism, discipleship, and church growth, complete with contact names that Montserrat had mentioned in her letters.

Mr. Everett presented my proposal to the mission board, and within a few weeks, the mission accepted my plan. I couldn't believe it; I would be in Spain by September, and would get to stay there through Christmas.

There must be a reason God had answered my prayers.

⁓⁓⁓

I wasn't just pretending to get a free trip; I had convinced myself that Spearhead actually should branch out to Europe. I could see no reason not to try. Thomas worked with a different international mission group and was serving in Germany, and I wanted to do something similar. Growing up with Thomas, I'd often felt I was competing with him and somehow always losing. He was perpetually one step ahead of me. This time maybe I could show him up, I told myself.

I also convinced myself that God had called me to be an ambassador abroad. I believed my motives were legitimate; getting to see Montserrat was just the cherry on top.

At the conclusion of my third summer in Central America with Spearhead, in September 1980, I flew from Mexico City to London.

In the busy Heathrow airport, Montserrat's beaming face emerged from the crowd, almost as if by magic. "*Mi amor*, Sharon. It's so wonderful to see you again."

We held each other in a tight embrace for a long time, though it felt like only two seconds. She stepped back and stared at me. My heart leapt for joy. Then she noticed my luggage.

"How in the world are we going to travel with that big yellow suitcase?" she demanded. "And it doesn't even have wheels, does it?" The softness of her embrace was replaced by the scraping of her criticism.

"I need my stuff. My Bibles. My raincoat. Extra shoes..." My voice faded. I felt like a child who'd just been reprimanded by her mommy. "I can carry it just fine."

"Of course you will, because I certainly am not going to drag it around for you."

Why was she angry with me all of a sudden? Wasn't she happy to see me? Her sharp words were like needles in my heart. We had written letters and had the occasional (very expensive) phone call while I was in Central America, but we had not seen each other for over two years—and now here she was, yelling at me already. I'd had no idea what a burden it would be to haul that stupid suitcase into train cars and up and down flights of stairs in metro stations and such. Montserrat, in comparison, had a small black suitcase and a small backpack. I felt so stupid.

I struggled through the airport tugging my cargo behind me, trying to keep up with her. She turned around abruptly to say something, and I froze like a little girl about to be rebuked.

"I am so sorry I barked at you, *cariño*, but it's going to be tough with that heavy bag," she said. "I don't want it to ruin our trip.

Let's decide to have a marvelous time. I'll help you with it if you need me to." She gave me a quick hug and a peck on the cheek.

I exhaled with relief. We exited the airport and she hailed a taxi to the train station.

I was relieved that this taxi ride wasn't as terrifying as the Mexican ones. We arrived to the train station in just a few minutes, and yes, I had to struggle to extricate that heavy yellow bag from the car when we got there, but I put on a happy face, my excitement replacing my sore back muscles. It was now Montserrat's turn to show me around her part of the world.

First-class Eurorail train tickets for three weeks took us through England, Belgium, Germany, Austria, Italy, and Switzerland. We were hosted by Montserrat's many European friends until the last night, when just the two of us enjoyed a private bed-and-breakfast somewhere in Switzerland.

I stretched out on my back in the cozy bed, lying close (but not too close) to my lovely Barcelona lady, recalling our camping trip across the US only three years before. Studying the rustic wood ceiling of our small room, I murmured into her delicious, Maja-scented ear, "Little chilly tonight, eh?"

Under the colorful down quilt, she scooched closer. It was exciting to have our own private room and not be separated by individual nylon sleeping bags. She turned toward me, our warm bodies melding together.

"Sharon, my love..." Her lips were feathers against mine.

I had kissed a girl once before, as a teenager, but I'd never before loved someone like I loved Montserrat. It had taken me until age thirty to experience this feeling for the first time.

I draped an arm just above the curve of her hip. I was simultaneously terrified and wet with desire.

"Sharon," she whispered, her lips barely grazing mine. "I've been wanting to say something to you." Her smooth fingers interlaced with mine. "If one of us were a man, I'd ask you to marry me."

Her words ricocheted inside my skull, scraped their way down to my heart, and sliced it into bloody chunks. How could she say such a thing?

I had fallen wildly in love, but I had no idea how to express that love. So I just lay there in that bed, completely at a loss for words. At a loss for any understanding of who I was.

~

Later, I would fantasize about how this scene might have played out differently.

"Sharon," she would have whispered, her lips barely grazing mine. "I've been wanting to say something to you." Her smooth fingers would have been interlaced with mine. "If one of us were a man, I'd ask you to marry me."

Then I would have said, "You're the love of my life, Montserrat. Let's live together in Barcelona and get married soon after. I don't need to return to the mission in Mexico. I want to stay with you." I would have slipped my hands around her face and kissed her deeply, and we would have spent the night fulfilling what we had wanted to do since we had met in Columbus, Ohio, three years before. We would have begun a life together.

What actually happened was that I said nothing, and we eventually fell asleep. In the morning, we awoke at that bed-and-breakfast and, after enjoying delicious sweet French crêpes with strong coffee, we caught the morning train headed southwest.

It was an overnight couchette sleeper car through France. At a train stop in Bern, Switzerland, our train car was uncoupled from the other cars and had to wait a while to connect to several freight carriages. That's when I became impatient, got off the train, and left Montserrat hanging out of the window.

When the conductor waved me away, he was yelling at me in German (which, of course I didn't understand), telling me to wait, that those train cars would reappear five minutes later on the other side of the same platform.

I was still standing there like an idiot, thinking about how the waiting passengers still on the platform must have enjoyed watching my failed sprint after the train, when the cars returned on the other side of the platform. The conductor's ample belly bounced with stifled giggles as he motioned for to me to ascend the steps, safely this time.

I crept into our cubicle, tail between my legs. Montserrat gave me a scolding and I promised to be a good girl.

Somewhere deep down, I knew I had missed getting onto another, more important train—one that would have taken me into building a life with Montserrat. But neither of us knew how to do that. After all, we were good Baptist girls. Both of us had been steeped in evangelical theological dogma that had taught us our love was not valid. The things our religious leaders had impressed upon us had smashed our true identities to bits, and even when we tried to retrieve some of the broken pieces and hold them close to our hearts, we didn't know how to glue them together again.

At this point, I had no understanding of the words *gay* or *lesbian* or *bi*. I had lived such a sheltered Christian lifestyle, I hadn't even been aware of the Stonewall Riots of 1969 when they took place. It is remarkable to me now that I, an educated person, could have lived each day, each year, and even decades with such over-whelming blindness, but I did—and I would continue to do so for the next ten years of my life. Bamboozled by profound misinformation and ignorance, I would make a fool of myself on various train platforms time and time again before finally figuring things out, missing opportunities for love and disrupting other people's lives along the way.

◦⊸ℓℓ⊸

My three months in Barcelona were filled with failed attempts to contact Baptist churches, half-hearted Bible distribution in front of Antoni Gaudí's La Sagrada Familia Church, and sporadic communication with my mission in Mexico. Montserrat and I rented separate rooms in an Episcopal convent where we spent evenings holding hands, sitting side by side on her bed studying the Bible, and praying. Very frequently, we lay down together and hugged, but my chaste hands never strayed far.

I retired to my own bedroom each and every night, and every morning I awoke alone in my bed, feeling the unfulfilled passion of my dreams throbbing between my legs. I'd rush to the bathroom to take a shower and try to focus on one more day, hoping, *Please God, just for today*, I could annihilate my sinful appetites.

The impact of Montserrat's marriage proposal to me faded with time, but her words were never completely extinguished from my heart and imagination.

∽∾

After my return to the US, Montserrat and I continued to write many letters to one another. In a letter dated May 1982, two years after our Eurorail trip, she wrote,

> *In my mind you are the same Sharon I met back in Ohio. Capable, independent, happy, takes initiative. With the "problem" that we have discussed previously [she never could name it for what it was, but neither could I], I don't think that you have completely explained to me the emotional trauma that you have suffered, and its consequences. This "subject" torments you. It's like a cycle. You fear handling human relationships. You have talked about your "problem" on the surface, but you haven't gotten down to the deep reason for it.*

She then said she hoped I'd be able to find a good psychotherapist and that God would eventually give me the gift of healing for my "problem." I wondered if she had been in therapy herself. She never volunteered the information, and I never asked.

She and I both were trapped in our evangelical straitjackets, so much so that neither of us could sort out the dynamics of our relationship or how to walk forward with it. Because of that, our only option was to pretend that we didn't even have an option.

Sharon Wulfensmith

CHAPTER 6

THORNS

In January 1981 I returned to my mission in Latin America to re- sume my role as Team Leader. I soon discovered that the twelve Spearhead volunteers had weathered my three-month absence with- out a hitch and weren't thrilled to have me back.

While doing evangelism in rural churches outside of Mexico City, Joy Berg, nine years my junior, asked to speak with me privately.

"No offense, Sharon," she said, "but you lead our team with such a harsh hand. You were gone last fall, and now you want to take over." Her gentle, light brown eyes probed mine.

"God has appointed me as a leader for this team," I replied curtly, sitting erect in my chair.

From my point of view, I was doing a good job—monitoring my team members' every move, controlling them as much as possible. Being efficient, I had even created a checklist for the daily devotions, reading, and prayer time I thought everyone should do. I was frustrated that my team members refused to hand it in to me weekly. I was following the training I'd had in the Navigators group during college. I was too busy being in charge to notice that my approach was snuffing out the creativity of the other team members.

"Something tells me that you have been deeply hurt or disappointed in some way," Joy said, her words soft as rose petals. "I'd like to be your confidant. Your friend. Let me know if you'd ever like to talk." Her face lifted as she tried to get me to look her in the eyes.

I couldn't. Instead, I bolted to my feet, my fury rising up like a fire during dry season. "Who do you think you are, telling me how to lead this team?" I snapped. "You don't have the experience that I do!"

Later, I would wish I could have a do-over on this one. Had I allowed just one of her kind words to soothe my dripping, toxic wounds, I might have been able to begin a journey to wholeness. Instead, I dug in my heels and led with an iron fist for the next few months.

In March, our team of ten crammed into our VW bus and left Mexico City, bouncing along roughly paved roads south to Oaxaca, east through Chiapas and on to Guatemala City. We spent three months there living in homes hosted by the churches we served in, eating fried plantains, black beans, and *huevos pasados por grasa* (eggs passed through hot grease; they were warm, but still raw. Ick!). We did the normal mission work, connecting with evangelical churches and helping them increase membership through outreach to children and teens.

One morning, we each stuffed a week's worth of belongings into pillowcases and drove northeast out of Guatemala City to the damp lowlands, where descendants of the Maya still lived. We parked our VW van near a riverbank and waited for our contact person there. (Someone must have communicated by mental telepathy to arrange the meeting points, because there was no electric means of connection whatsoever. Not even telephones.)

Oftentimes my prayers to God sounded like an administrator's list of requirements and goals. *God, send two men within two hours to this very spot to meet us. Keep us safe and healthy. Amen.* More often than not, I believed, God followed my specific instructions. Why weren't my team members cooperative like that?

Miraculously, two hours later we were met by three men paddling three long *lanchas*, canoe-like boats carved out of huge tree logs. They maneuvered them near a clearing so we could embark. Crouching to enter the canoe without tipping it over, small groups of us sat or knelt on our belongings for the ride as each man paddled and poled his passengers for about two hours down the river.

The banks were crammed with overhanging vines and thick foliage. I tried not to imagine what beasts lurked just under the surface of the opaque water, bright green algae lacing the edges. It was challenging enough for me to sit in a crouched position for such a long time and another feat to unfold my body again as we disembarked on a muddy edge of the river.

Just when I thought our journey was finally finished, the men showed us how to hold our bags up on our heads in order to walk the rest of the way. At least it was a relief to move my limbs.

We started out walking in ankle-deep water along the river's edge but soon took a path that led us away from the water. For what seemed like two hours more we walked on pathways of rocks, dust and dirt, fronds of colorful flowers and plants tickling our legs and sandaled feet. The mosquitoes descended upon us like the purple flying monkeys in *The Wizard of Oz*.

Upon finally reaching the home of the Q'eqchi' (Kekchi) tribe, we saw a clearing with huts and fire circles sheltered under the dense jungle canopy—a paradise of enormous flowers and plants I had never imagined possible. Even more beautiful than Kauai. The Q'eqchi' people were gracious and giving; they motioned for us to sit down on logs and tree stumps and heaped ceramic bowls with mounds of delicious sticky brown rice and black bean paste.

One of the men who had paddled was bilingual in Spanish and Q'eqchi', and was our only translator. I was a little embarrassed to tell him that I needed to pee in the worst way and had to find a bathroom fast, but there was no way around it, so I quietly asked him where I could go.

Leaning over to whisper my request to one of the women, he translated my request into the Q'eqchi' language. I heard the women chatter, and then burst into uproarious laughter. It wasn't funny to me; I had to pee!

A torrential tropical rainstorm began just as a woman approached me and beckoned for me to follow her. She led me to a banana tree, where she removed one enormous leaf, and then led me to a tree a little ways away and motioned for me to squat while she held the banana-leaf *paraguas* (umbrella) over my head. Relief! The *paraguas* leaf folded in on itself as the rain pounded on my head, plastering my hair down and making it impossible for me to focus through my fogged-up glasses. I could actually see better without them by this point, so I tucked them into my bra.

As I was finishing my task, I noticed a group of giggling children peeping out from behind a nearby tree. I would later learn that the children were laughing not because my butt was exposed but because they had never before seen skin the color of clouds. Their skin was the color of coffee.

The sun eventually came out and dried our clothes. There would be no need to wash clothing by hand that week.

After an evening meal of tasty boiled plantains wrapped in banana leaves and more black beans topped with white cheese, our hosts served us delicious goat meat flavored with burning hot chile that warmed the heart and cleared the sinuses. Already I felt like I had gained five pounds.

Golden spears of evening light thrust their warmth through the dense forest canopy as we sat on fallen logs around a roaring fire and sang songs in Spanish for the Q'eqchi' and they sang their native songs for us. What a beautiful exchange! The light had long since faded and our cloud-white skin had become a sumptuous meal for the evening shift of mosquito hordes swarming around us by the time we finished.

Our translator informed us that the women in our group were to sleep on the dirt floor in the chapel, a small structure with walls of small tree trunks two to three inches in diameter bound together with vines. Branches and sheets of banana leaves thatched the roof, effectively keeping out the torrential afternoon rains. An altar raised up onto a few rocks graced the front of the room; upon it sat a wooden cross and communion cups waiting for the next Eucharistic feast.

Making sure that no little eyes could see me through the window openings, each night I carefully took the blue-flowered plastic tablecloth that covered the altar and laid it on the floor so as not to sleep directly on the dirt. Each night I shared that altar covering with my teammate, Jessica. During the night I would sleep pressed close to her, not fully aware of what I was doing or of how she might feel about it. In the morning, when she awoke, she would push me to one side and I'd say that I was sorry, that I had accidentally rolled into her. I could not admit my craving to feel the touch of a woman's body next to mine in the night.

My ministry had become my identity. I clung to it as tightly as the thorns cling to the stem of a rose, but in grasping the stem, I was bloodying my hands. Losing control of what I knew made me feel like I was losing control of everything. Pain and shame were trying to speak to me, but I didn't know how to listen.

Years later, I would find several journal entries written during those months:

> *Now we're in Honduras. I feel a void within me. I fill it with activity and chatter. Each day I wake up here in Tegucigalpa with dread. I don't know what the dread is, though. I take a brisk run in the chilly morning air. My stomach clenches with uncertainty at lunchtime. I'm just hungry. I'll fill up with spicy tamales. Yum. I'm glad I don't vomit so much anymore.*
>
> *I ride the bus daily for hours. The Hondurans struggle to live each day. Babies wrapped in rebozos [blankets] wound around their mother's bodies. Chickens cluck wildly, struggling to escape the confines of the cloth bags sitting on women's laps. Men stand on weary legs. Their weathered hands steady themselves on the bar overhead as the bus lurches forward in spits and starts. I clutch anything to keep my balance. No seats left. I usually stare out the window. I'm still working on holding a book in one hand to read on the bus. That's what Kev Davis does. I feel so tired. Goodnight.*

The next day I wrote some more:

Tonight heat is rising up my right leg like a ribbon of fire, searing and stabbing. I have to shift and turn in my soft, lumpy bed. Better to sleep on the floor. Fold the bedcovers into a strip to cushion my bones from the hardness of the concrete. I'm never comfortable. Too much pain. I don't have trouble sleeping because I'm so fatigued all the time. Survive! Pretend there's no pain. Put on a happy face. Be cheerful, sensitive and kind to others. Don't take too many Tylenol tomorrow.

I know God has called me to be here, but I'm homesick. How I wish that M were here with me. Lying together. Sleeping together. I miss you M.

I made no space inside myself to recognize the emotional pain interwoven with my physical discomfort at the time. I lived like I had little brush fires dancing up my legs, along my back, and around my neck—fires that sent flares flying from my eyes and fierce words spewing from my mouth.

My pain was screaming at me through my nerve endings. It was eroding my fragile inner spirit. And pain can only wait so long. A volcanic eruption can't wait; it just spews out hot lava when the time comes. My pain would soon burn me up with a vengeance. But I wasn't paying attention. I missed all the warning signs.

CHAPTER 7
WOUNDED

Our time in Honduras was done. Back in our VW van, we drove north for twelve days, through Central America and back to Mexico, to join the 1981 summer Spearhead group. On the way, we enjoyed visits to the ancient Mayan ruins of Copán in Honduras and the ruins of Tikal in Guatemala.

During those countless hours in the van, I wondered why my right leg burned as if a firebrand had been stuck through the bottom of my foot. Most of the time I was wedged between Kev and Tamara in the middle bench seat, hoping to distract myself from my discomfort with my enjoyment of their friendship. Even if I wiggled my leg, rubbed it, or even stood and walked to take a needed break, the searing pain persisted from my foot up to my waist.

That summer marked the last months of my three-year Spearhead commitment. I felt confident that I was a highly effective leader, and often reminded others of this fact. Back in Mexico City, the mission director, Gordon Everett, chose me to assume a huge responsibility: coordinator of the ten team leaders for the fifty new summer recruits. My assignment was daunting, yet I tackled my task with gusto, determined to prove to the world that my talents were indispensable.

In an unconscious attempt to alleviate my growing emotional pain, I sought out those with whom I could laugh heartily. Alan Yale, a beach bum from Southern California, who gifted me with a Spanish grammar book, *Knowing the Naughty*—which taught me that the word *fuck* is said differently in each Latin American country—was one of those people. Our evangelical mission group certainly hadn't taught us these Spanish variations. Using these words during our free time gave us the pleasure of engaging in

47

impish but harmless behavior. We didn't dare share our new vocabulary with Mr. Everett.

One evening, I went to a fair at Chapultepec Park in the central part of Mexico City to eat *perros calientes* (hot dogs) and enjoy the rides with Alan and Patrick Dell, a guy from Berkeley. Remembering the fun I had as a kid, I immediately spotted the *montaña rusa*, a lightning-fast roller coaster that looked higher than Mexico City's Popocatépetl, the volcanic peak we could easily see to the southeast on a clear day.

"Let's get on the very first car so we can peer over the edge as we go down!" Patrick yelled through the din of tamale and taquito vendors, loud *corrido* music, and a million Mexicans.

As I climbed aboard the miniature car and looked in vain for a buckle where the seat belt should have been, a little voice screeched inside my head, *Hey, Stupid. Your right leg has a ribbon of fire down to your ankle.*

I ignored it.

"Alaaan!" I screamed, flailing my hand as if swatting flies. "Over here!" We three jammed our bodies inside the tiny, wheeled box—the first car—and seconds later, the creaky little vehicle click-clacked its wheels up, up, and up.

When it crested the highest hill on earth, I looked downward. *Yes!* It paused for just a second, and then—*Wheee!*—the segmented snake plummeted to the bottom, where a hairpin curve thrust us upwards again, mashing our butts against the hard wooden seat.

At that moment, my brain seemed to have left my body and was floating above us. I could see myself below with my two crazy friends screaming and laughing hysterically as the little train continued its wild and dangerous journey around the track. But the brain above wasn't laughing. Dread was filling it up like a balloon about to pop.

"Wasn't that fun?" Patrick grinned at me and dragged me by the hand to lead me to our next ride.

"I think I lost my hair barrette." My tousled long red hair draped over my eyes. "I have to find it. Right now." I scanned the littered ground under the trestle of the little train.

"Just forget it. It's lost." Alan gripped my swaying shoulders to steady me. "Hey. You okay?" He was looking right into my face but I didn't recall seeing him.

I commanded my feet to take steps. "Can we go home now?" I weakly managed.

⌒ℓℓℯ

I have no recollection of what happened over the next couple of hours following that moment. Later, I would learn that sometimes when a person goes into shock, they experience it as an out-of-body feeling.

Arriving at home later that evening, in contrast, I had an acute *in*-body feeling. Exploding fireworks illumined the sky inside my cranium.

The impact of the little car's descent and hairpin upswing had burst my already bulging L4-5 and my L5-S1 lumbar disks, just below my waistline. But I didn't know that quite yet.

During the night I cried and screamed in pain, my voice unheard by my Mexican host family in their main house. My little rented quarters, the servant's room, was set apart.

In the morning, I managed to scoot across the floor, close enough to reach the phone, and I called the family to ask them to take me to a doctor. I had never experienced so much pain.

They took me to the American British Hospital in downtown Mexico City. "The doctors are good," they said. "Educated in the USA."

At the hospital, I watched the bright ceiling lights whiz past. My wheeled gurney, guided by two green-gloved hands, sped down the narrow corridor. Dizziness engulfed me.

An enormous mosquito injected my spine with a proboscis full of dye.

A huge eyeball looked inside my bones.

A white coat said, "Lumbar laminectomy as soon as possible. Two discs exploded on impact."

A plastic cup sucked on my face. The bright lights faded away. Blackness. Nothing.

Until a familiar voice screamed, "Get me out of here!" Frantic hands grasped at a knot of venomous vipers coming out of my face. "Help me!" the voice cried. "Snakes!"

A disembodied voice called from a distant fog, "But she wasn't *supposed* to wake up in the middle of the procedure and pull those breathing tubes out of her throat."

The gurney ride again. The lights flickered on and off this time.

More screaming.

Another voice saying, "Sorry, the sheet ripped under you when we tried to transfer you from the gurney. You didn't fall very far."

Then a white triangle saying, "I don't even have to know your room number. I just follow the sound of the screams."

I opened my eyes for a few moments and saw a black-and-white TV suspended in the corner of the room. A drugged voice I vaguely recognized said, "I want to watch the wedding." It was July 29, 1981. I was referring to Princess Diana and Prince Charles's wedding.

Valium was my best friend. A week of torment and hallucinations followed.

In my unstable condition following the surgery I wasn't able to return to the United States for several weeks.

～ﻞﺲ

It would take me years to grasp the degree of emotional pain I endured during my years in Latin America. My attempts to conceal my *homosexual proclivities* had made me so fragile that my body shattered into pieces. The loss of the love of my life, the fear of my attraction to women, the pressure of performance, the absence of self-confidence, and now the searing physical pain of my broken lumbar discs plummeted me over the precipice.

I would later discover that the roller coaster had not caused my catastrophic physical carnage as much as the botched Mexican surgery had. Maybe those "doctors from the USA" had failed their board certification exams back home.

Whatever the case, there would never be a way to reverse the damage.

We all experience different types of pain in our lives. Sometimes it crashes on the shore like a big wave and then recedes. At other times, the waves continue crashing, offering no relief. Pain takes a lot of time and energy.

I was thirty-one. My future would never be what I had hoped. Following that back surgery, I would have to make various ergonomic modifications to help manage pain so as to limit my use of medication. I would have to curtail sports I loved to play, limit travel, and learn to use the term "handicapped."

I would also become an expert at self-flagellation. *You idiot. Why'd you get on the roller coaster in the first place if you already had a bit of a back problem?* All my self-criticism, the *shoulds* and *shouldn'ts*, couldn't ease any of the pain.

Someone once told me that physical maladies—a broken leg, a cold, even cancer—could be a result of deep-seated emotional/spiritual dis-ease. I'd always thought that ideas like that were nonsense. In my case, that yellow suitcase of mine was too heavy, and contributed to my herniated lumbar disks. The damn roller coaster was too high! The Mexican doctors were incompetent! Get it?

No, I didn't get it. Not then.

It would take me another couple of decades to admit that my broken lumbar discs may well have been related to my struggle with my sexual orientation. At the time, if anyone had suggested this connection to me, I would have rejected the idea as preposterous.

When I was well enough, I returned to California, where I spent a paltry three weeks before embarking on a master's program. I continued to be careless about my body's limitations, and to complain about them.

Eventually, I ditched the yellow suitcase, but I continued to haul a thousand pounds of deceit and denial and shame around with me, like a ball and chain, for years to come.

CHAPTER 8

HOME AGAIN

I don't know how I managed to endure sitting on a flight from Mexico City, but I did. I planned to stay a few weeks at my parents' house to rest before beginning my graduate studies.

My mother and father met me at the LAX airport. Their faces were ashen and serious as they beheld their broken daughter standing next to the baggage carousel. My big yellow suitcase had gone around hundreds of times before they arrived, but just staring at it hadn't lifted it off the belt.

My father grunted under its weight as he picked it up and set it on the floor. "We're so glad that you're home and finally free of that back pain." He gave me a gentle side hug.

"We got your telegram after we arrived in Germany," my mother said. "Thanks for being sensitive to us on our trip. If we had known you were going to have surgery in Mexico, we would have gotten a plane out of Barcelona and gone directly to Mexico City." She gently rubbed my shoulders and brushed her hand down my back. The lines on her face betrayed her worry for me.

I had withheld the news of my surgery from my parents, knowing that it would spoil their vacation in Europe. The last week of July, they had gone to Spain to visit Montserrat for a few days and then flown to Germany to spend a week with Thomas and his family. He was still working with Inter-Varsity Christian Fellowship there. I had sent a telegram to him so he could share the information with my folks when they arrived at his house. I would later learn that they had wept and prayed together for me, and that Thomas had been especially comforting to them, as I'd hoped he would be.

Still standing near the baggage carousel, I explained how things unfolded.

"Everything happened so fast, I had to have the surgery right away. My back still hurts a lot, but I'm sure it will be fine after a few weeks."

"I'll go get the car and drive it closer," my dad said, and hurried off.

He returned a few minutes later, hoisted up my battered yellow suitcase, overstuffed with all that I owned, and carried it outside. My mother gently wrapped her arm around me and guided my steps out to the waiting car. My dad had put a camping cushion in the back of their Volvo station wagon so I could lie down.

I wished my mind could switch off the relentless, stabbing pain, but it had settled in to stay like an uninvited, angry mother-in-law.

⁓

My parents had always been present for me. As a young woman, when I brought home girlfriends instead of boyfriends to introduce them to, they'd been gracious and friendly, never asking too many questions. During college, when the 1970 riots happened and Kent State University was closed, I'd had a home to shelter me from the storm. When I had to confirm my final decision regarding the mission to Mexico, my father had traveled from Santa Barbara to Columbus, Ohio, my home then, to discuss it personally with me.

About two months before I was born, Thomas, just a toddler at the time, had almost died from drinking a deadly poison. Curious, he had wandered out of the gate for just a moment, found a little bottle near the trashcan, and drank it down. Carbon tetrachloride.

My mother heard his choking sounds and rushed outside to find him unconscious. My parents were fraught with fear, not knowing if their firstborn would live or die. It was 1949.

"Your little boy is not responsive at all." The doctor's voice, dry and steady, was hardly comforting to my mother. "He will be severely impaired if he lives. Pray that he will die. Maybe you can have another child as soon as possible." The doctor's dull eyes stared at the pile of papers on his desk as his fingers fiddled with folders and files.

Beneath his messy desk, my mother's hand fluttered to caress the bulge under her black linen dress. She felt she couldn't breathe. She leaned forward in her chair and inhaled enough of the stuffy air to say, "I *will* have another child. In six weeks! Haven't you noticed I am pregnant?" She rose to her feet and, attempting to hold in her sobs of despair, bolted from the small office.

For two weeks, she visited the hospital, begging God for her firstborn son to be spared. "Our Father, which art in heaven . . . *Thy will* . . . No!" She wasn't even able to even say those words. But finally, several weeks later, when she was able to choke out, "*Thy will be done*," something miraculous happened.

The doctor phoned. "Mrs. Smith? Your little boy has rolled over in his bed and is crying normally. He seems to have snapped out of it. He can go home now."

After a frantic drive to Alta Bates Hospital in Berkeley, California, my mother burst through the doors, dashed down the hallway and into his room.

Her precious toddler was up on wobbly legs, holding on to the rail. "Mommy up," he pleaded, reaching for her waiting embrace.

Her fearful tears had been all used up during those previous weeks. Now she wept copious tears of gratitude as a little voice whispered, "No cwy, Mommy. No cwy."

Four weeks later, I would be born.

When I was old enough to understand, my mother told me this story, explaining that when I came into the world, my parents felt like they had experienced two births: Thomas had been reborn from sickness into life. I had been born just because I was.

She also told me that she had looked forward the chance to do mother-daughter activities with her little girl that she could not do with her sons (In addition to Thomas I had an even older brother, Kobe, a son from my father's previous marriage who my mother had adopted). She had high hopes, she said, that in time she could make me into a pretty little girl.

After the grueling trek on the freeway from LAX to Santa Barbara, I lay on the floor in my parents' family room, in too much pain to sit in a chair.

We Smiths, at least, were never at a loss for words. We could tell stories to each other until the cows came home and the sun had set.

"On the mission in Mexico were you allowed to wear pants?" my mother asked.

"Usually, it was just too hot, Mom," I answered from the floor. "Only skirts or dresses. No pants at all. We weren't even allowed to wear shorts. I always wore those wraparound skirts you made for me before I left. They came in quite handy."

My mother began to chuckle. "I remember when you were a little girl called Shawnee I could barely get you into a dress!"

"Oh, come on. Really?" I smiled.

She laughed and shook her head. "Yes, really!" She began to tell a story of the time in 1955 when I tore off my frilly yellow dress.

I laughed. Now I recalled that incident. "I always thought those darn fancy dresses were too scratchy, anyway."

⁓⧫⁓

My five-year-old voice could have shattered the chandelier overhead. "Mommy! Pleeease don't make me!"

"Honey, we're going to church. C'mon, Shawnee. Get your pink panties pulled up. Now up, up with those arms. Yes. I'll pull your yellow dress down over your head like this..."

"Stop!" I wailed. "It makes me itch. Like when I had those welts on me." I tried to squirm away.

"Those welts were the hives. This dress won't give you the hives, for heaven's sake!" She yanked the dress down over my flailing body.

As soon as it was on, I sprinted away, tore it off, and flung it onto the floor. Then, wearing only my pink panties, I dashed down the stairs to the basement, figuring that this was the perfect time to finish constructing my toy boat. My brother and I often made our own toys out of wood, using our father's vise, a small saw, a kid-size hammer, and nails.

When I heard the clomping of my mother's high heels coming down the basement steps, I scrunched into a ball under the worktable. *She'll never find me here*, I thought.

Two swats on my frilly pink bottom got me moving upstairs again, and another swat convinced me to let her cram the dress back over my head.

"Why do I have to wear dresses?" I complained. "Tommy doesn't have to."

"Maybe this afternoon you can play nicely with your little friend Sally," my mother said. "She will have a pretty dress on today too. Maybe playing together will help you act more like a g—"

"I don't care about Sally. She's a girl! She's dumb," I stated matter-of-factly.

Sighing, my mother simply offered her hand so we could walk together to church. I had on my yellow dress, but my hair looked like a rat's nest.

I held on tightly to her strong hand. I knew that she loved me. She held me on her lap. She read me bedtime stories. She scratched my back. She smiled. She laughed. She was a happy Mommy.

And I was a happy daughter.

Sometimes.

Somewhere within the hollows of my little-girl self I sensed that something inside was terribly wrong. I had no words to describe it. I wanted to play like a boy, fight like a boy, wear Thomas's hand-me-down clothes, and I would scratch like a wild baby tiger when my mother tried to dress me in girl-clothes.

I wonder what direction my life could have taken had I been born three or even four decades later than I had been? What if, as a second-grader, my parents had read to me the children's book, *Is*

That For a Boy or a Girl? by the transgender author S. Bear Bergman? What kinds of conversations would my parents and I have had knowing that this author believed in God, just like we did?

What could my world have been like if those courageous people who call themselves "transgender" had been the presence they are today when I was a little girl? Those people who experience a coming home to themselves, a metamorphosis to align their bodies with their true being? Those people who have a medical procedure called "Gender Confirmation Surgery"? How might things have been different for me?

Who could I have become?

CHAPTER 9

TOMBOY

I was still hanging around on the family room floor, chatting with my mom, when she asked, "Sharon, hand me that basket of sewing stuff, will you?" My mother often did mending while we talked. She was preparing to fix a frayed collar on one of my dad's brown plaid shirts.

I watched her quick movements and noticed how the veins on her wiry hands still popped out. "Mom, I love your hands."

"Why do you say that, honey?" She held out both her hands, turning them over and over. "They've got bigger veins than the Mississippi River." She laughed softly.

"I like how they look," I said. "Remember when I used to poke at them? Like this?" I reached to get a hold of her left hand to squish a vein.

"Stop that!" She swatted me away, chuckling.

It was 1955. Rushing to get to church on time, my mother had forgotten to put on her glasses.

"Mommy!" I cried. "What's wrong with your face? I'm not going to church with you looking like somebody else." I froze in place, my feet glued to the shady sidewalk.

Still holding my hand, she bent down to my level and said, "You should see what *you* look like without my glasses on." She smiled and laughed a little as she straightened back up.

I didn't think anything was funny, and I wailed loudly as she dragged me along, my black patent leather Mary Janes scuffing along.

We squeezed into a crowded pew and she wrapped her big hand around my tiny one. I pressed on a fat blue vein on the back of her hand until it got bigger and bigger. It looked like it would burst! I pressed until the blue river emptied out, then let go and watched it fill up again. At least her hands looked the same, even if her face looked different.

When we were home again, she perched me on her lap and put on her glasses. "Better?" she asked, facing me.

I smiled. "Yes, Mommy. When you let me play with the blue rivers on your hands, I always feel better."

"Remember, I will always be here to comfort you when you need it."

"I'll remember, Mommy." I wished I were Baby Roo so I could climb inside my mother Kanga's pouch.

Now, after my back injury, I needed my mother's comfort once again.

"That story about your hands always makes me get emotional, Mom," I whispered from my place on the floor near her.

Just then the light caught a glint in my mother's eye. Was it a tear?

Without saying a word, she finished up her little sewing task and went to the kitchen to prepare lunch. "Stan?" she called. "Your shirt's mended now. I'm making some turkey sandwiches. Want avocado?"

"No thanks. Never did like it much," responded my father from his makeshift desk in the corner of the room.

"Ha!" I called from my position on the floor. "I used to hate that stuff. Love it now, especially after eating all those Mexican avocados." I got up and started setting places at the dining room table for our lunch.

"Do you guys remember the story of when I first tasted avocado at Uncle Frank's dinner table?" I asked.

"Yes, I remember hearing about it," my mom's voice drifted out from the kitchen. "Stan and I had parked you and Thomas at Uncle Frank's avocado farm in Camarillo when we went on vacation to Japan in 1958. Didn't you have a little run-in with Grandma and her sisters?"

My dad interjected, "Tell us the story again. It's a doozy."

"Yeeech..." I crossed my eyes to try to see what I had on my tongue, which was thrust out as far as Fisherman's Wharf in San Francisco. "Dis duff taesh like shoap." I grabbed an embroidered cloth napkin beside my plate and chucked the green glob into it. Wiping my mouth on my sleeve I said, more clearly, "This stuff tastes like soap."

"Mind your manners," Grandma Lula told me, straightening the laced collar of her flowered dress. A discussion amongst my great-aunts ensued regarding how a young lady should act at the dining room table.

"Young lady," Grandma Lula said, frowning so hard I thought her white eyebrows would touch in the middle. "You may not spit that out." I always wondered why her eyebrows weren't blue. Her hair was.

I sat tall in my chair, chin up. "Already spitted it out. In the napkin. Besides, my name is Sharon. Not 'Young Lady.' I'm big now. I am eight years old." I unwadded the napkin. "See?"

Aunt Lora pushed my napkin down with one hand as she patted her stiffly sprayed, purple-hued hair with the other. "We don't want to see it. It's called avocado. All you have to say is, 'No thank you' next time."

Tears spilled into the uneaten mashed potatoes and gravy on my plate. I kept my words tucked in under my chin. "I love my grandma and everybody, but I miss my mommy and daddy."

Uncle Frank reached over and fluffed the back of my already messy, tangled red hair. "After dinner, I'll need some help outside." His blue eyes crinkled at the corners in his very round face; his bald head was as smooth as a bowling ball. "You'll need to change into some old jeans and a long-sleeved sweatshirt. You can't work on a farm in a dress, can you?"

Maybe Uncle Frank understood that I loved wearing *boy* clothes. *He* never brushed my hair. *Never* put me in a dress for church. He just liked me the way I was. Just me!

I ran upstairs to change into Thomas's old pants and a T-shirt my mother had packed for me for such an occasion. After dashing down the stairs two at a time I announced, "Readyyy!" and laughed freely. "Don't say anything important while I'm outside," I called in to the dining room crowd.

Uncle Frank and I would pick a thousand avocados that day.

Sixty years later I would discover several letters between my grand-mother, great aunts, and my mother that expressed their consterna-tion with me. The correspondence was dated 1952. I was only two years old at the time. My relatives loved me, but they could see something unusual about me and none of them had the vocabulary to name it. My family had no framework to know what to make of a little girl who wanted to be a boy.

When I went out with my uncle to pick avocados, I imagine that they talked about me when I wasn't in the room. The scene might have played out like this:

"What is going to become of this little girl?" Aunt Lilly asked, squinting through her thick, wire-rimmed glasses. "She acts like a boy and wears her brother's clothes every time she gets a chance." She wagged her head from side to side.

Grandma Lula's voice cracked a bit. "When Sharon was only two I took care of her and her brothers for a spell." She cleared her throat. "She wouldn't let me put a dress on her. She wouldn't let me brush her hair. I wrote to her mother, Bernell, telling her that she should arrange play dates with the little girl next door. It doesn't appear that the *girl* rubbed off on Sharon at all." She dabbed at her eyes with her embroidered napkin.

Uncle Red, whose hair was wavy and redder than mine, said, "She'll grow out of it soon enough. Don't worry so much."

Aunt Lora clucked her tongue. "Just wait until she's a teenager. Some young man will sweep her off her pretty feet. She'll change."

Grandma Lula quickly finished the conversation when she heard me stamping the dirt off my shoes out on the back porch. "She looks so much like a boy now," she whispered. "There's got to be a little girl inside, waiting to come out."

In Santa Barbara, sitting at the table at my parents' house, I finished telling that story. It felt good to express these things with my parents, even though I still didn't understand what the implications were. I told myself that I still had some growing up to do, and that hopefully I'd meet the right man to marry at seminary and all this boy vs. girl confusion would get ironed out.

My father swept the crumbs of his turkey-without-avocado sandwich into his hand and said, "I still don't like avocados to this day." He lifted his eyebrows. "Are you still a tomboy, Sharon?" He chuckled his deep little chuckle.

I didn't like that one bit.

My father had a talent for lancing words with laser-beam accuracy. As a little kid, those words carved holes in my self-esteem. Even as an adult, my mind was still all a-jumble with questions about my gender and why I acted like a guy sometimes. Because of that, I detested the label "tomboy," but somehow my family had a way of always bringing it up.

My father could be so loving at times, but belittling at others. During those moments I would construct a high wall and hope against hope that no one climbed up a ladder and peeked over.

With shame I recalled my friendship with Montserrat, and how we had behaved while alone in that pup tent on our camping trip. I also remembered my anger toward Melody, my roomie that first summer in Mexico. What was it that she could have known? I hoped that my parents couldn't see the parts of me that I felt I still needed to hide. But as my mom and dad, couldn't they see right over my wall, no matter how high I built it?

As a kid, playing hide-and-seek was always one of my favorites, especially on a hot summer evening. It was thrilling to crouch in a cramped crevice just under an overhang on the side of our brick house, sure that no one would find me.

One summer in 1962, when my little brother Greg was about four and I was twelve, we let him play with us. He would hide for six seconds, then run out.

"You have to stay hidden!" I chastised him.

"I want to know if somebody's coming," he said.

"Greg," I explained, "if you don't want the other kids to see you, then you have to hide."

"Doesn't matter," he called as he scrambled out over the lawn. "They can see me anyway!"

It would take him a couple more years to learn to hide. I already knew how.

As a young child I hadn't cared so much about the reactions of others. I'd been aware that I was different, yes, but not until I was about twelve did fear become a part of my fabric, like a bright red thread woven into the tapestry of my life. I was under the impression that I could hide from others, but maybe I was really hiding from myself.

CHAPTER 10
ONWARD AND UPWARD

During those few weeks at my parents' home in Santa Barbara, I felt stronger every day. I was glad that my new orthopedic doctor had put me into a corset-like back brace so I could actually sit, stand, and walk.

"Do you realize, Sharon, that you've made some pretty good decisions on your own?" my father said one night as we relaxed in the living room.

"What do you mean?" I asked.

"College, a job, Mexico, now grad school at Fuller Theological Seminary. Sometimes I'm proud of you." He smoothed back the reddish curls above his untamed eyebrows with his hand.

Only sometimes?

"Thanks, Dad," I said. "I've appreciated your perspective when decisions were hard for me. Gads! Look at those eyebrows of yours!" I needed to find a little humor to deflect the sting of the word *sometimes.*

I watched him extend one eyebrow hair out about two full inches. He stood and headed towards the bathroom. "Come here," he beckoned to me. "Look at this one!"

I grabbed a ruler from his desk to measure it. "Three inches and a half!" I exclaimed. "Mom, look at this! Dad's gonna go blind when these copper wires coming out of his forehead poke out his eyeballs!"

Mom and I laughed like silly teenagers while Dad leaned closer into the mirror, searching for another hair gone wild.

Family members and even friends often commented on how much I resembled my dad: freckle-faced, red hands, red hair, and bushy eyebrows. Unfortunately, his critical spirit had a way of displaying itself through me as well. The Spearhead volunteers I'd worked with in Latin America over the previous three years could certainly attest to that.

I fluffed my own red hair with my hand. "It was Kev Davis from Spearhead who convinced me to consider Fuller Seminary. Honestly, I feel scared that I won't be able to keep up with the work."

My mom's voice wafted in from the kitchen. "You're a lot smarter than you think. Just make sure you don't waste so much time like you did when you went to Taylor University." She shook her head and laughed softly. "You failed a few classes back then, didn't you?"

It was true: as a seventeen-year-old college freshman, my grades had been even worse than they had been in high school. I resented her bringing this up again. I wasn't feeling too good about myself this evening for some reason. As my mom reminisced about my bad grades, my mind started to whir with reruns of several sexual encounters I'd had as a teen—stories that I would never share with my parents.

⁓

I chose Taylor University because my friend Lilly Kvork, from Cleveland Heights, was going there. When she and I arrived at Taylor, however, we realized that we'd been assigned to different dorm rooms.

We were just freshmen then—still "wet behind the ears," as the sophomores liked to remind us. Lilly was pretty and feminine, quite unlike me. We had hoped to be roommates because we had been best buddies in our Baptist youth group.

I quickly settled into my room and skittered across campus to see Lilly's room. "Nice job!" I praised her. "I like how you arranged your stuff. Which bunk bed is yours?"

As soon as she pointed to the top one, I jumped up there and beckoned for her to join me, and we began giving each other backrubs.

"Aaah, a little to the left, up, that's it." She sighed. "You're really good at this, Sharon. We should invite other gals in the dorm to enjoy this too."

Soon, my services were in demand. Sitting on a girl's butt as she lay face down worked best. Sometimes my hands slipped down the sides just a little bit, but of course that must have been by accident—at least, that's what I'd tell myself.

The first time I'd become aware that another girl turned me on sexually was at a high school summer camp. Through back rubbing, arm rubbing, and feet rubbing exchanges, another girl and I had pulled ourselves into an arena of forbidden feelings that I just didn't know how to handle. I'd managed to convince myself back then that I was only sweaty because it was a humid day.

I didn't know if Lilly Kvork felt sexually aroused by our back-rubs but I certainly was. If she felt something, she sure hid it well. I certainly hoped that my feelings would never be discovered by anyone.

I was a music major at Taylor, and I enjoyed playing clarinet in the marching band. One afternoon during practice, the guy sitting in the back row poked me with his trombone slide.

"Hey! Watch it! You hit me!" I twirled around in my seat in the rehearsal room to stare down the offender.

A pimply face, greasy hair, thick glasses, and a warm smile over crooked teeth peeked out from behind the trombone bell. "Hey, Miss Clarinet. What's your name? I'm Paul."

"I'm Sharon," I said, blushing and fiddling with my clarinet reed.

After rehearsal, he said, "Want to go for a bike ride this Saturday?"

Paul Sinclair's laugh was infectious. It was easy to feel attracted to him because of his interest in sports, bicycling, and other outdoor activities. And during our first semester, most of my girlfriends had found boyfriends—even Lilly (I was so jealous). So I figured, why not? Soon, we began to date.

Not having dated much in high school, I wasn't used to being with a guy. I enjoyed Paul's company, and it helped me to feel what I thought was normal. Listening to stories from my girlfriends, I knew it was normal to kiss and fondle boys. So, one evening, I agreed to go *parking* off campus in Paul's car. I'd experienced that with Charlie when I was fifteen, but I hoped things would be different this time, three years later.

They were. Paul wanted us to get to know each other, so we talked a lot. I appreciated that. I enjoyed hearing his stories about working on a farm with his father, and other adventures of rural Indiana life. And when, after we'd been sitting and talking for a while in his car, Paul asked if it was okay to touch me before trying anything.

I told him yes. He was tentative and slow. I liked his respectful manner. When he began fondling my breasts, he proclaimed, "A handful is enough."

I would carry that statement with me for years, happy that my small breast size was just fine.

Even though Paul's face was scratchy instead of smooth like Lilly's, I managed to acquire the ability to enjoy kissing him. This was the first time I had actually explored the fascinating things a guy's body offered. Sitting together in his red GTO convertible, his bulge would grow, especially when I rubbed it. One night I thought I had peed in my pants, but actually it was my first orgasm. Ever. Paul explained that to me after I freaked out.

One late evening in his GTO, we got quite involved petting, and time flew away from us. It was 2:00 a.m., four hours after curfew, when Paul walked me to my dorm. When I rang the bell, the Dorm Matron, whom we called Miss Pit Bull, yanked open the huge wooden door.

"Go to your room!" she barked. "First thing in the morning you must report to the Dorm Council. Goodnight!"

In the morning I awoke to a loud rapping on my door. It was Miss Pit Bull. In the light I noticed that it really did look like she had bowling pins for arms with five little stubs at each end, just as I'd heard other gals in the dorm giggling about before. I followed her down the hall, watching her rump jiggle like Jell-O that had been left in the fridge too long.

The Gestapo-like interrogation lasted an hour in a miniscule, stuffy, dim-lit room, each council member wanting to hear juicy details about what I had been doing in my boyfriend's car.

I answered their queries with silence.

One council member, with big shoulders and huge breasts, stood up and glowered at me. "You have to answer every question or your punishment will be more severe. Get it?" Her huge ass made a noise like a fart when she plopped it back into her narrow chair.

I remained silent. Miss Pit Bull waved at me with her left bowling pin, barking, "You are grounded for six weeks! You can go to classes, the library, dining hall, and that's it."

It wasn't what I'd call an encouraging learning environment. I would only last two years at Taylor University. And even though I would date Paul during those entire two years, I would also continue to spend time in the dorm with my girlfriends, giving and receiving much-desired backrubs and also taking afternoon *naps* with Lilly. The sexual attraction I felt toward her could not be acted upon, of course, but it did have the effect of arousing a sexual fire that I funneled into my time with Paul.

That said, I also spent a lot of energy tamping down the guilt that was building inside me like an underground fissure needing release.

༺❦༻

From his desk area in their Santa Barbara home, my father's voice broke through my private musings. I felt some relief that my parents couldn't read my thoughts.

"When do your seminary classes at Fuller begin?" he asked. "We can drive you down."

"Next Monday," I said. "Jerri Wilkins and I will be renting a room off campus in a building near Fuller. Remember her parents from your Methodist church?"

"Yes, and she's a nice kid besides." He nodded in approval. "Say, how will you get around in Pasadena?"

I shrugged. "I can ride my bike. It's only a mile."

The following week, my parents dropped me off at Fuller Seminary in Pasadena.

CHAPTER 11
BACK TO SCHOOL

"Whew! It's really hot down here in Pasadena," my dad commented as he unloaded some of my things from the Volvo.

"Where are the mountains? I thought your school was near the foothills," my mother said.

"I don't know," I said, turning 360 degrees. "They're supposed to be north, but I don't see anything." I reached for one of my bags. "I can take my stuff in just fine. Thanks for driving me here."

"Oh no you don't! You'd better take care of that back of yours," my mother cautioned. "Let us help you carry your things in."

In the end, my parents made not one but several trips into the building where I'd rented a room. It was right across from Pasadena City College, a mile east of Fuller Seminary. The San Gabriel Mountains were, in fact, to the north, but they hadn't been visible all summer. All we could see was a grey window shade pulled down over the skyline; the smog was that thick.

When my things were safely inside, I hugged my folks, said a quick "Love you both!" and disappeared into my new little home.

⁓ele⁓

At Fuller, moving on with the next phase of my life, I acted as if I hadn't survived the trauma of a major surgery less than a month before. Hauling my bicycle up and down a flight of stairs every day to bike to classes did further damage to my back, as did pedaling the mile to school through the smoggy air with a backpack full of books. In fact, I constantly engaged in activities that were injurious to my body, mind, and spirit, oblivious to what it would cost me in the long run.

The first week of classes, I looked over the students sitting near me in the small lecture hall for a Systematic Theology course. I was glad to see that we were of many colors and cultures, and both men and women were well represented.

I had a lined yellow tablet and a pencil to take notes with. Even though I carried a small pillow to stuff behind me while sitting in the uncomfortable contoured plastic chairs, there were many days that I had to lie on the floor with the little pillow under my head. When my professors heard that I'd had back surgery recently they were sympathetic to my prone position in class and even congratulated me for having the tenacity to pursue an MA program after such an ordeal. Still, my hand would ache after taking notes for two hours in this position, writing uphill.

Whether I was lying down, standing or walking, if I didn't have pain in one part of my body, pain visited another part. She was my unwelcome friend. What a shame I couldn't "unfriend" her.

I was proud to have the opportunity to attend such a reputable school. Fuller Seminary, the largest such school in the United States, was a multidenominational Christian evangelical graduate school. In 1947, its founders sought to change the anti-intellectual position of traditional fundamentalism and separatist Christianity that plagued evangelical church practice from the 1920s through the 1940s. Their vision was to establish an intellectually viable graduate program—"a Caltech of the evangelical world"—in Pasadena.

Fuller students could enroll in a master's or doctoral program in theology, world missions, or psychology. I chose a master's program in Missiology, the study of being an effective missionary. When people asked me, "What is missiology?" I enjoyed saying, "It's the study of female singleness. Get it? 'Miss' plus 'ology.'" I thought that was funny. Inside my own spirit, though, I was as scared as a little rabbit. I hoped to God that no one would ever find out about my attraction to other women. I knew I had no control over who might trigger it or when it would present itself. In my own mind I called it the *sweaty-down-there* feeling, because I just couldn't name it for what it might be, though I'd struggled with this dilemma since puberty.

I feared I would never meet the husband that God must have chosen for me. *Oh God*, I pleaded silently, *will I find him here at seminary?*

Would a husband be able to erase my same-sex attraction? I certainly hoped so.

⁓⁓⁓

Because I'd spent three years in Latin America doing mission work, the Missiology Program at Fuller seemed appropriate for me. I would study the practical theology that drove the call, the gospel and the goal of the Christian church to win the world for Christ. My Spearhead group had partnered with a number of missionaries associated with the American Bible Society, a group that translated the Scriptures into languages that weren't even written languages yet. I felt excited by the challenge of learning how the science of language itself could fuel accurate yet culturally appropriate Bible translation and interpretation. At Fuller I would study linguistics and anthropology, as well as wrestle with how the church had historically failed to respect different religious practice in various cultural contexts. Energized by these goals, I felt ready to face the challenge of studying hard.

One morning in Dr. Brewster's class, The Anatomy of Language, I sat next to Duncan Mwangi, a coal-black young man from Kenya. His Swahili accent made his English a bit challenging to understand.

After class we chatted a bit while gathering up our books and I ventured, "Did you learn English in school as a child?"

"No, I didn't," he said quietly.

"When did you start? Your English is very good."

"Three months ago." His perfect white teeth gleamed behind his dark lips.

I cleared my throat, feeling like I was asking too many questions. "But this quarter started last month."

The white cowrie shells sewn to his earth-toned Kikuyu long shirt made sounds like tiny, laughing castanets. His broad chest bounced with his words. "Yes! Last summer, when I decided to come to Fuller Seminary, I started learning English!"

"What?"

My wide-eyed stare made him laugh all the more.

"You Americans don't get it, do you? I grew up speaking more than twelve languages. When you walk along the beach gathering a pocketful of pretty shells and you notice another beautiful one, you pick it up and put it into your pocket. English is just another beautiful shell."

I had no English words with which to respond.

I had many more intriguing conversations with Duncan over the months to come; over time, we became good friends.

⁓

During the early 1960s, more and more black people moved into our East Cleveland neighborhood and into our church. White flight was in full swing, but our family would stay.

One Sunday, when Pastor Taylor finished his sermon, he put both hands on the sides of his tall wooden pulpit and announced, "We have noticed that Negro people are coming to our church now. We also notice that fewer white people are attending. I can only be sure of one thing. No *real Christians* are leaving this church!"

The Lutheran church I grew up in believed that Jesus had called us to make a difference in our world. We would be involved in the civil rights movement of the 1960s. But that did not yet include an awareness of the rights of LGBTQ+ people.

⁓

I hoped going to Fuller Seminary would fulfill my dream of becoming someone who would make a difference in the church, whether as a pastor, a lay worker, or some kind of missionary or activist. During my time with Spearhead, I'd seen many women pastors and leaders. Fuller seemed like the right place to be right now.

One semester, I met Finja Vogel in Professor Heibert's Anthropology and Mission class. Another woman on her way to ministry! I felt a surge of happiness. That afternoon at the bicycle stand, we began our first conversation.

"So you ride a bike to school too," I began as I secured several books on my rack with a bungee cord. My backpack on my back was already full. "I'm Sharon."

"I recognize you from class. My name's Finja. From Germany." Her curly, light brown hair fell over her pink face as she bent to unlock her bike and adjust her backpack on her bike's rear rack.

We exchanged pleasantries and then had lunch together the next day.

My friendship with Finja grew quickly. Because she had no family to go to in the States for holidays, I invited her to come with me to Santa Barbara to spend vacation times with my family. As we got to know each other, I was thrilled that my body never once manifested that sexual pull when we were together. This helped to convince me that I was *normal* after all.

In another class Finja and I shared, Evangelism and Church Growth, Dr. Wagner told a little story one day:

> *The pastor came home, taking off suit and shoes, and, sitting in the living room to rest, called out, "Honey, please bring me the paper and a cold lemonade."*
>
> *The voice from the kitchen responded, "Right away, dear, just as soon as I finish feeding the baby."*
>
> *"Thanks, Ralph," said the pastor.*

Upon hearing this story we students burst into laughter. It was funny because most of us assumed that the pastor, by default, would be the husband, and the wife would be in the kitchen with the baby. This role reversal sounded quite unusual to us.

We weren't progressive enough to capture the idea that this story could have meant that there were two husbands. Or even two wives. It had taken decades for Fuller to even admit women into its ranks and train them to become pastors. The school would never become so progressive that it would accept openly gay and lesbian couples to train them for the pastorate. After all, it was evangelical; same-sex relationships, according to the people in charge, were outside the scope of correct Christian doctrine and practice.

CHAPTER 12
BLUE, NOT PINK

I learned Bible stories in Sunday school, and as a teenager I participated in Bible-Drill contests to see who had memorized the most
verses. During my time with the ultraconservative Navigators at
Kent State University, I memorized hundreds of Bible verses. And
on the mission in Mexico, I studied, taught, and preached from the
Scriptures every day. Nonetheless, when it came to being able to
comprehend the context of who had written what, when, to whom,
and for what purpose, I was pretty much in the dark. My spiritual
leaders, especially the Navigators, had often cited portions of stories
or particular teachings out of context to prove whatever point they
wanted to make about marriage, the family, women's place in the
home, sexual relations, and so on. I would later realize that this
practice, called *proof texting*, is widely used in many evangelical
groups and churches.

For thousands of years the Bible has been misinterpreted to
support the idea that women are second-class citizens and should
obey their male leaders. In my experience with the Navigators, that
kind of patriarchal teaching was of paramount importance. For
example, I Timothy 2:12 states, "I do not permit a woman to teach or
to assume authority over a man; rather, she must be quiet." Christian
men who claim to believe in a literal interpretation of the Bible use
such passages to make sure that women are not allowed in any
position of leadership—not in church activities, not in business, not
in the home. Many conservative ministers conveniently leave out the
context of the Apostle Paul's words, which were written to Timothy,
a pastor in the city of Ephesus, who was dealing with specific issues
within his congregation during the first century. Without proper
historical and cultural context, the Scriptures are worthless.

Some say that you can prove anything you want to if you can pick out the right Bible verses.

At Fuller, I would learn that the Bible had been written by hundreds of different authors to various audiences over more than a thousand years. The stories and historical records represented many cultures, epochs and languages, and didn't necessarily have only one interpretation. The teachings were not a dogmatic system meant to dictate to all people for all time a list of do's and don'ts. One of my favorite professors, Dr. Daemon Fanger, taught a course called Contextual Theology that opened my heart and mind to how the Bible's message of God's love and Jesus's life could be transformative for those who engaged with their Creator.

I was glad I took Dr. Fanger's class during my first semester at Fuller, in 1981, because it helped me understand the other theological courses I went on to take during my three-year master's program. Dr. Fanger would shout, "Who wrote this letter to Timothy? Why did Timothy need to hear these words? What was the church's problem at that time? Why did they get into such a mess? If Paul wrote these words to Timothy, then why did he say something else to a different church in another city?"—sending us students scrambling for answers.

Dr. Fanger's class revolutionized how I read and thought about Scripture. My theological paradigms rearranged themselves into new shapes and colors, and gave me a new sense of freedom regarding women's role in ministry. What a shame I hadn't made these discoveries before the Navigators squashed me just because of my gender.

It was a shame too, of course, that I was not yet able to adjust my theological paradigm to recognize that God had created me as a woman who could love other women. It would take a cataclysmic adjustment—and another wasted decade—before I would reach those conclusions.

At Fuller, I decided to surround myself with women friends who were likeminded and who wanted to become leaders and pastors. I was making new friends like Finja Vogel, Bethany Knapp and

Beatrice Pugh. All of us were pursuing a master's in Missiology, but each with a different focus. Bethany was studying ethnomusicology with the goal of ministering in African countries to record and preserve the native music of tribal groups instead of teaching them Western hymnology. Finja would work with the poor and homeless peoples of downtown Los Angeles. Beatrice didn't know yet what her mission calling would be. I, meanwhile, wanted to become a pastor in a Latin American country someday.

My friends and I spent much of our time in a secluded area of the fourth floor of Fuller's library. There, we could study, take naps on a padded bench seat, and talk and laugh without disturbing other students.

While we were studying one afternoon, without thinking about how my request might be perceived, I leaned over to Bethany's study carrel and said, "My back really hurts today. Can you give me a massage?"

A sideways glance and a two-minute neck rub was all she offered as we took a break. Could she sense that my request might have involved more? I didn't think so, but just the mere thought made me self-conscious.

Finja had joined me several times at my parents' house for holidays during the past year and a half, but no backrubs had ever been requested or offered between us. I was thankful that I didn't have to deal with my secret issue while with her.

As for Beatrice? I wouldn't have wanted her to touch me anyway. She was a bit rough around the edges.

It frustrated me greatly that I had to figure out each relationship and its ramifications to my cursed body. For each new female friend I made in seminary, I had to test out whether she was safe for me to be around. *Safe* meant that we could just be friends and I wouldn't have to deal with any unwelcome passionate fire igniting inside of me. I certainly didn't want to have to bring this up for discussion with any of these women at Fuller. It felt like an unfair burden to secretly bear.

These three new friends were not like Lilly Kvork at Taylor University, who'd made my heart race when we napped together. These ladies were not like Sarah Szabo at Kent State, who'd just plain turned me on and then turned away from me when I confessed my feelings about her.

I never seemed to be able to put my finger on why some women triggered a sexual arousal in me, and others did not.

When did I first notice that I was wired differently than others?

In college? No, earlier.

In high school? No, earlier still.

Junior high? Go earlier.

Elementary school days?

Go back farther. Way back.

An alarm bell went off in my head while I was at Sky View Camp near Kent State for a Navigator weekend retreat during my senior year of college. One morning, my good friend Harlin Fox preached from the book of Proverbs, saying, "The eyes of man are never satisfied!" He leaned over the small pulpit and continued, "Do not look upon your Christian sisters in an unholy way."

I listened, convinced that he was speaking directly to me. *Oh my God! I do look at my sisters that way! I felt that sexual spark with Sarah last year!*

Unable to endure my shame, I ran from the chapel, angry with Harlin and angry with God. Why did I have the eyes of a man? I kicked stones out of my way, raising a cloud of dust. I was a dirty misshapen stone on that clay path.

God, did you make some colossal mistake when you created me?

Harlin's words continued stabbing at my thoughts.

Other female friends had come to my mind during that sermon:

Barb. My Navigator discipleship trainer. What would it feel like if she and I could walk along the pathway holding hands?

Judy. Another backrub gal in The Navigator group. It felt tantalizing when her hands slipped down the sides just a little bit and almost touched my breasts.

Terisa. From my sophomore year in college. She had those hairy arms, and when they brushed up against mine when we shared a songbook in chapel, my heart would practically leap out of my chest.

I needed help. Badly. I decided to go talk with my Navigator Bible Study leader to confess my curse.

Sheepishly, I approached her little cabin at Sky View and knocked on the door.

"I need some advice from you, Sue," I told her. I tried to explain, and finished by saying, "I somehow feel like there's a guy's passionate desire inside of me, but I'm a gal. I guess I have the eyes of a man, like Harlin says. I can't help it; I feel lust for other girls."

She leapt up and away from me as if I would infect her with impetigo. "You are choosing despicable sin!" Her trembling finger pointed to the doorway. "Get. Out. And don't ever talk like this again," she hissed through clenched teeth.

Her words were like a bulldozer; they crushed me entirely.

I possessed no vocabulary that might allow me to express my feelings to the right person—and after that day, I wouldn't even try to do so. In fact, I would never speak of this matter again to anyone for the next twenty years.

When I was only sixteen, I went to summer camp with the Holiness/Pentecostal Church. Several youth groups met at the forested Camp Sychar in northeast Ohio. When Brenda, also sixteen, held my hand in prayer I got wet down there between my legs. When she gave me a backrub, I got soaked. I nearly drowned when, one evening, with no one else around, she came up on me from behind, turned me around, and planted a sensuous kiss upon my lips. Unable to control the urge, I returned the gesture, and our tongues twirled deliciously until we finally broke apart.

That kiss stayed imprinted in my being for years to come. No boy's kiss had ever made me feel the sexual excitement that Brenda's kiss had. I had no idea why.

When I was in tenth grade, I used to stay after school to do projects in the biology lab. I enjoyed the dissection of little creatures; I found their physiological systems fascinating.

I waved for my teacher to come and take a look. "Miss Brainard, I have two frogs cut open here, a male and a female. Watch this!" I carefully lifted the egg sac out of the female and nestled it into the male's body. "Ta da-a-a! The boy frog just became a girl frog, and—"

"Stop it, Sharon. That's not even funny." She told me to put away my specimens and go home.

I was disappointed. I thought it was *so cool* to change the gender of the little froggies. At the time, I had no clue that human beings could change their gender too. So, at fifteen, I erased my child-like thoughts and prayers of wishing I'd wake up one morning to discover that I'd been transformed into a boy.

When I was a freshman in high school, I noticed that all the other girls had boyfriends. Except me. I was almost fourteen when Andy—also fourteen, a family friend who was visiting our house in East Cleveland—pulled me behind a door and kissed me on the lips. His kiss was wet and slobbery. Maybe it was because of his braces. I wondered how in the world girls could say that they liked boys' kisses? *Eeew!* I thought.

I should have noticed that I was a bit different from my peers when I fell in love with the Beatles. I was fourteen, and saw their first concert on the *Ed Sullivan Show* in 1964. I loved them so much that I wanted to be just like them. I wore my brother Thomas's suit coat and tie so my father could take pictures of me with a Beatles haircut. Alone in my bedroom, I danced to their music in front of the mirror with a big sock stuffed in my crotch. Later, I did learn to play the guitar; but I couldn't exactly grow a dick.

When I was thirteen, my friends made fun of me and called me Flatty because I had no breasts yet. They humiliated me—forced me to take off my T-shirt and laughed hysterically upon seeing that I only had little pink nubs for breasts. I beat up the ringleader, Mary Ellen, because she had mocked my body, jeering, "Are you a boy?" At least I knew how to fight like a boy. When I got home to tell my mother what they had called me, she acted as if it was nothing and brushed it off. Her lack of response ate a little hole in my trust. I resolved then to withhold from her any painful experiences or deep questions I had. I would never share with her how being different plagued me every day.

If my mother couldn't understand my shame at being called Flatty, then there was no one in the whole wide world who could hear my anguish. Lying in bed each night, I'd pray that God would somehow hear my voice. Sleep escaped me. I devised a fantasy: I'd climb to the tippy top of Terminal Tower in downtown Cleveland and throw myself off. My body would crumple into a heap on the busy sidewalk below, my limbs broken and all akimbo. A crowd would gather. People would bend down close to me. "Is she still breathing? Is she dead?" they would ask. They would gasp and sigh, press in around me, not knowing what to do. Lying in my bed, the fantasy of receiving all this attention soothed me, and I would go right to sleep. I wanted so badly for others to look at me with compassion instead of ridicule.

When I was just ten, I went to my favorite shoe store because I wanted to buy boys' high-top combat boots. I was in fifth grade and would often drop into the store after school because I knew the owners, the Harveys. When the clerk refused to bring me the shoes I had requested, I found the desired shoebox all by myself, put those leather lace-ups with the thick-treaded Vibram soles on my little feet, and paraded proudly through the store. Why wasn't anyone smiling at me? I was confused. And when Mrs. Harvey wouldn't let me buy them, I ran home in my socks, crying all the way. Why couldn't I have those boots? I was convinced that I looked fantastic in them. My brothers had shoes like that. Why couldn't I?

Many times during puberty and after, I would wonder if I had been born into the wrong body. But I never understood why I felt that way.

I wonder if I realized my different-ness when I was only seven. One day, my brother Thomas, some neighborhood boys and I all crouched in a big cardboard box in the basement with a flashlight. They took turns touching one boy's penis with a small tree branch, and we all watched in awe as the fleshy stick grew and rose upwards, holding its position like a little soldier standing at attention. I didn't want to touch it. I wanted one of my own. Why didn't I get to have one?

Quite possibly, I wanted one of those fancy bodily attachments because I had learned already that those who possessed a penis could wield a kind of power that eluded those who didn't. In my short years of life I had already seen with my own eyes that boys had priority, privilege, potential and prestige that little girls, and not even some grown women, could possess. Perhaps this was what percolated inside my brain to convince me that being a boy would be better than being *just* a girl. At seven, I had already absorbed this male-dominant poison, and I hated the impotence that had already enveloped me.

But my recognition of my being different goes back even farther than that—to when I was only three and my pre-school graduation was about to begin.

"No, nooo!" I held tightly to a post at the back of the aisle in the sanctuary of First Presbyterian Church, Berkeley, California. "Not pink! That color is for girls! I want a blue one!" I wondered why in the world anyone would try to force me into a little pink paper graduation robe, complete with a little pink flat hat.

"Sweetie pie," the elderly Sunday school director murmured into my ear.

I peered up, past the massive bosom of the flowered dress and into the red-painted mouth above the layered, fleshy folds of face.

The mouth spoke again, this time through clenched teeth: "The pink robes are for the girls; the blue ones are for the boys. Understand?"

"I don't care!" I wailed, wrenching my skinny three-year-old wrist free from her vise-like grip. "I want a blue one!"

"But you're a little girl. Pink is for girls," the mouth said, and at its expulsion of the word "pink," a tiny drop of spittle landed on the back of my not-so-dainty little hand with the chewed dirty nails.

I angrily wiped it on my stiff blue gingham dress. "No! Then I will stay in the back and I won't graduate from stupid Sunday school. You can't make me wear pink. Pink is for girls... and I am a b..." I couldn't say the word.

But I knew one thing: I wanted blue, not pink!

My mind swam with questions:

Aren't Sunday school teachers supposed to be nice to their little students?

Can't Daddy or Mommy hear me screaming? Why don't they come running to help me?

Though only three, I had somehow already absorbed that I was different. Inferior. My little brain had no vocabulary to describe the powerlessness I felt. My inner pain found no release through words. Rage rose up to fill the void, giving me the illusion of the power I needed to survive. Adults who attempted to quell my temper tantrums only added fuel to the angry flames. My only recourse was to strike back with a vengeance, which often meant hurting those who loved me the most.

How different my life would have been had I heard the simple words, "Honey, here's a blue robe just for you."

And now, here I was, at Fuller Seminary, thirty-one years old, studying to be a minister of the gospel, and I had yet to resolve my personal issues regarding my gender identity, or sexual orientation, or *whatever* it was called. I was trapped in a dark closet that I couldn't see out of; I didn't even know what freedom might look like.

CHAPTER 13

PASTOR

My on-campus roommate in Fuller Student Housing my first year was Jennifer Dillaha; after that I lived with Patricia Hurst. I was thankful to have good friendships with both roomies but none of that *chemistry* that complicated some of my female friendships. For a few months I even had a boyfriend, Roger Crest, whom I'd met in a theology class.

During my brief relationship with Roger, we engaged in some sexual play, but we didn't accomplish much—guilt was too present in the bedroom. Nonetheless, Roger served a purpose: he moved me back toward the concept that I was indeed normal and interested in guys.

During my last year at Fuller Seminary, in the fall of 1983, the Housing Office allowed some of us to move into a nice condo building on Del Mar Avenue in Pasadena. I had never lived with access to a swimming pool and Jacuzzi before. Relaxing in the hot tub with other grad students was soothing after so many hours in class and the library.

Sedric must work out a lot, I thought as my eyes noticed his rippling chest and arm muscles while we relaxed in the bubbly water one day. He was in the School of Theology, preparing to become some type of pastor, and asked thought-provoking questions in the theological discussions we had through the rising steam on those chilly evenings.

Spending time in conversation with Sedric was like watching crocuses break through the dirt in my garden. The bulb had been planted long ago, but it was as if that Jacuzzi water had encouraged a sprig of new life to burst forth. I told myself that I must be a heterosexual woman after all, impressed as I was by Sedric's muscular frame.

The next spring, a month or so before graduating from Fuller, my old roommate Jennifer told me about another student, Jose Dido, who was finishing his master's in theology. She had mentioned that he was hot and charming, and I looked forward to meeting him sometime soon.

"Hey Sharon," Jennifer's voice called to me over the busy tables out on the quad during lunchtime. She approached me, flanked by a brown, muscular man with a confident stride. "This is Jose. The guy I told you about."

Jose extended his hand as my eyes landed on his dark, angular face and perfect teeth. "I'm Jose Dido. You can call me Joe." The crush of his handshake hurt a little, but I noted that his hands were beautiful—not callused but smooth, like someone who worked with his brains, not his hands. "Jennifer told me that you're one of the women in seminary who wants to become a pastor." His coffee-colored eyes met mine.

"Nice to meet you, Joe." I wondered what that zing I felt just then was. "Yes, someday I'd like to be a pastor. Hopefully in Latin America. Where are you from?"

"Cuernavaca, Mexico. I graduated from la Universidad Nacional Autónoma de México in Mexico City with a degree in history."

Jennifer cleared her throat and said, "I have to meet somebody in fifteen minutes over in the psych building, so I'll be going now. See you soon, Joe, Sharon."

Joe and I sat down at one of the little tables and continued talking about Mexico. He told me about his family business in Cuernavaca with a tour company and how he'd worked as a pastor in a Lutheran church while finishing his BA. I told him how I'd worked on the mission with Spearhead for three years before attending Fuller. I couldn't believe how much we had in common, especially when it came to ministry.

We met the next day for lunch, and then a few days later for dinner, and then the following week for a walk at Huntington Gardens. Before long, we were going on dates about once a week, sometimes more.

⌒ℓ⌒

"We're so proud of you," said my mother, beaming at me.

It was a glorious June day in 1984, and my parents had arrived in Pasadena that morning to see their daughter graduate with her MA in Missiology. The ceremony had taken place in the cool of the auditorium, and now we were spilling out into the sunshine of the garden and open-air chapel area to mingle with the many students and their families.

My face was radiant with pride and streaming with sweat as I stood there in my graduation gown on that in the sweltering heat. "I can't believe I did it! Thanks for your encouragement for the past three years."

We gave each other sticky hugs and I introduced them to a few classmates as we mingled in the crowded area.

"What do you plan to do now that you have all this education?" my father asked.

A little distraught, I didn't answer his question right away. My eyes were scanning the crowd, my head flitting right and left. A ripple of nervousness ran down my body.

My mother could usually read my signals of disquiet. She smoothed her hand down my back, like she always did. "Is everything okay? You looking for someone, honey?"

"Yes, Mom. I thought he'd be here. There's a guy I'd like you to meet today. Sorry, Dad, I didn't answer your question. Actually, I'd love to marry a pastor and plant a Hispanic church, now that I'm fluent in Spanish. Or maybe go back to Latin America and be a pastor there."

"That'd be great. Got a lucky man in mind?" My father gave me a wink.

"Maybe." Just then, I spotted him. Our gazes met, and Joe sauntered over to stand next to me. "I'd like to introduce you to a man I've been dating for a short time." I put my hand on Joe's arm. "This is Jose Dido, from Mexico."

"Hello, Jose. So you're also graduating," my father said, gripping his wide hand in a firm handshake. "Did you study pastoral theology?"

"*Sí*—oh, I mean, yes. I am already a Lutheran pastor," Joe replied, his smile a ray of sunshine beaming from his handsome, dark face. "You can call me Joe."

"It's a pleasure to meet you, Joe," my mother said.

Joe's dark eyes looked into my mother's blue eyes as she told him about our family's involvement in the Lutheran church during the civil rights movement of the '60s. "You have beautiful black hair," she said, grinning, as she finished her little story.

"Thanks," said Joe. "Sorry, but I need to meet someone at two o'clock, so I have to get going. It's a pleasure to meet you both." He shook my father's hand again and gave my mother a typical Latino polite hug and peck on the cheek, then hugged me, sneaking in a butt-cheek squeeze, before disappearing among the other grads.

I beamed with pride having such a handsome man to introduce to my parents. I thought I might even be falling in love. However, I did sometimes feel a little uncomfortable with Joe's machismo. He would tell me that even though women could be pastors, they had to be obedient to their husbands. I'd heard that shit from the Navigators many times, and wasn't about to buy it any more. Often, during conversation he'd insist that his point of view was the "right" one, and I'd feel that my opinion was less-than. But I explained it away by telling myself we just needed to become better acquainted; we'd only been dating for about six weeks, after all.

Our conversations, which we conducted in fast-paced Spanish, challenged my fluency. And though I was thirty-four, I had not dated a man since my college days. Going out to dinner with my new beau, walking in Pasadena together, strolling on Huntington Beach... all these experiences were welcome adventures for me. Our physical relationship had begun quite early in our relationship, and my head was still spinning with the newness. His kisses were passionate yet somehow his fierce embrace sent titillating shards of fear down my spine. Joe's intensity was like an overcharged electric current.

⚘

That August, Joe and I went to Santa Barbara to spend a Saturday with my parents. My grandmother Lula, ninety-one, lived with them. When I introduced them, Joe, such a charmer, bent down to where Grandma was resting on the sofa and brushed his lips to her cheek.

"My, what beautiful big brown eyes you have, young man," she said, her fading blue ones twinkling like little stars. "Sharon, I am so proud of you. Graduating with your master's degree, and then you bring home such a handsome young man." The ancient queen's head melted back onto her cushions, a broad smile gracing her face.

To me, it felt like a benediction.

Joe and I excused ourselves from my parents' house after dinner and walked hand in hand through a rose garden in the cool Santa Barbara evening. For the first time, I felt proud of how my body was made. I was a woman! And Joe liked my body. Just the way it was. No shame. No guilt. I felt free as a butterfly flitting among those red and yellow roses.

I stopped to admire a cluster of yellow roses about to spring free, my thoughts prancing inside my head.

"Sharon!" Joe's insistent voice pulled me my attention back to him. "I was telling you about one of my professors, Dr. Smedes. Weren't you listening?"

"Sorry," I whispered. I hoped I hadn't made him angry. Sometimes he had a bit of a sharp edge. I wanted to redirect the conversation so I blurted out, "Hey Joe, did you know that I have an interview with Pasadena Covenant Church this week?"

"Wonderful! For the pastoral staff?" His beautiful teeth gleamed like a pearl necklace.

"Yeah!" I said, glad he was letting me talk about myself; I often felt overpowered by his strong personality. "I really want to be a pastor."

Joe swooped me up into his arms, laughing with joy.

The crocuses in my garden were more than sprigs now; the vibrant pink and purple buds were peeking out into the sunshine. I willed myself to believe that my dream was coming true and some-day I'd share a ministry with a husband.

Just two months after Fuller's commencement day, in mid-August 1984, I stood in front of a mirror, using my curling iron to make sure my strawberry blonde hair framed my face just so and examining my makeup to ensure that my light blue eye shadow wasn't too severe.

I felt like I had barely shed my graduation robe and already I was going to an interview at an evangelical church—and I wanted to present my most feminine self. This could be the beginning of a real professional chapter of my life.

I arrived a bit early at Pasadena Covenant Church, wring-ing my hands like I was putting on hand cream. As I waited to be called into the pastor's office, I forced them to stay still and folded in my lap.

When they called me in, I entered what looked like a library. I sat across from Pastor Graydon at a small table as he peppered me with questions about my faith, my experience and my goals in ministry. I focused on his round face as he spoke.

He seemed impressed as he summarized my interview. "So you have experience in Christian Education, cross-cultural missions, youth group leadership, evangelism and discipleship, and you are fluent in Spanish!" Looking into my eyes, he folded his hands over his desk and leaned forward. I wondered if his perfectly combed grey toupee would slip off and plop onto his desk. "Can you give us at least a five-year commitment? We'd like to extend an invitation to you to join our pastoral staff here."

Feeling a twinge of nervousness, I perused the tall bookcases of theological tomes—Bibles of every English translation, commentaries and church history books. *He sure must read a lot*, I thought.

Pastor Graydon explained everything about the church. It was easy for me to affirm that I followed Jesus Christ and believed that the Bible was the Word of God, a perfect rule for faith, doctrine and conduct. He told me that the Evangelical Covenant denomination had freedom of interpretation on certain theological issues, like the method of baptism. As a person who had attended a range of evangelical denominations over the years, this flexibility seemed like a good fit for me. He also mentioned that after one year he would like me to start a Latino church. "As you probably know already, Pasadena has a large Hispanic population, and we'd like to begin a Latino church right here in our neighborhood. Your mission experience will serve you well in this endeavor." He went on to explain that for my first year, as youth pastor, I'd work with young children and teens, and through them reach out to their families to draw them into the church.

Had I just landed a tailor-made perfect job? As I shook his hand I looked into his deep-set blue eyes and said, "I'd be glad to minister with you for the next five years, and maybe more!" I looked forward to working with this man and his team.

"Wonderful!" he said. "We'd like you to start your position in ten days. That should give you enough time to tie up anything you need to, then hit the ground running when you arrive."

⁓

When I began my new position I connected well with the assistant pastor, Carl Goodwin, also a Fuller grad. He became my go-to person when I had questions. I worked most closely with Inez Kunz, developing various outreach projects for children and youth. There were two more assistant pastors on the team, one for counseling and another part-time person who worked with very young children and their parents. I had never been part of an evangelical church that had so many paid employees. I decided the church members must contribute a lot of money.

I was a full-time employee. My salary was modest, but it at least paid my bills and gave me health benefits.

On days off, Inez and I spent many hours together, going cross-country skiing together and developing a group of mutual friends. My back condition had improved enough so I could participate in fun activities, but I was vigilant about not reinjuring myself. I felt so happy to be incorporated into what felt like a grand family doing a grand ministry in Pasadena. Inez and I enjoyed time together, and even though we shared an occasional backrub, the fingers did not slip, the wet remained dry, and Joe and I were still dating. My life was finally falling into place like I'd always dreamed.

My parents were also quite pleased with how my life was taking shape. They were happy that I'd found a job so quickly after graduation, and that I was dating a pastor.

By the time Joe and I marked three months of dating, I found myself questioning whether this relationship was the *real deal*. Was I actually falling in love, or was I just trying to fall in love? I didn't know the difference.

Joe seemed happy about my new job, and our time together often included pastor-to-pastor discussions about our respective churches, but there was always a little lizard of fear lurking in the grass when I was with him. I wasn't sure why. Sometimes his hands would meander over my body as we embraced, sending bits of excitement downwards. This still felt like scary territory for me. Once in a while, I would wonder if I was in over my head. Were we moving too fast? What might happen if we went farther?

One afternoon, I felt the need to redirect his wandering hands—we were standing on campus behind The Catalyst, Fuller's coffee and sandwich shop, and I didn't want to do something in public that I'd be embarrassed about—so I began to tell him a random story from my childhood.

⌒ℓℓ⌒

My little arms cradled my doll. "You're as big as I am, Booby Baby. Let's dance. La-la-laaa," I sang and swayed with her, the elastic bands on her feet securely tucked around my shoes. "You can always be my favorite dolly."

While I was dancing with my dolly, my father came into my bedroom.

"Why did you name your dolly *Booby Baby*?"

His tone of voice frightened me. Had I done something wrong?

"That's what it says on the tag on her leg," I said, my voice trembling. "See? I can read it all by myself, Daddy."

He walked away, leaving me alone to struggle with the little elastic bands that held my dolly to my shoes. "Is dinner ready, honey?" he called to my mother.

I ran after him. "Daddy, look. Look at the tag." I had Booby Baby upside down, and I held her up as far as my little arm could reach so he could see the tiny words sewn to her leg.

He came back out into the hallway where I was standing, grasped the doll, and frowned, looking at the tag. "Booby? That's not a nice name for a dolly, Shawnee."

"But Daddy... that's her name," I insisted, my voice quavering.

"Do you know what booby means? Or boob? Not a nice word. And it's not a nice name for your dolly."

He handed my dolly back, turned away, and walked toward the kitchen.

Confusion swept through my little body. What did I have to be ashamed about? I'd done nothing wrong.

"But Daddy . . ." I began to cry. "That's her name." I ran and buried my tear- streaked face in my mother's dress.

~~~

I had grown up on a diet of guilt and shame, though I hadn't known that as a little girl; I'd only known that my father loved me but could sometimes be cruel. He had shamed me about something I couldn't comprehend. I hoped against hope that Joe would never do something like that, though I didn't understand why I would even have such a thought.

As I finished my story about the doll, Joe and I walked to where his car was parked—on Oakland Avenue, close to Fuller. We got in and cranked up the AC.

"Why would your father say that? There is no shame in your breasts, uh . . . your *boobs*, as Americans call them. They are beautiful to me." His large hands gently reached up and inside my blouse. His skilled touch molded my breasts like an artisan shapes the clay. My spirit was transported to a planet of ecstasy, even as I hoped that no passerby looked into the windows of the car.

Being with Joe was exciting and sexual, but deep down I had to admit that I didn't have that sense in my spirit that I was actually falling in love. With him, I didn't feel the profound connection I'd felt with Montserrat. I could only conclude that with men, love must feel like something else. Sort of like a boat tied loosely to a dock. Rocked by the slightest wave, the rope could come undone.

I wished I could follow the old adage about trusting your heart. But I didn't know my heart well enough to be able to trust her.

CHAPTER 14

SHAME

After graduation, Jerri Wilkins—my friend and very first roommate at Fuller—and I decided to move in together. We found a rental house in Altadena and fixed it up, putting new carpeting in the living room and painting some walls. By fall of 1984, it felt like home.

The house was located on the hill behind JPL (Jet Propulsion Laboratories), and I often rode my bicycle past the enormous complex and up into the mountains. Now that I was working full time as a pastor, I needed to recharge my batteries on my day off. My back injury had healed enough for me to ride, and even to hike a little. I was extremely thankful to God for the days when I had less pain and could do more. However, pain was still a constant companion.

One hot Southern California September day, I invited Joe Dido to my lovely home for the first time. We'd been dating for several months now.

I gave him a tour of the interior and then led him out to the back patio. "And this is our little picnic area," I said. "Let's sit out here, in the shade."

We sat together on the little bench, and in just a few minutes, his hands were massaging my breasts again and our legs were entwined like the honeysuckle climbing the lattice on the back fence.

Joe and I had never had a discussion about sex. I assumed that we could fondle each other—just a little of course, like I had done in college with Paul—and that would be it. We were unmarried evangelical pastors, after all.

"*Vamos adentro*," Joe finally suggested. "It's too hot out here."

I was happy to go inside where it was cooler. He followed behind me as I stepped through the door.

"*No tengas miedo, mi amor.*" (Don't be afraid, my love).

His voice was like warm honey, but I wondered why he was telling me not to be afraid.

"*Te voy a enseñar algo muy bonito. Muy grande.*" (I'm going to show you something very beautiful. Very big.) Once inside, he gently turned the deadbolt, twirled around to face me, unzipped his fly, and let his *muy bonito* spring into view. "*Tócame.*" (Touch me.)

The honey in his voice was gone. This was a command, not a request. Still standing in the living room, he pulled me toward his *muy, muy grande* thing. My arms were glued to my sides, my hands too heavy to lift.

What was happening here in my home? We had been inside less than three minutes.

"*Tócame!*" his voice was now a knife poised above me. His dark eyes became daggers. Clucking his tongue and hissing out a breath, he pushed me in front of his body, held me around the waist from behind, and pushed my feet ahead of him, so I was taking each step like I used to make Booby Baby do with me. I could feel his hardness bobbing against my butt. He guided me toward my bedroom. My legs were robotic. My mind began to shut down.

Now a hungry jaguar, Joe flung me down onto my own bed and pounced on me like I was an innocent doe. Seemingly unable to hold himself back, he began to pound his hammer relentlessly against the doorway of my virginity.

I couldn't—wouldn't—let him in, even though he was doing all he could to pry me open.

"Stop!" I begged. "Do it to yourself. Not to me."

But it was too late.

I'd never expected that something like this could happen. This was not consensual sex—not at all. Was this what they called rape? My rational mind imploded like a dynamited building.

"The Bible says that masturbation is a terrible sin," he growled. "Just let me in."

Time folded in on itself. From a faraway place, I heard someone breathe, *Let me go. Please!* Her shallow gasps went unheard.

Spent and still panting, Joe emptied his despicable, warm goo on the girl's thighs, then leapt from the bed to gather up his clothing. Before he exited the room, he muttered, *"La puta de mierda me hizo pecar."* (The shitty bitch made me sin).

He slammed the door as he left the house.

I lay on my back. My eyes studied the pattern of cracks in the ceiling. A shitty bitch? And was it me who'd made him sin? My frantic heart, the size of a watermelon, throbbed all the way down to that spot between my legs that he'd violated. Guilt grabbed at the little sense of self that remained. Shame swallowed me whole. I spent a long time in the shower, trying to wash it all away with hot water, and then collapsed onto my bed, unable to cry.

❦

That evening, my housemate Jerri came home late. I tapped on her bedroom door a few minutes later. "Can I please come in?" I begged.

She opened the door, frowning. "It's past midnight now."

"Something happened to me while you were gone." Tears finally came as I choked out my words between sobs and explained what had transpired.

"I'm so sorry! And in our house! Come here, let me hold you." She patted her bed.

Lying next to her, her safe warmth wrapped around me like a child's blanket, I felt comforted. Like a child soothed by her mother.

After a long while, I retreated to my bedroom for the night. In my dreams, a jaguar chased me, pounced on me, tore my flesh to pieces and broke my bones with each crushing bite.

In what seemed like less than thirty minutes, my alarm clock jolted me awake.

Church staff meeting in an hour? Nooo!

I dragged my aching body to the church that morning feeling like a filthy slut.

"Sharon, you okay?" Inez asked.

I reached for a cup of steaming hot coffee. "Huh?" I shook my head. "Just tired."

I was usually bouncy and cheerful in the morning. Inez knew something was amiss.

"You don't look too good," she said. "What's going on?"

"I'm fine."

I felt as vacant as an abandoned warehouse, and each hammering heartbeat pounded my still-aching vagina. I couldn't participate in the morning's discussion and left early, saying that I must be coming down with the flu.

When I arrived home, I called out for Jerri. I hoped that she would be there, but of course she wasn't. It was barely nine in the morning. How I yearned to crawl into bed with her. Not just once but every night. There was just something about her that Joe didn't have. Why could a woman fill my void like no man could? I felt like a house with a sagging porch, broken windows, and a main beam that was about to collapse.

When Jerri did come home later that afternoon, she just went to the kitchen, fixed a snack, and retreated to her room.

Later in the evening, yearning for her company, I told her that I wanted to talk.

She sighed. "Sharon, please don't depend on me. I know that you're hurting and I sincerely hope you can get the help you need.

But I have my own problems." She went back into her room and gently closed the door.

The assault had made me completely lose my bearings. I felt like I was hiking alone on a dusty desert trail, rattlesnakes coiled in every thorny bush, ready to strike.

Could I have prevented what happened? I felt so ashamed. Surely it must have been my fault. This was the worst sexual sin I had ever engaged in. Jerri knew, but I resolved I would never tell anyone else.

There was only one way to walk on this pathway fraught with guilt and self-doubt. I had the perfect idea. I would accomplish great things! I would be the best pastor, the best teacher, the best counselor, the best translator, the best guitar player and singer, the best of the best in my ministry and beyond. No one would ever suspect that I carried secret sins. I would hide my trauma under layer after layer of sedimentary rock so that when people saw me, they saw only the beautiful colors and patterns of the stratified layers on the surface. That way, I could avoid having to confront my pain, guilt and shame.

I had to avoid the painful things that gnawed at me at all costs. Avoidance had become a part of me. It would stand between me and the world like a sentry guarding a castle.

Sharon Wulfensmith

CHAPTER 15

BURYING SHAME

I needed to accomplish a lot in a short time if I wanted to be the best of the best. I had to focus on productive goals.

I decided I would expand the church's mission in the world—that any doubt, pain, guilt, or shame I felt had to be buried under the layers of the good deeds of my ministry.

My ministerial responsibilities had now expanded to include the planting of a Hispanic church group, so I would focus my efforts there. First task: helping Hispanic people get their immigration documents in order. This effort would seed the future Hispanic ministry outreach Pastor Graydon had spoken of during my interview for the job with the church less than two years earlier.

The Immigration Reform and Control Act of 1986, signed into law by President Ronald Reagan, granted amnesty to about three million undocumented immigrants in the United States. Seizing on this unprecedented opportunity, my responsibilities at Pasadena Covenant would now focus on English as a Second Language (ESL), history, government, and citizenship classes for the Hispanic people in our neighborhood—amnesty classes, as we called them.

Pastor Graydon called me into his office one afternoon. "I have a surprise for you, Sharon. This is Jude."

I shook hands with a young man who looked barely twenty, and we all sat down around Pastor Graydon's table.

"Jude Renner is a Fuller student whom I met at a special forum led by Dr. Palmer, Professor of Preaching. He needs some hours for his theology internship and wonders if he could help us at Pasadena Covenant."

"This is great news," I said. I loved my job, but it was daunting. Extra help would be fantastic. "We're starting up a Hispanic ministry and certainly could use an intern. Do you speak Spanish?"

"Sí," Jude said, and then he launched in to tell me, in Spanish, about a mission he'd done for a year in Central America. It seemed so unlikely that this young, blond, blue-eyed young intern would know Spanish as well as he did, but I was thrilled.

Pastor Graydon stood and extended his hand. "I trust that the two of you understood the last paragraph of whatever was said in Spanish." He laughed a bit. "Welcome to our ministerial staff, Jude. Sharon will make sure you know what's going on, but feel free to drop into my office any time."

⁓

Within a week, Jude had become an invaluable partner to me in my new responsibility as Hispanic Outreach Pastor. He was shy, but that didn't stop him from doing excellent outreach. Over the next few weeks we spent many hours together doing door-to-door evangelism in the largely Hispanic part of northwest Pasadena, sharing information about our church and telling people about our upcoming ESL classes. To advertise our ESL/Citizenship classes, I painted two six-by-six-foot posters on canvas and we hung them on the church bell tower at the corner of Lake Avenue and Santa Barbara Street. We also organized rallies, dinners and Latino music concerts at the church and handed out flyers at laundromats and shopping centers. People were grateful to see amnesty classes offered for free so close to their neighborhoods.

Working alongside a young man like Jude and keeping a very busy schedule helped me to push away any shameful feelings about my assault.

When we opened the registration tables in the fall of 1986, crowds of Latinos stood in a line that snaked around the building. My volunteers registered over a hundred people on the first day. I was deeply proud of my efforts, as were my mother and father, who came to visit from time to time.

A church member who was also a leader with the San Gabriel Valley Literacy Council, Ellen Herring, allowed me to utilize her materials in addition to worksheets that I created to help teach the classes. I was continually impressed with the perseverance of the students, some working at their jobs ten or more hours a day, who never missed our evening sessions, and managed to complete all of their homework assignments. Some only had a sixth-grade education from their countries of origin and struggled to read and write in Spanish.

Our goal was to respect each and every student, meet them at the level that they brought to us, and raise that ability level up to the standard required by the 1986 amnesty exams. At the end of each class quarter, we celebrated with potlucks and music. My face ached from so much smiling after each of those parties. To my surprise, I had found my calling in the ministry right in my hometown of Pasadena.

The following year, I was invited to participate in a weekend interdenominational conference for Hispanic pastors at the famous Crystal Cathedral near Disneyland in Orange County. Over a thousand brown and black pastors and lay workers from Los Angeles County attended the event. As a woman, and especially as a white woman, I was definitely in the minority there.

On the second day of the conference, while making my way through a crowded doorway, I noticed a familiar face about ten feet away. My faith unwavering, my heart galloping, I asked God for a miracle—*not right now, Lord, but in an hour. Amen.*

As the session concluded, when the throng pressed back outside through the small doorway, that same face saw mine, at close range.

He smiled, his deep brown eyes looking into mine. *"Hola. ¿Cómo estás? Un gusto verte de nuevo."* (Hi. How are you? It's great to see you again).

I looked Joe Dido right in the eye and said, quite loudly, "*¡Me violaste, Joe! ¡Eres un chingado hijo de puta!*" (You raped me! You fucking son of a bitch!)

The whites of his eyes widened around his dark pupils and he snapped back, "*Lo quisiste, puta estúpida.*" (You wanted it, stupid whore.)

I whisked myself away, shame enveloping me like a damp dark shroud. Had I wanted it? Was I dirty?

After that conference, I made sure that my ministry consumed my whole life. My good deeds would build additional layers of stratified rock, the colors of avoidance, and protect my vulnerable true self.

⁓·ell·ᴈ

After a Pasadena Covenant Church special workshop one evening in the fall of 1987, a man about my age approached me in the foyer. His short-cropped hair and steel blue eyes caught my attention. He didn't ask, but rather made a statement: "I'd like to take this beautiful young lady to dinner sometime soon."

Was I being asked out on a date? It had been three years since the rape. My voice a soft croak, I managed to respond, "Sure, thanks."

"Ethan Collins," he said, extending a beefy hand. "I really love how your hair looks this evening." He grinned. His gentle voice pulled me in.

As a professional person on the pastoral staff, I labored long and hard on my appearance every day now, using the curling iron each morning to carefully coif my shoulder-length hair, regularly applying a subtle pink nail polish on my now-longer nails, and enhancing my blue eyes with soft light blue eye shadow and mascara. This particular evening, I'd worn a cream-colored, round-collared blouse under a sky-blue blazer with a matching straight skirt.

Still, I wasn't accustomed to being flattered. "You like my hair?" My red eyebrows raised an inch. "Thank you very much,

Ethan." I studied his black polished shoes, too shy to look him in the eye.

A few days later we sat in a small café in Montrose, sipping lemonade and eating burgers. Ethan leaned in over the small table. "I like pretty women. And you're a pretty pastor woman. Y'know, I used to be a policeman in La Cañada, but now I'm a chiropractor. I even have a portable treatment table and make house calls."

I perked up. "A chiropractor? House calls?" I'd never heard of a chiropractor that made house calls. "I've had a back problem for several years now. I was badly injured in 1981 and still have a lot of pain. Think you could help me?" Hope swelled inside me like a sunrise.

"Sure I can help you." He almost took my hand in his, but pulled it back. "Where do you live?"

"I rent a house in Altadena up behind JPL."

After that day, Ethan began coming to my house several times a week.

I loved his strong, thick, healing hands on my body. "Strrretch out those muscles," he said, pressing gently on my back to help me bend over farther.

Wearing that damned back brace for a couple of years had caused my back muscles to atrophy. The old scar tissue from my Mexican surgery four years earlier, meanwhile, had become inflexible as a stick of beef jerky. I still couldn't bend down enough even to touch my knees. It was a major challenge for me to get dressed in the morning.

"I'll help you to become flexible again."

He was true to his word: his treatments, adjustments and exercises twice a week began to give me the mobility and strength I'd thought I would never regain. Could this chiropractor be the miracle worker I'd prayed for?

I imagined that one day I could feel healthy again. Strong again. Free of the persistent back pain that had been my constant companion for the past few years. I fantasized that one day I would marry Ethan and have my own personal chiropractor for life. How I wanted to find a husband. I was already thirty-six, and I feared my childbearing years were passing me by.

More and more often during his home treatments, I wondered what it might feel like to kiss Ethan. With him I didn't feel the zinging shards of fear that I had felt with Joe—I felt safe.

During one of his home treatments in the middle of my living room, as Ethan worked the muscles on my upper back, his hands slid around to almost cup my breasts. "Would this be okay with you, Sharon?" His unshaven chin nuzzled my neck, igniting a shockwave down past my abdomen.

"I like it."

It felt exciting. Not frightening.

Over the next few weeks, my chiropractic treatments began to include muscle work on both sides of my body. It worked better with my blouse off, so he could touch my breasts. That narrow, portable chiropractic table became a place to enjoy sexual play.

Ethan taught me what a man wanted. He would lie on the little chiropractic table face up and tell me what to do. Giving him a hand job was certainly a new experience for me.

This kind of activity led me to believe once again that I was a "normal" heterosexual woman. I'd finally grown out of my *phase* of same-sex attraction. Ethan and I began to go out to dinner and movies, and to attend the Pasadena Covenant Church together. I felt proud to be seen with such a handsome man. After a few months of dating, I even took him to Santa Barbara to meet my parents one weekend. They were gracious and friendly to him, as they always were to my friends.

Back home in Altadena one evening, shortly after Ethan left my house with his fold-up chiro table, my housemate, Jerri, burst through the back door. Whew, was I glad she hadn't come home any earlier. I wondered what she'd say if she'd caught me and my chiropractor nearly naked together.

Her voice could have shattered the living room window as she exclaimed, "I have been waiting out in the driveway for about an hour for you guys to, um, finish up! Don't you know that this place a fishbowl? We don't have any curtains on these huge glass windowpanes in the living room!"

"Sorry," I said, studying at the floor. "Won't happen again." With that, any past thoughts of lying in bed with Jerri popped like a soap bubble. I'd always hung on to a feeling of attraction to her but had never acted on it. Now I felt I never could.

Later that day, I phoned Ethan and asked if we could start doing the treatments at his apartment instead of my house.

＊＊＊

At the church the next day at work, I popped my head in to chat with Alex Monde, Pastor of Counseling.

He invited me in to sit down and, as he closed his office door, said, "Sharon, I've been aware for a time that you seem to be struggling with some personal issues. I'm not one to judge you for anything, but if there's something you'd like to share, I'm all ears."

I wondered what he thought he knew. A shiver of shame ran down my spine.

Even though Alex was younger than me, I'd always respected his quiet demeanor and depth of understanding in meetings. I felt I could confide in him.

Fidgeting with my hands under the table I began, "I've been dating this chiropractor for a few months now, and he does adjustments at home, and..." I told him what had happened the previous day.

"Well," he said, "it sounds like you're wanting to have sexual intercourse with this man. Is that true?"

I hated that he had said it so directly. Me? Have sex with a man? My body yearned to have consensual sex with Ethan, yet my

Christian beliefs clearly told me that this was sin. The dissonance between those opposing forces was deafening. I couldn't decide which way to go.

"You need to listen to your desires, and then try to make a rational decision as to whether you're going to follow those desires or obey what you feel the Bible says about sex outside of marriage," Alex said.

We talked a bit more. Eventually, I promised Alex that I'd be a pure Christian woman and not cave in to my fleshly desires.

Alex wasn't convinced. "The way you talk, Sharon, I bet that in one week you will find yourself in bed with this man."

He was wrong. It didn't take a week.

That very evening, driving up the 210 Freeway from Altadena to our fave spot, Montrose Café, my body throbbed in anticipation of what might happen. I didn't have to guess; we'd been dating for four months now, and although Ethan and I had never discussed having intercourse, I figured that was where we were headed. I decided to trust him.

At the café, the evening late, sandwiches long gone, fries cold, he softly said, "Sharon, tonight I'd like to... Uhh... Been waiting a long time..."

I raised my hand, like I was in school. "Waiter! Another beer for me. Dark." I wasn't a drinker, but I wanted a buzz for this anticipated event.

After I finished my beer, we drove to his place. Upon entering his small apartment, we walked directly to the bedroom.

Ethan's double bed was soft, clean and smelled like the oak barrel scent of Bourbon Cologne. He'd clearly planned this evening's encounter. He removed my clothing, and I his.

"I'll be gentle, honey," he said. "Just lie back and let me be in control. I don't want to hurt you."

It did hurt, but it was a consensual, positive experience. Unlike Joe, a fierce jaguar, Ethan was a gentle housecat, one that rubbed and purred.

After it was over, we lay together on his mussed-up bed, hugging and talking. Later, in the bathroom mirror, I saw a woman with tousled red hair and a glowing face. The face smiled. *You're not a virgin anymore, Sharon. You're grown up now. You are a heterosexual woman. Believe it!*

Over the next few weeks, we continued our intimate play. I was amazed by how Ethan's body responded to different stimuli; sometimes I would act like a kid in a toy store, testing out the mechanical dolls. I would ask him questions about why his penis did this or that, poking it instead of stroking it, and he would tell me that those kinds of questions and actions made me sound like a teenager who'd never had sex before.

When we began dating, I think he assumed I'd had sexual experiences with other men. I was such a novice I probably frustrated him more than anything else. Over the next month or so, we continued to engage in sexual play but never had full-blown intercourse again. We dated for a couple months more, but our encounters always ended with arguing: Ethan would tell me that I didn't satisfy him and that I just plain didn't know how to act, which made me feel incompetent and ashamed for being so stupid. The initial thrill of being with a man quickly faded. I felt like a total misfit.

For years my sexual desires had sprung up, unbidden, and invaded the space that I tried to maintain between certain girlfriends and myself. Now I had an attractive man who wanted sex and I just couldn't perform. It didn't occur to me that this was because I didn't really love Ethan. And I definitely didn't love him. If anything, he was an experiment for me to see what it felt like to be with a man.

One evening, I phoned him. "I think that we should stop seeing each other, Ethan." I was beginning to quote some god-awful Bible verse when he cut in.

"You don't know what you're doing when we're together. You'll never be able to get married if you act like this. You're a failure."

His words pierced my fragile heart.

Things didn't quite end there. On several more occasions, we hurled stinging insults at each other. What had happened to the calm, soft-spoken man I'd met a few months before?

Maybe he was right. I was a failure. I'll never be able to know how to act with a man. I gave up trying to repair things between us. Clouds darkened the sky and we parted ways.

Only seven years earlier, what had been the key to my love with Montserrat? What might have happened if we had been able to express our deep love and explore one another's bodies with total abandon?

Who was I, really? When would I ever figure this out?

I didn't really enjoy being with a man, but I believed that to be with a woman was homosexual sin. The constant, pelting rainstorm of my guilt was weathering down my protective rock layers. Who would listen to what I longed to say but couldn't find the words for?

CHAPTER 16
CONFESSIONS

A flesh-eating bacterium of guilt was gnawing at my insides. I couldn't hold it in anymore. I needed to tell at least *some* of my secret sins to someone I could trust. But who?

My parents had friends in Santa Barbara that were taking some classes to become intern pastors in a local church. I had met Kelly and Dan Sims several times, and engaged with them in discussions about the Bible and the church. I respected their theological perspectives on a number of different issues. I decided that Kelly was a person I could confide in. She didn't know any of my Pasadena friends or church contacts.

I called her.

"Hi Kelly," I hoped my voice didn't quaver too much. "I'd like to discuss some things with you . . . personally." I hoped she couldn't read my Guilt-o-Meter through the phone line. It had quite a high fever.

"Sure, Sharon," she said. "Let's meet at the Beach Bluff Cafe near Shoreline Park."

We made a date for the following week.

Sitting with Kelly at a table for two near the back, I twisted my napkin into knots, hoping that others couldn't overhear our conversation, as I took a deep breath and related my experiences with Joe and with Ethan.

"I have sinned," I said. "With two men. I need absolution."

There was no way I was going to tell her about my secret sexual inclinations toward other women. I figured that it had indeed been a phase, and was no longer a problem.

Kelly Sims laughed out loud. "Absolution for getting raped? That's crazy backwards. And absolution for having sex with Ethan? Ha!" She leaned across her cup of coffee and whispered, "Did you like it with Ethan?"

I wished she'd keep her voice down. Ashamed, I confessed, "With Ethan, yes, I... I liked it." I wouldn't tell her that I really felt like a total failure.

She smiled and took both of my hands into hers. "Why don't you chalk this second one up to helping heal you of the pain of the first one?"

I was shocked; I hadn't expected that kind of answer.

Kelly said a prayer, and that was that. Done! She flagged down the waiter. "Can we have the bill please? I'll pick up the tab." She scraped her chair back from the little table and stood, ready to go.

Kelly didn't seem to grasp how I felt inside. I still didn't feel that my issues were resolved. My confusion festered under my skin like a pus-filled cyst. I needed an excision. Why was my life such a mess? On one level, I was glad to have had one positive sexual encounter with a man, but on another level, I knew that previous female friendships had been more satisfying, albeit not overtly sexual.

I'd never been naked in bed with another woman. Just the idea scared the shit out of me. I didn't even know how to consider such a concept yet. But I also knew I wanted more than what I'd felt with Ethan.

Even though Ethan had helped me immensely with his chiropractic treatments (the legitimate ones), I still had significant and debilitating back problems. After we broke up, I found another chiropractor in Pasadena who was able to help me a lot. One afternoon in his office, Dr. Field asked me who my previous doctor had been, and I told him. During my treatment session, he mentioned that he had known Ethan from their chiropractic college and added, "Did you know that Dr. Collins just passed away? I heard that he had a heart attack." His hands pressed down, giving me a crunch on my right side. "Now roll over onto your left side so I can give it a scrunch."

His words were like a slap. Even though I'd known Ethan for less than a year and we'd broken up with harsh words, I was shocked to learn of his death. And Dr. Field had delivered the news like he was talking about the weather outside.

I took a deep breath. "I didn't know that you knew him. He was one of my first chiropractors after my botched Mexican surgery. He helped me to become more flexible."

"In school, Dr. Collins used to brag about taking his portable table to women's homes for so-called 'treatments,'" Dr. Field said with a snort. "I hope you didn't fall into his trap." He chuckled and shook his head. "Now slide over this way so I can adjust your neck."

My face growing hot, I said, "All I know is that he helped me bend, stretch and be freer from pain." I hoped he wouldn't see my embarrassment. "Thanks for telling me the news." I kept my face turned away, the words *took his portable table to women's homes* echoing hollowly in my head.

Leaving Dr. Field's office, my mind whirled. I had to ask myself if Ethan had used me. Had I just been an object to him? How many women had he taken to his bed? This was 1987, and the news was full of reports of HIV infection. Could Ethan have carried the virus? Oh no! It had never occurred to me to ask him to use a condom.

It had been several months since I'd been with Ethan. I needed to get an HIV test. On the way home, I stopped at Planned Parenthood to get a blood test.

I breathed a sigh of relief a few days later when the results came back negative.

How stupid of me to fall into his lair. I would have to learn to use my brain more and my body less when it came to my love life.

Several months later, Pastor Graydon called me to his office at Pasadena Covenant for an annual review of my ministerial accomplishments. He told me he was pleased with how the ESL and citizenship classes were going. He seemed impressed with how these strategies brought Hispanic people into the church. Jude had helped me establish regular Sunday afternoon services in Spanish with an attendance of about twenty people. By this time I had baptized, married, and buried members of our congregation as a Hispanic Outreach pastor. I was proud of what I'd accomplished.

"I think you would be a good candidate for ordination in the Covenant denomination," Pastor Graydon told me. "Can you add graduate classes to your already-full schedule? We might be able to help you with tuition."

Even though I was considered a pastor and was a member of the pastoral staff, I had never been officially ordained by any denomination. I was dumfounded that only three years after my graduation from Fuller Seminary, I'd be on a track leading to my ordination as a full-fledged pastor. More grad school? Why not?

"Our denomination encourages candidates to study at North Park Seminary in Chicago," he continued. "Would you be willing to relocate there for a year or two? We'd be waiting for you when you return." His round face beamed and he patted me on the shoulder. Pastor Graydon could be quite fatherly to me at times, and that made my heart fill up, even though his request terrified me.

I tightened my lips so he wouldn't see them trembling. My thoughts tumbled around like pebbles in a polisher. How could I relocate now? I was in psychotherapy for all the confusion and emotional turmoil that I had going on under the surface, and didn't want people to know how much I was struggling. "I . . ." I stalled. "I'll need some time to think and pray about this."

"Take your time, and let me know."

During my time at Fuller Seminary I had taken a class called Emotional Health for Ministers. As we explored how our spiritual lives interconnected with our emotional lives, I came to the conclusion that I could benefit from psychotherapy. My back pain and weakness tainted my daily life in all aspects and I needed help to find ways to cope.

I began to see Connie Doukas, a therapist who'd graduated from Fuller's School of Psychology. I hadn't counted on the fact that through therapy I would discover so much more. I discovered I really didn't know how to communicate effectively with the male species and that my relationship with men in general was a disaster. I'd grown up with the tumult of sibling rivalry and bullying at the hands of my brother Thomas. My relationship with my father needed some fine-tuning to help resolve some past hurts. I was pleased with how he and I were growing closer together, because Connie helped me learn skills to be able to better express myself with him when his bristly side came out.

I knew that if I went to the seminary in Chicago I'd lose the momentum of my healing processes; I wanted to stay the course in Pasadena.

So, two weeks after Pastor Graydon made his offer, I went to him and hesitantly asked, "May I begin the required theological classes right here in town at Fuller?"

Please say yes...

His familiar, broad smile gave me courage. "That sounds like an excellent idea! You can continue your Hispanic ministry and take one or two classes at a time. Then, the following year, I'd like to see you at North Park Seminary."

Even though I felt flattered that Pastor Graydon would give me such affirmation, I had some conflicting emotions regarding the prospects of becoming an ordained minister in the Evangelical Covenant denomination. On one hand, I felt honored that he would believe in me and encourage me to reach that mountaintop. On the other hand, I wasn't sure that I even believed in myself enough to be able to climb up this ministerial Mount Everest. I did know, however, that I was capable of taking those first steps in the foothills so I went ahead and enrolled in two classes that Pastor Graydon had suggested.

Here I was, back at Fuller in late 1987 for another round. In my Theology of the Gospels class, I struck up a friendship with Xavier Rosas from El Salvador. He was studying to become a pastor in the Assemblies of God denomination, similar to Pentecostal but not as conservative.

Could Xavier be another *experiment* for me? His black wavy hair and deep dark eyes were similar to Joe's, but his personality couldn't have been more different. He had a quick sense of humor but always maintained good taste. A solid Christian and a respectful man, he was five years younger than me but was already working part time in a church in East Los Angeles and on a track with his denomination for ordination. Often after our class, he and I would spend time chatting in the Catalyst coffee shop on Fuller's campus. After a month or so, we spent more time together—having dinner, attending lectures or musical events, or just plain walking together holding hands.

Here I was, dating a man again, convincing myself that I was heterosexual. We were attracted to each other, weren't we? We looked cute together, didn't we? I would find myself repeating such statements in my own mind, a litany of wishful thinking.

One evening while Xavier and I were walking hand in hand in Old Town Pasadena, we stopped in front of a store window.

"*Mira*, Sharon! Look! *Chocolate y vainilla!*" He held up our interlaced fingers. Dark brown, white, dark brown, white...

We both laughed and continued walking. I enjoyed his playfulness.

When I spent time with Xavier, I dressed up, usually in skirts and dresses. I felt that he deserved it. When I was with him, I didn't ever want to appear to be tomboyish. After my somewhat positive sexual experience with Ethan, I understood that I was a woman, and wanted to express my best, God-given, feminine side with Xavier. I resolved that I would be a respectable woman with this respectable, and respectful, man.

Each time he saw me, a huge smile spread across Xavier's face and he'd say, *"Luces bien bonita hoy."* (You shine very pretty today.) And I would swell with satisfaction.

My friends Jude and Finja married one another the year that Xavier and I began dating. I was honored that they asked me to play guitar and sing at their wedding. I selected my outfit carefully for the event: a matching yellow cotton blouse with a straight skirt slit up one side. I never wore heels because of my back problems, so I figured my Birkenstock sandals would do the trick for the wedding event. The people would be looking at my face anyway, not at my feet, I reasoned.

As we were leaving the wedding, Xavier commented, "I couldn't believe that you wore those clunky brown sandals today. Don't you have any pretty heels?"

The joy I'd felt over singing beautifully slipped away like a minnow in the rushes. I had worked hard to put in a good appearance. I'd failed. What was it about men that required women to please them at every turn?

⌒ℓℓ᳕

Just about every evening, Xavier studied in the Fuller Library. He liked a particular secluded study carrel on the mezzanine. Often I'd sneak up on him from behind and slowly let my hands and arms envelop him. He'd reach around, a big smile on his face, gently extricate himself from my clutches, and ask me not to do that there. I would feign kissing him, making quiet little sucky-sounds, but he'd swat me away like an annoying fly.

When we finally had a real talk about why he reacted that way, he explained that he was a Man of God and needed to keep up an appearance of purity while in public.

Sheesh!

Sometimes I'd wonder how I could ever learn to behave in a way that some of my Christian friends called *godly*. Especially with Xavier. He said needed to keep up a certain appearance. I had no clue what was really going on inside me, so had no ability to keep up appearances. I was trying so hard to discern what would be an "appropriate" way to act with Xavier, but I just wasn't very good at acting, I guess.

Often, Xavier and I held hands as we sat cramped together in my little red Toyota on Oakland Avenue and talked for hours. His hands never strayed. No spark ever ignited. His lips were only for speaking.

Maybe I wasn't good enough for him, I thought. Maybe he could see past my dresses and makeup and knew the truth about me. Maybe I had offended him in some way.

Slowly but surely, we saw each other less and less. I would tell myself, *He must have had to study more. I had to work more at my church. Maybe someone told him something about me.* Whatever the reasons, our supposed romantic relationship gently faded like the early-morning fog. Surprisingly though, we remained friends.

I still couldn't figure how to put the pieces of my puzzle together. In spite of all my attempts to deepen my walk with God, to read my Bible, and even to preach as a pastor, I still couldn't *get it* that I was wired differently than the people around me.

CHAPTER 17

SIN

It was now the summer of 1988. I was thirty-eight years old, watching my childbearing window of opportunity closing and fearing I would never marry. The deep disappointment over my three failed attempts to develop a serious relationship with a man festered inside of me.

As I finished up another theology class at Fuller in the summer quarter, the prospect of going to North Park Seminary sat in my belly like an undigested meal. I would postpone the Chicago idea as long as possible. I couldn't leave Connie, my psychotherapist. By now I was seeing her two times a week, and though I wasn't making much progress in understanding my life's underpinnings, I was convinced that one day I would experience a breakthrough and everything would finally make sense. Chicago would have to wait.

I was successful in ministry—or so I thought—and people were coming to our little Hispanic church, some of them getting saved (accepting Jesus as their personal Savior). Jude Renner had finished his internship, so a part-time Puerto Rican volunteer preached on occasion, giving a more Latino flavor to our gatherings. Pastor Mateo could roll his R's like a drum roll and had an infectious laugh and a passion for saving souls. Every Sunday that Mateo was around, I felt like I was drinking a Red Bull full of spiritual caffeine.

I dropped in to Pastor Graydon's office one morning and told him that I needed to stay on in Pasadena for a while longer.

He motioned me to a chair, then smiled and listened attentively to the reasons I was able to reveal to him. I focused on my connections to Fuller.

"Your ministry here is what we've always dreamed of in our outreach to the community," Pastor Graydon said when I was done explaining. "The Lord is pleased with all that you've been doing. Don't postpone Chicago for too long. The Evangelical Covenant denomination needs bilingual pastors like you. Sharon, your passion drives your success." He tapped his leg. "If you can spend at least twelve months in Chicago, get the required theological classes under your belt, take specific classes in Covenant history and polity at North Park, you could probably get ordained by the end of 1989."

"Give me another six months to take classes at Fuller, and then I'll be ready for North Park," I said. "Please." I hoped it didn't sound like I was begging. I was trying to convince myself that I would be ready, but deep inside I was terrified.

Not only did I not want to interrupt my psychotherapy, I didn't want to live so far from my parents, even if it was for only a year. Even though I'd lived on my own for years, when I returned to California from Mexico I felt like I was engaging with them on a deeper level. Perhaps it had to do with how fragile I felt at the time, and needed my mother and father to be ready "in the wings" in case I had a breakdown.

Pastor Graydon reached out to pat my shoulder in his fatherly way. "In three months I will no longer be here. I'm retiring. I believe you will work well with Pastor Raymond Howard, who will be taking my place. Carl Goodwin, the assistant pastor, will still be here, as always."

My heart sank. Pastor Graydon was a good listener, and he believed in me. I would miss him terribly. I determined that I would take advantage of his fatherly advice for the remaining time before his retirement.

⁓⁓

During Pastor Graydon's last week the pastoral staff had a special Goodbye/Hello luncheon and introduced Pastor Howard, a man in his fifties, from Minneapolis. He was handsome, gregarious, and eager to live in Southern California. I liked how he looked me in the eye when he asked me what my role on the pastoral team was.

The following week I went to his office. Pastor Graydon's books had been replaced with newer tomes of Bible commentaries and historical reference books. I determined I would learn to work with this new senior pastor. I'd show my best face and muster the energy I needed to do an excellent job in ministry.

"I am glad to meet a bilingual female colleague." Pastor Howard shook my hand and I sat down. He didn't feel fatherly, but was pleasant. "Share with me what your responsibilities are. In Minneapolis we don't have as many Latino people as you have here. Go ahead and tell me everything." He smiled and waited.

I told him I knew the neighborhood streets of northwest Pasadena as if I lived there myself. I loved speaking Spanish every day, singing and playing guitar to lead worship with *Coritos de Alabanza* (praise choruses), and the ESL/Citizenship classes were going great. Overall, Pasadena Covenant Church was expanding, and this brought joy to my heart. I explained that sometimes I couldn't believe that I was doing a missionary kind of ministry right here in my own city.

During our conversation, a wave of excitement washed over me. I couldn't believe that soon I would be a full-fledged ordained pastor in a mainline evangelical denomination. I felt proud of myself. And I knew my parents would be proud too.

❧

Many ESL students in our citizenship classes had applied for amnesty and were on track to receive their legal papers. Sometimes, however, the immigration process didn't seem to be working very well. I determined I had to be creative to help things along.

One student, Eduardo Casas, needed my help. It was already 1988, and he'd started his ESL classes two years before. I invited him up to my office at the church.

"Can you figure out how I can get my legal documents?" said Eduardo. "The US isn't giving Peruvians amnesty right now."

"Sure, whatever it takes," I said without hesitation. I had become familiar with a number of case studies of failed amnesty applications and felt frustrated with the broken, inconsistent system the US government used to deal with the multitude of immigrants flowing over our borders to seek a better life. I had no qualms about trying to beat the system to better serve the people in our ESL classes and in my congregation.

I had an idea. "I could teach you to speak a Mexican accent and you could lie your way through your interview with *La Migra* (Immigration)," I suggested.

I was a Christian who had been taught the commandment *Thou shalt not bear false witness*, meaning don't lie, but I felt that this was a justice issue. Justice would have to trump the damning truth. At eighteen, Eduardo had fled an oppressive political system in Peru. Yes, he had come into the US illegally, but now he had a job, paid taxes, and wanted to go to college and begin a new life here. Passing the amnesty exam would give him the opportunity to reach his goals. God's ways were not man's ways, I reasoned.

Eduardo and I worked together for a few months, until he was ready to pass the inquisition of the immigration officers' interviews. Sooner than we could have even hoped, he was able to take a bus to Calexico, very near the Mexican border. He'd go to the immigration office there.

A week later, my phone rang.

"Yes, I will accept a collect call from Calexico," I breathed anxiously into the receiver.

Eduardo's voice came on the line. "I wanted to tell you the good news. They believed my story and granted me amnesty. See you tomorrow in Pasadena."

"Thank God!" I smiled into the telephone. "I can't wait to hear how you pulled it off."

He became a US citizen the following year.

Hearing stories of civil war, poverty, gang violence, threats, and death of family members, I would do anything and everything necessary to help these members of my community stay in the US. Several churches in Pasadena were already Sanctuary Churches, but ours was not.

When we had started ESL classes back in 1986, I'd met Michell Zurreva and she'd told me, "*Yo quisiera aprender inglés.*" (I want to learn English.)

She was the first one in the long line at the registration table. I looked up into the brown face of a young woman with perspiration glistening on her forehead—it was a hot afternoon.

"The civil war in Nicaragua just keeps on going," Michell told me. "My sisters and nephews are in danger. Hopefully, I can bring them to the United States before tragedy strikes our family." She lowered her gaze.

A lump rose up in my throat and I thought, *I'll do anything to help these people. That's what Jesus would do.*

A few years later, after Michell had learned English, processed her legal papers, and brought several family members to the US, she would tell me what went through her mind the first day she saw me. "When I saw a redheaded white lady sitting at the registration table, my heart sank. How will we communicate? Then you greeted me in perfect Spanish! I knew at that moment that my life would change forever. It has! *Muchísimas gracias.*"

These kinds of encounters always solidified my resolve to continue in ministry. This was where God had called me. Where I belonged.

My close relationships with the Latino people at my church made me feel like I was part of their family. I wanted to assimilate into their culture. Someday, I'd have a Spanish surname. I had not let go of my hope to find the husband God must have waiting for me—and I hoped he would be a Latino man. Until I found him, I would continue to dress and act as feminine as possible.

My definition of "feminine" at this point in my life included wearing dresses, hose, attractive flats, longer hair, and makeup; sitting, walking, and moving my hands in a particular way; avoiding certain vocabulary; and so on. Girls looked and dressed like *this*, not like *that*, according to my parents, my church, and broader society. And during my college years, if I so much as crossed my legs *like a man does*, the Navigator leader would slap my leg down and harshly rebuke me in front of everyone. In that world there was no wiggle room, no space for variation, and no self-expression. Gender had strict rules and regulations.

Most of the time, my ministerial duties kept me so busy I could toss little prayers up to God while still running at full speed. *Listen up, God. My ministry is going well. I'll go to Chicago soon enough. About that husband you've got planned for me—somehow I'm not finding him here. I'm being the best woman I can be, not bothered anymore by attractions to other women, and open to your direction in my life. Don't let anything get messed up. Amen.*

However, there were moments of doubt that caused me to check my motives and monitor my own behavior carefully. I could suppress that same-sex allure/inclination up to a point, but I had to tell myself to be cautious around certain women—in particular, Bela Chaco, a woman from Guatemala. She was probably in her mid-twenties and I was thirty-eight, not quite old enough to be her mother but old enough to feel the gap between our ages. Still, I sometimes felt that pulse, like bubbles beginning to boil up inside, just from sitting next to her. Her beautiful brown eyes and winsome smile too often caused me a visceral reaction. Another prayer to toss heavenwards: *Hey God! I can't afford to stumble. I am a pastor in an evangelical church. A woman of God. I am a normal woman. I need a husband. Where are you, God? Amen.*

Bela lived in the gang-dominated area of northwest Pasadena. Many of the houses there were large two-story homes, built in the 1920s, with six huge bedrooms. Families or friends of four to six people could rent one bedroom with a lock on the door, sharing one bathroom per floor. Bela rented a second-floor room in one of those big houses on North Raymond Avenue. The shared kitchen and living room for the entire house was a place of fellowship, laughter, food, and late-night conversations. I felt at ease visiting these homes, sitting on front porches and just hanging out with people. Perhaps because I was known as the *white-lady pastor*, I didn't even think about my safety, I just thought about the people I knew and the God I represented. Those evenings were an enjoyable part of my ministry duties.

After Bible study sessions at the church, I would make my rounds taking people home in my little red Toyota Tercel. I thought it was cute that Bela called my car *El Bomberito* (The Little Fire Engine). Sometimes, she would request to be taken home last so she could ask me questions about God or about some personal issue. I wanted to listen to her, but I didn't want to be alone with her, afraid of what might happen. Often, she invited me into her house and we sat in the shared living room space with other folks, all of us talking together. But sometimes we would sit in my car in front of her house and she would tell me about her family and their situation in Guatemala.

Bela came from a poor rural area, and had come without documents to the United States to work so she could send money home for her sick mother. Because she only had a sixth-grade education, she struggled with the ESL amnesty class material. Sometimes I would tutor her either at the church or in her living room, trying to help her absorb the information needed to pass the exams.

After the Latino church service one Sunday, Bela and I clasped hands and prayed for her mother.

Bela pleaded, "*Oh Dios mío, cura a mi madre. Tiene cáncer.*" (Oh my God, heal my mother. She has cancer.)

Overcome with spiritual emotion, Bela and I both began to weep, and I reached out my arms to comfort her, holding her in what I thought was a motherly caress and gently rocking her until her crying subsided.

My logical self told me that comforting her was a pastoral, sensitive gesture, but my passionate sexual self set off clanging bells and warning sirens. I could feel her breasts pressed against mine. *Why is that such a big deal?* I asked myself. But it was.

Driving home later that day, my unwelcome dreaded sexual pull attacked me with a vengeance. What was it about Bela that made my body respond in this way? *Please God, answer my prayer already. Heal this defect I have.* I felt I was drowning in a tempestuous sea, yet I dared not scream for help. I had learned my lesson years before; I needed to keep my mouth shut about this topic. What should I do? I suffered in silence, too embarrassed to even share it with Connie, my therapist.

～ele～

Bela started asking me over to her house with greater frequency over the next few months. During these visits we would talk, read the Bible together, engage other people in conversation, and pray at the end. It wasn't a formal Bible study. It was just a "pastoral visit." Each time, I made sure that we stayed in a common area and that I kept my distance. My body was already doing things I hated. I couldn't admit to myself that I was wet with desire every time I was in her presence. Damn again! I resolved not to fall into sin.

I wasn't aware if anyone in our little Latino church group had noticed that I was paying these extra pastoral visits to Bela. My normal ministerial responsibilities included many house visits to various people, and I made sure that I had a reason for each visit to Bela's house. I was too deep in denial to acknowledge to myself that my body might harbor a hidden agenda.

One morning, Bela called me. *"Estoy enferma. ¿Puede venir?"* (I'm sick. Can you come over?)

Mustering my best pastoral voice, I lied, saying, "I have appointments all day. Can I come around six this evening? Hope you feel better. God bless you."

Talking for one minute with this demure, lovely woman with the tantalizing voice, my body was already reacting. *Help me, God!* I needed the day to pull myself together. Were my little tossed up prayers falling back down again?

～ele～

At six that evening, Bela answered her front door wearing only a robe.

I braced myself. *"Buenas tardes.* How can I help you now that I'm here?"

I was hoping to have the usual visit with her in the house's common area, but she said she needed to go change and, to my surprise, invited me to ascend the stairway with her.

I agreed, telling myself that I'd be upstairs for less than five minutes. I said stiffly, *"Ojalá que todo esté bien con usted."* (I hope all is well with you). I had to be polite. Formal. Right?

I followed Bela from the living room to her bedroom. Once we were inside, she gently closed the door. She didn't look sick at all. She looked very fine. Very beautiful, in fact.

She met my eyes and crooked her finger. *"Venga aquí."* (Come here).

The light switch of my resolution to keep my distance from Bela clicked to OFF. My sexual attraction to her clicked to ON. My body swelled with desire. What might it feel like to kiss her? To see her naked?

God, help me! I pleaded silently.

She turned around and let her bathrobe fall to the floor. Her sheer nightgown didn't do a very good job to cover her plump breasts.

Paralyzed, my eyes scanned her figure. She moved so close her warm Amber fragrance bathed my nostrils. Standing motionless, I allowed her to remove each piece of my clothing as if she were gently plucking petals from a daisy. She let them slip through her fingers to the floor. Then her nightgown slid down her smooth bourbon-colored skin and we came together before falling onto her bed.

Accusing voices off in the distance screamed at me, *You filthy sinner. Your ministry is ruined!* But I couldn't bring myself to care.

⌒ℓℓ⌒

On my drive home that night, I wondered when we could do that again. I craved more.

I also dreaded facing Connie at our next therapy session. Now I'd have to tell her what I'd done. I was tumbling into a bottomless chasm of no return.

When I arrived at the church office the next morning, I couldn't concentrate. I couldn't interact with my colleagues. I felt that every eye in the universe was looking at me. I was sure that everyone knew that I was a sexual pervert. I was naked before the entire world.

"Hey Sharon," Inez greeted me. "What's with you? You look like you've seen a ghost."

She had seen me stumble into a staff meeting before, like after the rape experience with that *puto* Joe. Today I must have looked even worse.

I stammered something, and then closed myself into my office. Everything around me had some deeper meaning: The rustle of the papers and letters on my desk... *They're all laughing at me.* The slam of the file drawer... *The gunshot that should kill me.* The theological books on the shelves... *They're screaming Bible verses at me.* The light coming in through the window... *It's exposing my sin.*

Inez knocked quietly on my office door. "You okay in there?"

I yelped like a puppy with its tail slammed in the door.

She knocked more loudly on the door. "Hey! You've been in there all day without coming out. You even missed lunch." She slowly opened the door.

I was sitting at my desk, staring at the wall.

"C'mon. You sick?"

I couldn't respond.

"I'll walk you down to your car," she said, gently but firmly. "You need to go home."

The robot behind the wheel guided my car to its destination. I went into my apartment. Sat. Stared. My body automatically breathed in and out. In and out.

CHAPTER 18

CONDEMNED

After my crash day of withdrawal from the world, I called in sick to the church office.

Then I called Bela. "Hello?" I offered no pleasantries; not even a *Cómo está usted.* "You and I committed a terrible sin last night. Stay away from our church. Never call me again."

She didn't speak. I could only hear muffled sobs. But I felt nothing. I sat like a cardboard figurine. No depth. No feeling. Only a painted façade.

I was totally focused on how to get Bela out of my life once and for all. If the cancerous cells were completely removed, the cancer could not return—or so I thought. I needed to get her out of my community, my congregation, my context. I wasn't able to imagine how she herself might feel about our experience together.

I called in sick again the next day.

The following day I phoned Pastor Howard to make an appointment. I couldn't just keep calling in sick.

Sitting in his office, I wrung my hands. "Pastor, I've been sick. Not physically, but spiritually. Sorry I've taken a few days off. I did something terrible, and I feel so guilty that I can't function. I..." Words failed me.

"You look like you're having a tough time right now, Sharon," he said kindly. "Maybe you should take some time off work, sort things out, and come back when you're ready."

I sat motionless, studying a speck of dirt on the toe of my left shoe.

"Do you have a therapist?" he asked.

I nodded. "Yes."

"Tell your details to him, or her. I don't need to hear them." He didn't ask me anything. He didn't offer a rite of absolution. Actually, a spiritual flagellation would have felt better, but I didn't get that either.

I hadn't gotten what I wanted after any of my relationships ended. After Joe raped me, I had heaped guilt upon my own head, but no one I'd confided in had done so. After, Ethan, I'd wanted to be absolved from my willful sin and instead received that surprise response from Kelly Sims: *Did you like it?* My relationship with Xavier, meanwhile, had been as sterile as a gauze pad. Nothing to feel guilty about. Was that what a pure relationship with a man was supposed to be? I felt like a rat in a labyrinth—confused, no way out.

"Thank you for your kind words, Pastor." I stood and left, my tail of shame tucked between my legs.

⌒ℓℓᴈ

I had never before willfully engaged in a physical sexual encounter like this with another woman. I knew it was wrong. I knew what the Bible said about sexual activity outside of the bonds of marriage. I knew what the Church taught about faithfulness to a spouse. For God's sake, I was a pastor. I preached this stuff on a regular basis. Yet I had lain in a bed of passion with one of my female parishioners. Would I burn in hell for this?

Following Pastor Howard's advice, I took a leave of absence for two months. Never before had I fallen so far from grace. Where was God? I started seeing Connie three times a week.

It took many therapy sessions for me to be able to articulate what had actually transpired with Bela. Guilt and shame were drowning me. Daily, I visited my fitness center for slow swimming and unfocused gazing at the walls. At home, I just sat. I couldn't read. I couldn't even concentrate enough to watch TV. Never having been depressed before, my foggy mind, dull emotions, apathy and lethargy were foreign to me. I was a walking dead person.

Denial had cloaked me with a thick layer of darkness, even as I professed The Light as I preached from the pulpit. In her poem

"The Uses of Sorrow," Mary Oliver writes, "Someone I loved once gave me a box full of darkness. It took me years to understand that this too, was a gift."

It would take me two years more to understand the gift God had given to me.

⸎

As the date of my planned return to my ministerial duties came closer, I tried turning on the TV at home a few times. One evening, to my horror, I thought I saw my name appear on the ABC breaking news. Was I going crazy?

The next afternoon, standing in line at Vons, I was sure that it was *my name* headlined in the *Los Angeles Times* papers neatly stacked near the checkout. Then, driving home in my little red *Bomberito*, I believed I heard the radio announce my sin to the whole world: *"Sharon Smith Steps Down After Public Confession: Evangelist Admits Moral Sin, Leaves for Indefinite Period."*

I was convinced that I was that sinner. Destined to be publicly humiliated. Who would answer my cries for help? Why was the world talking about me?

Arriving at home, I clicked on my TV. As the tinny voice of the news announcer filled the room and the stories unfolded in the dancing blue-grey light of the miniscule box, I saw Jimmy Swaggart's sweaty face, not mine. Maybe I wasn't crazy after all.

Staring at the TV, I saw the repentant fire-and-brimstone televangelist weeping openly from his pulpit, and learned that he'd stood in front of 7,000 of his followers in the World Faith Center of Baton Rouge, Louisiana, that day and confessed that he had sinned, although on public television he had declined to disclose the exact nature of his sins. The announcer explained that an investigator had taken pictures of Swaggart with a prostitute at a motel.

Oh my God! What if someone took pictures of Bela and me? What if... ?

I hoped and prayed that no one actually knew the nature of my sin.

Swaggart publicly admitted to his wrongdoing and begged for forgiveness from his congregation and from God. He also offered to step down from his position for a period of time.

I had already stepped down for a couple of months. Did I now need to step up in front of my Iglesia Cristo Vive congregation at the Pasadena Covenant Church to confess my sin? I could not. I would not. Ever! I was convinced that I was worse than Jimmy Swaggart, anyway. I had willfully engaged in sexual behavior with a woman. Homosexual sin was the worst kind—and I had enjoyed it! Hell must be stoking its fires. Could God forgive me? Could God cleanse my guilt? Could God erase the desires that had plagued me since I was a little girl? These thoughts and questions consumed my entire brain. I couldn't imagine returning to my church in this condition.

Pastor Mateo could continue to fill in for me for now. I added another few weeks to my ministerial leave.

⁓⁓⁓

Finally, Pastor Howard phoned me. "Sharon, I don't want to pressure you," he said. "But we need you to come back soon. We will welcome you and respect you."

I trusted his word, though I was scared shitless. How could I go back and face anyone again?

The Sunday morning I was scheduled to return to my congregation, I had to run to the bathroom immediately after waking up. My nerves were so frazzled I had diarrhea.

I chewed up three Pepto-Bismol pills, had oatmeal for breakfast, got showered and dressed—and then stood inside my apartment door, unable to open it.

Methodically, I took ten slow, deep breaths to calm myself. *God is with me. He loves me and forgives me. I must go back to my ministry.* Before I could change my mind, I forced myself to go outside, get into my car, and drive to the church.

⁓⁓⁓

I arrived in fifteen minutes. Sitting in my car, I took a series of calming breaths again. Then, willing myself to hold my head high, I walked in smiling.

As the members of my congregation filtered in, filling the chairs of our little worship space, every face held a welcoming smile. Many came close to wrap me in bear hugs, and more than a few gave me kisses on my cheeks. These were the comforting caresses I longed to feel. I had been welcomed home.

My congregants had no idea why I had been gone so long. After our worship time, they told me they had missed me and were very glad to have me back. Even though I was still inwardly burning with shame and sadness over my own failure, I couldn't help but feel pleased that these people were still treating me like family.

Nonetheless, as my guilt gnawed its way through my mind and soul, I found that I could no longer prepare sermons. How could I preach about the love of God if I felt like my God was punishing me? How could I preach about the forgiveness of Christ when I felt like putrid scum skimming the surface of fetid waters? How could I preach about the healing hands of Jesus when Jesus's hands had never healed me of anything?

To maintain the appearance of a faithful pastor/preacher, I had to talk about something from my little lectern, didn't I? Anything. Anything at all. So, every week, I went to the Fuller Seminary Library, found old Presbyterian or Methodist preachers' sermons, and plagiarized them.

Standing behind my small pulpit each Sunday reading those sermons made me feel like I was just reading a script for a play. I'd look out over the eager faces of the twenty or so parishioners God had given to me, and I'd feel like I was lying to their faces. These people were coming to Iglesia Cristo Vive to meet God. To worship. To make friends like family. Couldn't I provide that for them?

One Sunday as I was presenting one of my concocted sermons, I caught the eye of a female parishioner who was looking up at me expectantly. Even though my mouth was saying the words I was reading, my mind began racing in another direction, under its own power.

Leticia. From Ecuador. Grad student in science. Smart. Talented. Attractive. Sexy. Sharon! STOP!

I had to grip the sides of the little lectern, look down and take a deep breath. I hoped that my little congregation thought I was praying. I was... but for self-control. Another toss-up prayer. *God! I am trying so hard to be pure. I am in therapy. Why does this temptation feel so overpowering? It's just not fair! All Leticia did was look at me.*

I don't know how I made it to the conclusion of that sermon that day. My thoughts had grabbed Leticia, flung her onto my sofa at home, and I began to make love with her. My imagination was just plain slutty.

I'd been involved in the lives of most of those people present in my little congregation for several years. There was Eduardo, whom I had helped become a citizen of this country. There was Michell, whose family sat in the congregation. They often thanked me for opening their doors of opportunity. There was Suyapa and Berta and Rosalia and Jaime and Esteban and Juan and Bonita and Santiago and Guadalupe and Socorro and Salvador and others. But not Bela. She had been banned.

I didn't hear from nor hear about Bela for over two years. Then one day, out of the blue, I got a phone call that brought back a horde of unwelcome memories.

"*Hola, Sharon. Soy Bela. Necesito verla a usted.*" (Hello, Sharon. This is Bela. I need to see you).

Why in the world would she be calling me now? I certainly do not want to see this woman. Ever again. But against my better judgment—propelled by a repulsive broth of guilt, remorse, curiosity, and stupidity—I agreed to meet with her. Maybe I should ask for forgiveness, I told myself. Maybe I would find some kind of closure.

I drove to her apartment near downtown Los Angeles. She rented a cramped room on the third floor of an ancient brick building. Common restrooms were down the hall.

As I willed my legs to walk in, my nostrils were assaulted by the musty smell of unwashed clothing draping the sparse furniture. Personal items cluttered the floor. I perched on the edge of what must have been a roommate's bed. Bela didn't look beautiful anymore. Her eyes didn't sparkle. Her uncombed, greasy hair fell limply over her shoulders. Her words were distorted. One side of her face drooped like melted wax, paralyzed with Bell's palsy.

It took all my strength to sit and visit with Bela for what felt like an hour but probably was only ten minutes. I listened to her talk. Guilt crept over me and seeped into my pores along with the stench. I couldn't bring myself to ask for her forgiveness. I had to flee.

Had I somehow contributed to her present condition? Did she too feel guilty for what we had shared during those unthinkable fleeting moments of sexual intimacy a couple of years ago? Had someone found out? I would never know.

What could her life have been had she never met me? How had my choices impacted her?

I thought I'd been broken enough by guilt and shame and my back injury, but my next malady would be far worse.

Sharon Wulfensmith

CHAPTER 19

PUNISHED

In the summer of 1989, I believed that God's wrath had finally caught up with my secret sins. I was in Santa Barbara to see my parents and Thomas, who was visiting with his family for a week from Wisconsin.

One morning the bright sunshine invited all of us to play at the beach.

"Let's build a sand castle!" I called to my two young nephews and niece when we arrived at the shore with buckets, toy shovels and plastic yogurt containers—perfect tools for castle-making—in hand. Kneeling in the sand, we worked for a couple of hours, then let the waves gently splash away our sand creations.

Afterward, tired and sunburned, we returned home to my parents' house for lunch and a much-needed siesta, collapsing into a happy pile of arms and legs on the living room rug.

After about half an hour my youngest nephew, only six, jumped up. "Let's go outside and ride bikes! Get up, Aunt Sharon!" His little legs ran in place as he tugged at my arm.

Still groggy, I responded, "Sounds great!" But when I stood, my body collapsed back onto the floor in a heap. Were those red, elephant-size sausages my legs? What had happened?

"C'mon, Aunt Sharon! I'll race ya to the bikes!" He darted out the door.

Shaken, I managed to shout back, "Not now, Nate." I turned to his older brother. Hey Josh, you feelin' okay?"

"Sure! Why? I'm gonna beat ya." He and his little sister took off running too.

"You all go without me this time." My voice came out in a raspy whisper, too quiet for them to hear.

The kids were fine. Clearly, I was not. Could I have inadvertently knelt on a poisonous jellyfish? A sea urchin? My flesh was not pierced, but something was boiling inside my knees. Two hot-pink water balloons connected my upper and lower legs.

I took Advil and put on ice packs, and my parents called a doctor. He said it was probably just temporary and the swelling would go down by that evening. Not to worry.

But I did worry. A lot. I could only take a few steps at a time. I had to scoot on my butt to get up and down the stairs.

A few days later, my father took me home to Pasadena in his car and my brother followed us in my car. I couldn't drive. My legs were so weak I couldn't press the accelerator, let alone the brake pedal.

I wanted to see my chiropractor, Dr. Field. *He knows every-thing*, I told myself. *He'll fix this problem in a snap.*

My father and brother bought some food for me, dropped it off, and then left me. Alone. God, I felt so terribly alone.

That first evening back at my place, I melted onto the sofa, feeling like I had used up a week's worth of energy in that one afternoon. What was wrong with my legs? I hobbled to the freezer in the kitchen to get two of the gel-pack ice compresses I'd bought a while back from my chiropractor for my back pain. I tied the blue ice on each knee with bandanas. The coldness gave me relief, but the gel-packs felt like they weighed about nine hundred pounds.

Oh God, it has been hard enough to deal with my back pain, and now this? It's too much for me to bear. Please... please heal me.

I called Dr. Field and set up an appointment for the next day.

The next day Dr. Field asked me many questions, carefully examined my legs, took measurements of their girth, and then wrenched, pulled, twisted and just about yanked them out of my hip sockets.

140

They swelled further once I returned home. So much for Dr. Field and his so-called treatment.

Every day became a major challenge for me. The previous year, Jerri Wilkins and I had called it quits being housemates, and I had moved into a two-story condo with a different roomie. It was difficult enough to go from living room to dining room to kitchen. Getting to my bedroom on the second floor was torture. I had to sit and lift myself up each step of the stairway. At least coming down was easier: I devised a way to slide sitting on a pillowcase.

Several parishioners from my congregation came to bring groceries, cook, or take me to doctor appointments. If they had felt like family to me before, at this time they were demonstrating their care for me in the most beautiful way. I was deeply grateful for their friendship and love.

Unfortunately, I had to call in sick again to my pastoral job. This time I was sure to tell Pastor Howard that my affliction was physical rather than spiritual.

Over the next few months, I received varying diagnoses, from an allergic food reaction to chondromalacia (damage to the cartilage under the kneecap). I took lots of Advil, Tylenol, aspirin and other over-the-counter remedies. Medical doctors prescribed steroids and strong anti-inflammatories. My stomach reacted. I developed colitis.

I tried support groups for fibromyalgia patients. Self-help books taught me nothing. I was desperate to find an answer. Google hadn't been invented yet. No doctor knew what to do. I felt like I had aged so much that I needed geriatric care.

Small groups of people from the church came and prayed over me, laying on hands for healing. Finally, one orthopedic doctor ordered crutches. When that didn't help, another ordered a wheelchair.

Nothing eased my pain. I suffered alone. And because I was the kind of person who found a spiritual reason for everything, I threw myself more deeply into my feelings of self-hatred and blame, believing that God might be punishing me. For eight years I would wonder what had actually happened to my legs.

I felt like an unraveling tapestry with broken threads. Secret moths had chewed gaping holes into the fabric of my life. About a year earlier, my ministry had been thriving and successful. Now my life was in tatters. I needed to refocus my spirit.

~·~

I asked a friend to drive me to Casa Maria, a Catholic spiritual retreat center near Santa Barbara, where I planned to fast and pray for a weekend.

On my last afternoon there, I sat on a smooth fallen log in a secluded wooded area. Small birds flitted past and an occasional monarch butterfly fluttered nearby, her mysterious message eluding me.

I gazed upward through a clearing in the tree branches and focused on the contrast between the clear blue sky and the bright white, fluffy clouds floating in it. Those clouds didn't hold their shape for very long, I noted. They had no real substance; they were just vapor. Could my life be drifting by, disappearing into the mist, just like those clouds? Surely it must be because of my sin with Bela, I assumed. Would I have to stand up in public and confess to the whole world, like Jimmy Swaggart had done? I had set aside the weekend to listen to the voice of God. What was God's message for me?

Various passages from the Bible came to mind as I sat there:

"...Put aside the deeds of darkness... behave decently... not in sexual immorality ... Do not think about how to gratify the desires of the flesh." –Romans 13:12-14 (NIV)

"Now the acts of the flesh are obvious: sexual immorality, impurity, ... orgies... Those who live like this will not inherit the kingdom of God." –Galatians 5:19-21 (NIV)

"...God cannot be mocked. A man reaps what he sows." –Galatians 6:7 (NIV)

My physical maladies must be a manifestation of my unrepentant heart. Surely, I concluded, God was punishing my sin.

I would have to take responsibility for my actions and make some difficult decisions. First, I needed to move to an apartment with no stairs. And no roomie this time. Next, I would have to resign from my pastoral position. I couldn't work without being able to walk, and surely I was unworthy to be a pastor.

As for ordination? That was never going to happen now.

⸻

After returning to Pasadena, I quickly found an apartment on Lake Avenue. The friends who had been coming to pray for me got a truck and moved me, setting up my new small apartment in no time. I was so grateful for their loving help.

A few days later I called a Honduran pastor in the area and told him I had some sort of disease and couldn't work. Pastor Pedro Quesada, of the Iglesia de Amor evangelical church agreed to help out.

I went to see Pastor Howard that same day. My knees were on fire and my body was about to fold up into a heap, but I summoned enough energy to go to his office. "I am so sorry that I have taken so much time off, and have not completed my duties. I have come to submit my resignation, and—"

"Sharon," he interrupted. You seem to have an unusually heavy burden to bear with this illness. I wonder if some of it is caused by an inner turmoil, or . . ."

It was my turn to interrupt. "I'll beat this thing. For sure." I hoped he would agree, but my shaking voice belied the confidence my words suggested. "I spoke with Pastor Quesada this morning and he's willing to step in and work with my Hispanic parishioners." I pressed my eyelids closed to block the tears that wanted to spill out.

Pastor Howard's voice was calm. "I'm sure everything will work out. I'll call him this afternoon. I pray that God will give you healing. For everything." He stood, came to where I was sitting, and actually gave me a hug.

In the safety of my car my tears came out in a flood. The drive home to my new apartment was less than a mile but felt like a hundred. My heart was heavy as lead.

Unable to bring myself to publicly confess my terrible sins, I continued to languish for several more months, barely going outside. Depression yearns for sleep, so I spent more hours in bed than awake. I used padded knee braces and crutches when I had to leave the house, or had friends take me places where I could use my wheelchair. Friends came and went, helping me and praying for my healing.

Would it ever come?

CHAPTER 20

HOPE

A few friends from Pasadena Covenant who had been praying for me told me that I should go to the Vineyard Church in Anaheim, a charismatic denomination that focused on worship, healing, and the casting out of evil spirits. Even at Fuller, I had been told a few stories of miraculous healings and deliverance from demonic forces through the ministry of this Anaheim church. My favorite Fuller Seminary professor, Dr. Daemon Fanger, had spoken about it during several special class sessions in the evenings.

Desperate for healing, I figured I'd be a good candidate for this new type of religious experience. After all, I felt that my un-repentant heart, sexual sin, and pervasive guilt needed to be cleansed. I became determined to steer my expectations toward this new avenue of faith.

"There must be a reason you're sick," George Walsh, one of the guys from my church who'd come to my house regularly to pray for me, told me one evening. "Confess your sins and God will heal you. Simple as that."

When I first met George, I'd felt attracted to his positive spirit. He asked me how I was feeling, never seemed to judge me, and always promised to pray for me. He was in his early twenties and had the energy of an athlete. I thought if I hung around people like him, some of that positive energy might rub off. So I felt pleased and readily agreed when he suggested, "Come with me and my friends to the Vineyard next Sunday evening."

Does God still do miracles these days? I wondered. I hoped so.

⌒ℓₑ₂

It was still a physical challenge for me to drive more than just a few minutes, so I asked George if he'd take me to Anaheim.

For over an hour, he maneuvered us through the LA traffic that Sunday afternoon. The long ride solidified my legs and lower lumbar like brownies gone brittle after lying on the counter too long. When we finally arrived, it was a painful experience unfolding my limbs from the car—but once I managed, I stared at the vast parking lot in awe. I couldn't believe how many cars were still streaming in to find parking places.

Holding on to George's arm to steady myself, I hobbled into the building. People young and old flooded through the doors to find seats in the rows upon rows of folding chairs that lined the vast warehouse floor. Loud worship music accompanied by electric guitars and drums pounded painfully in my ears. Waves of people raised their hands, sang and swayed in dance-like movements. Some cried with loud sobs, others laughed or babbled in tongues, similar to what I had seen at the Holiness Camp Meeting when I was sixteen.

After an hour-long sermon, yelled by a preacher who must have had the loudest voice in his high school football cheering section, the congregation applauded wildly. Most of the content of what he'd said rang true for me—confess your sin and trust God's miraculous power to heal—but I had trouble swallowing his idea of thanking God ahead of time, even when you hadn't seen any tangible results yet. I wondered if it was like the elation I felt when a bank loan got approved but the funds hadn't been posted to my account yet. Sometimes the loan got snatched away, and you got happy for nothing. I had my doubts about my healing, so I wanted to play it safe.

I sighed and slumped in my chair, quite uncomfortable for my back. After another hour of singing, my body almost withered down to the floor. I just wanted to go home. I wasn't getting healed. I was getting exhausted.

When things seemed to be winding down, I grasped George's arm. "Is it time to go now? Please?" I was desperate for an escape from the pandemonium.

"We're just getting started," he exclaimed excitedly. "This is what you came for. We usually divvy up into smaller groups for prayer after the big service." Standing, he grabbed my hand and helped me up, then practically dragged me, limping, through the crowd to a special area off to the side.

"The prayers for healing are over here," he said as he delivered me to five Prayer Warriors. "I'll find you later," he called out through the cacophony of voices before disappearing into the throngs of people.

I stood amidst a small group of people, drowning in the chaos. Several Prayer Warriors gathered around me and asked me what I wanted healing for.

"My legs," I grunted.

Ten hot, sweaty hands pressed on my head, my shoulders and my back. "Jeeezus! Heeeal our sister Sharon this evening! Make her legs normal again. Right now!" implored a middle-aged man. He gazed at the heavens somewhere beyond the cracked white paint still clinging to the exposed beams and pipes of the unfinished warehouse ceiling. The others all prayed and swayed. They all went on for an insufferably long time, each soliloquy a mini-sermon in itself.

Finally, interrupting their prayers, I shouted, "I need to sit down! I can't stand up for much longer!"

"Have faith, Sister. We are praying for your healing," they persisted.

I raised my own volume to match theirs. "I do have faith. I just want to sit down. Right now!" Their insistence reminded me of a car salesman who won't let you think for yourself for even two minutes. Disheartened, I peeled my perspiring body out from under their healing hands and slunk over to a chair in a corner, the sinews of my knees almost unhinging before I slumped onto it.

The Warriors dispersed, finding a different victim in the crowded area to lay their sweaty palms on. "Jeeezus...!"

Near tears, I bowed my face into my hands to plead with God, *Why can't you just heal this? I'm only thirty-nine and I can hardly walk! Why me? I give up. I confess my sin of—*

"Hey Sharon!" Cutting through the noise, George's voice sounded almost harsh. "It's about time I found you! Been looking all over. Only about eight hundred people here tonight. Let's go. Hold my arm like this..."

I felt like a ninety-year-old invalid as I obediently shuffled back to George's car.

Over the next three months or so I returned to the Vineyard, each time hoping against hope for a miracle. Even though my first experience attending there had felt overwhelming, there was something that drew me back to it again and again. I had heard testimonies of people who had been miraculously cured of cancer, or of broken bones being mended. These people would talk about their CAT scans or X-rays showing normal results, and my heart yearned to be one of those people someday, waving my MRI films in the air and declaring that my lumbar vertebrae were normal. I wanted to prance down the aisle showing off neuro orthopedic scans revealing complete healing of my legs. Even as I fantasized about my healing, I regularly cried out to God in frustration and sometimes in anger, because my body remained the same with all its foibles and frailties. Still, I resolved that I would not cave in to my own doubt.

I purchased cassette tapes from the Vineyard and learned to sing their praise songs by heart. I bought their music books. At home, I played the praise songs on my guitar and sang. And sang. And sang. Maybe I could find the solution for my healing.

The repetitive music and lyrics seemed to bring me a semblance of peace. Yet the mysterious condition of my knees remained. Maybe I just needed to be more patient.

In time, God would surely heal me, I told myself.

During the time I'd been attending the Vineyard I had spoken many times on the phone with my parents about my incurable illness, and I knew they were concerned. However, they were unaware of the tincture of toxic shame that infected their daughter. I needed to tell them that I had resigned from my pastoral position at Pasadena Covenant and was attending a new church. It had been a few months since I'd seen them.

I called and let them know I wanted to come up for a visit. "I need to get away from here for a few days," I explained.

"You're always welcome to come and crash here. See you Saturday." My mother's voice had a way of pulling me in close.

When I got there, I went for a walk (or rather a gimp) on Hendry's Beach with my father. My legs still resembled cooked sausage. I hadn't counted on how challenging it would be to walk in soft sand—sort of like going through deep mud when you have to suck your boot out with each step.

"Your legs still look oversized," said my father. "Can you lift them okay to walk a little bit with me here?" His deep voice was soothing.

"I'll let you know how far I can go," I said. "I do feel a little better, but I really have no idea why I got this condition or what it is."

I changed topics, telling him how I'd had to resign from the Covenant Church staff. I tried to sound enthusiastic when I talked about the new church and how I especially liked the praise songs. I didn't want to reveal to him that the services lasted hours upon hours and that some of the people were peculiar, with their long prayers and strange utterances.

"People at the Vineyard have been praying for my healing," I said. "Maybe it just comes little by little." I stopped walking for a moment and stared out at Santa Cruz Island, barely visible through the cloudy mist—or perhaps the mist in my eyes was what was obscuring my view.

"I do believe that God can heal us, yes," my father said. "Just like he did when Thomas was a toddler."

I moved a little closer to him, recalling the story. "I remember Mom telling me about what happened when he drank that poison. She tried praying the Lord's Prayer, got stuck, and finally gave up. Dad," I said, my voice tight. "Sometimes I get so frustrated. First my back injury, and now this. It's just not fair!"

He turned to look into my face. "I guess Mom put it into God's hands because she ran out of words. Then, all of a sudden, the little guy was healed!"

"I wish it would happen for me that way, Dad, but it hasn't." My tears spilled out, adding more saltwater to the soft sand.

"We haven't given up on prayer or on you." He put his arm around my shoulder. "Let's just enjoy each other's company for these few days you're here. Sometimes God's timing isn't the same as ours."

We turned around and walked back in silence. It was better that way. Words. Sometimes they get all used up until there aren't any more left. I knew my dad loved me, and that was enough.

A few weeks later I went to visit my folks again. Being with them was like a sheltering in a refuge from the storm of my life. I could just be.

I sat with my mother in the family room as she finished up the edges of a baby quilt for her next grandchild, my niece or nephew, due to emerge into the world in another month. She looked up from her work. "Dad tells me you're attending a new church called the Vineyard. Do you remember that we have a Vineyard here in Santa Barbara?"

I shook my head. "I forgot. Where is it?"

"Down on Victoria Street near the Courthouse. How about if the three of us go together this Sunday evening?" Standing up from her Singer Featherweight machine, she unfurled the tiny baby quilt, stitched with intermingling pink and blue rectangles and squares. "This can be for a baby girl or a boy." She smiled, her blue eyes dancing and crinkling up at the edges.

Sunday rolled around and we went to the Santa Barbara Vineyard, housed in a large business building downtown. This group was smaller but had the same praise songs, the same loud guitar music, and the same yelled preaching. I had gotten used to it by now, but about halfway through the service my mother leaned over and shouted into my ear, "We'll see you out in the car when it's over!"

I wondered if there were different kinds of Prayer Warriors here in Santa Barbara. Ones whose hands weren't so heavy and sweaty. Ones who might listen to what I needed to say. But I didn't stay through to the end of the service, because I didn't want my parents sitting out in the car so long. I figured that I'd find out soon enough what the people in this group were like, and maybe get healed without so much hoopla.

Driving home, my dad said, "That was too loud for us. Say, did you notice that Dan and Kelly Sims were up in front helping to lead the worship?"

I shook my head. "I had my eyes closed most of the time so I didn't see them. I didn't know that they were involved with the Vineyard."

"They have Vineyard Bible studies in their home," my mother said. "Maybe we can try it out sometime soon. Surely it won't be so loud if it's just a small group."

"I'd love to do that. I especially like Kelly," I commented. Of course, I would never let my parents know what she had said to me when I'd confided in her about Joe and Ethan.

Sharon Wulfensmith

CHAPTER 21

HOPE SLIPPING AWAY

Even though I was making friends with some of the people in Pasadena who regularly attended the Anaheim Vineyard, I still felt like my life was slipping from my grasp. A dark tunnel was sucking me into its depths with the gravitational pull of a black hole. Nothing was getting healed. My physical limitations had made it impossible for me to work for the past year. I sold some of my mutual fund savings to pay bills because I was too ashamed to apply for disability benefits. I figured that I shouldn't get benefits for an ailment that was clearly my own doing.

My sausage-legs, meanwhile, remained the same: hot and weak.

My friends from the Covenant Church no longer came over to pray for me. I felt it was my fault they didn't come. I continued to find refuge at my parents' house whenever I was able to make the two-hour drive; they were always there for me and loved me unconditionally. Nonetheless, I felt completely alone. I guarded my secret sins well, sometimes trying to reassure myself that God couldn't really be punishing me like this. But deep down inside, I knew better. He was. I felt wretched—lost out in the cold.

One afternoon, I decided to fast and pray alone at my apartment. Perhaps a miraculous healing could happen after all. Tilting my comfortable La-Z-Boy all the way back, I sang the Vineyard worship songs and prayed for about an hour, making sure that I was praising God first and not asking for anything yet. That was what I had been taught. I believed that if I did everything correctly, I might find the magic formula for healing.

In the middle of one of my favorite praise songs I abruptly stopped and opened my eyes—and I saw a curious and frightful sight. A dark shadow was inching up the La-Z-Boy, slinking up my legs. The shadow became thick, like a flow of tar enveloping everything in its path. Its warm, dark stickiness oozed farther up and around my left shoulder. I cried out in fear, thinking, *Jesus my Savior! Help me!*

As I tried to say those words, the tarry blackness morphed into two hands with fingers that clenched around my neck. I struggled to breathe yet managed to squeak out, "I claim the cross of Jesus. You are a demon! I command you to leave me alone." My breath came out in short gasps, my words wheezing through my constricted airway.

Abruptly, a force flung me forward in the chair and I began to dry heave and spit onto the floor. I felt like I was going to vomit out my intestines, like I was being turned inside out.

Taking over my vocal cords, a shrill voice squealed from my mouth, sounding like a pig being slaughtered. It said, "I hate you, Jesus! You are not the Savior."

My body pitched downward as my hands clutched the chair's armrests. I pressed my eyes shut, trying to envision the cross of Jesus Christ, and again squeezed out my own words, though I was barely able to enunciate them: "Jesus! You paid for all my sins. I am forgiven."

My nails scratched into my own skin as I tried to free my windpipe from the grip of the tarry fingers clutching tighter and tighter around my throat. I couldn't get my breath; I was being strangled.

My brain separated from my body. From above, I could see myself in the La-Z-Boy, being murdered by a demon. Petrified that I would die right there in my own living room, I knew that no one would ever know the real cause of my death.

I managed to inhale one brief breath and yell, in between spasms of heaving and retching, "Jesus! Save me!"

Just as soon as I had enough air to speak, the demon again commandeered my voice box, screeching despicable curses against Christ. Of my own volition, I never would have nor ever could have uttered such blasphemous words. Some distant part of my brain registered shock at what I was hearing.

After about an hour of this turbulent storm, everything suddenly calmed. My vocal cords, raspy from the screaming voices that had hijacked my larynx, came back under my control. *The light of God is coming upon me*, I thought, and just then a brilliant yellow light came into the room, even though the physical light streaming through the parted curtain was the deep orange of the setting sun.

The light focused into a beam—bright and warm, like sunshine at the beach—that slowly wrapped itself around me, enveloping my weary body in a soothing embrace. As it did, I remembered how my legs dangled from my mother's lap when I was a child. I remembered how she massaged my back as my little voice pleaded for comfort. *Mommy.* Focusing upon this image, I inhaled the memory of her fragrance and I whispered to God, *Comfort me, Mama God.*

Physically exhausted, I stood up and made my way toward my bedroom. When I toppled onto my bed, hoping to fall asleep, a foreign, but this time not demonic, voice spilled from my spent lips. "*Bidda bidda gulu...*" I prattled.

Was this what speaking in tongues felt like? How foolish! I held both hands over my mouth, attempting to cork up the gibberish. Even though I was alone, I felt embarrassed by what was happening. After a short while, however, the whole scenario struck me as funny and I began to laugh. And laugh. And laugh. I couldn't stop.

Eventually, I was able to calm down and claim stillness. It had been two full hours since I had first sat in that La-Z-Boy downstairs. Was I finally healed now? And if so, of which malady? The back pain, the knees, or the sexual, sweaty-down-there thing? Or all of the above?

I'd never watched *The Exorcist* and never wanted to, but I guessed that this episode shared some similarities with a scene or two from that movie. The Bible is replete with examples of evil forces being overcome by the Spirit of God. Other religions have folklore of good versus evil as well. All of our traditions and stories come with some kind of a cultural and religious context, to be sure.

Had I actually fought with a demon? Or had I imagined the whole thing—a result of my involvement with the Vineyard sending the power of persuasion creeping into my psyche?

What had actually happened? I didn't have an answer. But I knew one thing: I wasn't healed. In the years to come, my illness and my pain would persist, guilt would rear its ugly head often, and I wouldn't even be able to bend my burning knees in prayer.

⌐⌐les⌐

Leaving a Vineyard worship service one evening, I perused the literature rack near the door. An attractive tri-fold flyer caught my attention: *Desert Stream: Healing the Homosexual.* My eyes flitted right and left, scanning the crowd. If my friends were to come by, I'd snatch up the flyer labeled *Playing Guitar for Worship Songs* or *Christian Home Decorating.* No one would know that I was really looking at a flyer for homosexuals.

I nervously touched several other flyers but kept my eyes on the Desert Stream tri-fold, mesmerized by the front cover. Could this be my breakthrough? Could this ministry actually help me redirect my life? Maybe hope was on the way. When I was sure that no one was watching, I quickly tucked the homo flyer into the pocket of my jeans.

⌐⌐les⌐

Riding home in the back seat of George's car that evening, I thought about what could happen if I aligned myself with such a group. What if Desert Stream could heal a deep, hidden part of me? Maybe I could be healed of my physical afflictions if my sexual sins didn't get in the way. The power of the Evil One had shown its repulsive face and had almost killed me, right there in my own living room. Even though I had privately repented of my sins, I felt that I could no longer walk with God the way I yearned to. I needed the power of Jesus Christ to reclaim my life once and for all.

Later that evening at home, I sat in my La-Z-Boy to carefully read about and contemplate the Desert Stream ministry.

Right away I identified with the testimony of Vivian, cited in the flyer. Her quote read, "I've had intense relationships with other women. During my twenties these relationships became sexualized, and I became ashamed and confused. I knew I had SSA (Same Sex Attraction), but didn't always act on it. There is no healing for this, or so I thought. I'll have to struggle with these desires all of my life." She continued, "I had some major problems, and then the wheels came off."

Reading Vivian's words, I thought, *This is exactly what is happening with my life right now.*

"I was in full-time ministry, but had to leave it," her testimonial continued.

Just like me.

"But just then I found a new church community that actually believed that God could heal my physical and emotional wounds..."

I thought about the past few months and the friendships I had developed at the Vineyard—the trust, laughter, tears, and prayers I'd found there. Like a family! Still, I wasn't sure I entirely fit in.

Smoothing out the colorful shiny tri-fold on my lap, I stared at Vivian's words. I examined my own living room, filled with family photos, my mother's paintings of flowers, my father's Japanese carving of a bird in flight, my bookcases full of theological tomes, Bibles, *Winnie the Pooh*, and *Calvin and Hobbes*. I stared out at the silhouetted giant palm trees lining the street outside my apartment windows. I sighed and felt the warmth of tears well up. Why did my life have to be so complicated?

Vivian had endured an unhealthy relationship with her struggling parents. She explained her "same-sex addiction" as being a result of her dysfunctional family. But that wasn't true of my experience. My parents loved me unconditionally. And I didn't have an addiction! I'd spent my life actively working to develop more feminine flair and trying *not* to have sexual feelings for other women.

In the end, Vivian described how she was now accountable to others and set boundaries to avoid unhealthy friendships with other women. She offered a list of rules to follow and scripted things to say or phrases to avoid. A formula for victory.

By now my mind was doing somersaults. I knew that on my own I couldn't get a hold of my female-attraction conundrum, but at the same time I couldn't imagine telling other people about it, like Vivian had had to when she joined Desert Stream. What if my family and friends all rejected me once they knew the truth? The thought terrified me.

I read another couple of testimonies cited in the tri-fold and then saw a familiar name on the bottom edge: Sedric O'Sullivan, Founder of Desert Stream Ministries. Had he been gay when we met in that Jacuzzi at Fuller Seminary housing back in 1983? Could he be a closeted gay man even now? Could people who suffered from Same-Sex Attraction actually be healed? Could they really become heterosexual?

If I chose to join a group like Desert Stream, I wondered, would I be throwing my body down onto the train tracks? Would I be asking to get run over?

I felt so weary of trying to find the right answers.

After reading the tri-fold, I let it slip from my fingers down onto the rug next to my La-Z-Boy. I was so tired of trying to be me. Who *was* I, anyway?

CHAPTER 22

VALENTINA

The money I had gotten by cashing out some of my mutual funds was running low. I needed to find a job. Sooner than later. I thumbed through the Yellow Pages and scoured the want ads in the local newspaper. The following ad caught my attention:

ESL Teachers Needed
English as a Second Language
Pasadena City College

I felt a bit insecure about my chances but went to the interview anyway, resume in hand. I wore the pretty yellow cotton blouse I'd bought for Jude and Finja's wedding with a dark, swishy, full skirt so no one would be able to see my thick knee wraparounds. My Birkenstocks, molded to my feet, were comfortable. I brushed and sprayed my short hair, hoping I'd look presentable enough. Oh yes, a splash of lipstick wouldn't hurt.

In the personnel office waiting room, I kept from picking my ragged cuticles by tucking my hands under my thighs. No one else seemed to be interviewing that day.

"Next! Miss Smith, please!" a shrill voice called out.

Taking a deep breath to calm myself, I entered the small stuffy office and sat down.

"Experience? Credentials?" The interviewer didn't mince words.

I handed over my resume, looking at horn-rimmed glasses perched on a narrow nose and a small hair bun perched above a tired, wrinkled face.

I puffed out my chest. "I recruited volunteer teachers and trained them to teach ESL by using curriculum that we developed, and many immigrant students were able to pass their amnesty exams. My Spanish language fluency helped me communicate with the Hispanic students."

"Have you worked with Asian students before?" she asked.

My throat clenched. "Not yet, but I am willing to work with students from any language group." I hoped I sounded like a pro.

"You will begin right away in Adult Education. Classes are non-credit, so you don't need a California teaching credential. You'll fill in for a teacher out on pregnancy leave." The interviewer slid a pen and a packet of paperwork toward me. "Complete this right now and I'll prepare your part-time schedule from now until the end of second semester." She paused momentarily. "No questions? Good."

I hadn't even had time to ask one.

I swallowed hard, took a deep breath, and began completing the forms. I decided I'd grab this opportunity. Over the past few months my still-swollen legs had gone down from 1,000 degrees to 99. They didn't throb with pain as much as they were flushed, swollen and hot to the touch, and the muscles just didn't hold me up. I figured I'd be able to walk from my handicapped parking space to a first-floor classroom. This part-time gig would pay me enough for rent and food. At least I wouldn't have to sell off more assets.

"Here's the attendance roster for your class." The woman's thin voice cut into my thoughts. The names were mostly Asian, as she'd said they would be. *Nguyen, Chin, Chiu, Dong, Fang...* How would I teach English to people whose languages I didn't know? It would be a steep learning curve.

But maybe this job would be a welcome distraction.

Monday came so fast I wondered what had happened to Saturday and Sunday. I arrived an hour early to assess the classroom and put my things in place. Grammar book, notebook paper, chalk, eraser, lots of sharpened pencils . . .

Was it eight o'clock already? Rapid-fire Chinese danced through the open doorway, and then I heard the tap-tapping of high heels clicking up the aluminum steps and into my pre-fab classroom trailer for Adult Ed ESL.

Middle-aged ladies in crisp business suits, balancing coffees in one hand and carrying their leather briefcases in the other entered through the door. My classroom quickly filled with thirty-five women talking quietly in Mandarin and other Asian languages.

No men? I thought. *Why?*

I would later learn that many of these women were the wives of men who owned businesses, corporations, and banks in Southern California.

"Good morning, students," I began. "I am Miss Smith, your new teacher. This is Basic ESL Level 1B. Today is February 1, 1990." I had written my name and date on the board. "Today we will review some English verbs."

Because the college had not provided me with a syllabus, I would have to lean heavily on what I had learned from the Pasadena Literacy Council when I had developed a curriculum for the ESL amnesty classes. I quietly huffed out a prayer under my breath: *God, help me to stand on these legs and not crumple to the floor. Make these students like me. I'm scared. Amen.*

After writing some verbs on the green-board at the front of the room, I mimed the meanings of the words, waving my arms and hands in the air, and chanted them loudly in present and past tense: "GO, go, WENT, went," and "DRIVE, drive, DROVE, drove."

The students all dutifully repeated after me.

"Now copy the verbs into your notebooks." My legs had returned to their temperature of 1,000 degrees by now and threatened to buckle under me. I leaned on the wall and shifted my weight back and forth to take a little pressure off. I couldn't wait to get home to lay ice packs on these damned sausages.

My skirt, though long enough to cover my knee braces, didn't quite touch my brown leather tie-up boots, which I had forgotten to polish. I hadn't had time to iron my white cotton blouse that morning either, and, with all my gesturing, it came untucked from my skirt. My short red hair was combed in one direction or another, I supposed; I had dashed out of the house without using my hairspray. And I wore no lipstick today.

Recently, a friend had made fun of how I dressed, calling me a dowdy missionary. I didn't care. After all, I *had* been a missionary in Mexico and Central America, hadn't I?

I continued the lesson. "I drive my car. I drove..."

As the students practiced the sentences with a partner, the classroom door banged open and then slammed shut and a young lady rushed in past me, looking for a seat in the crowded classroom.

A little out of breath, she said, "*Perdóneme por llegar tarde, Profesora.*" (Excuse me for arriving late, Professor.)

Not Chinese, not Korean, not Thai. She was blonde. White. Spoke Spanish. Where could her accent be from?

I motioned her to the only vacant spot, near the front, and responded, "*Siéntate, Señorita. ¿Tu nombre?*" (Sit down, Miss. Your name?)

"*Me llamo Valentina Esperanza Daiquiri Zamorro. Me dicen Valentina.*" (My name is Valentina Esperanza Daiquiri Zamorro. They call me Valentina.) Sitting down, she took out her grammar book, notebook, pen, and highlighter and leaned over to copy the verbs from a classmate's notebook to catch up.

She seems like a responsible type of student, I thought, watching her work. A shock of blond hair fell over her eyes. Slim fingers deftly held colored highlighters. She wore a sleeveless purple blouse tucked smartly into a black, straight skirt. She finished copying the verbs in record time. *Smart gal*, I thought. *In her head and in her style.*

And then, in an instant, my thoughts flailed out of control. *What's inside that purple top?* I wondered, and then immediately chastised myself. *Sharon, rein in your thoughts!*

I circled the students slowly, checking on those sitting near the back. *Focus! Verbs, spelling, short sentences.* I took a moment to take some deep breaths before returning to the front of the class-room, where I found respite behind my desk. My knees seemed to be telling me, "If you don't listen to us, we'll catch you on fire."

I felt ashamed and frustrated that my involuntary thoughts had taken me where I dared not go. How could this be happening again?

After two long hours, class concluded. As Valentina scooted out with the rest of the students, my eyes snatched a quick glance in her direction just in time to catch the movement of the curves be-neath that skirt.

Was I drooling?

The following Monday, I advised my students to wear loose cloth-ing, jeans and no high heels. Our lesson would be outside: How to change a tire.

As instructed, on Tuesday the women parked their cars in a line, trunks open. A Mercedes, a BMW, a Porsche...

Goodness! I thought. *These ladies have money.*

I explained where to find the tools, jack and spare tire. "In case you get a flat," I said, "you will need to know how to change it. May as well learn the names of the parts and the tools." At least today's lesson would be practical and, hopefully, interesting for them. I carefully noted all the verbs we would use in the English lesson after returning to the classroom.

I noticed that Valentina seemed adept at using the tools; she easily removed her right front tire from her shiny blue Nissan Maxima. I noticed another thing too: as she bent down next to her car, a gentle breeze billowed out her blouse. Instantly, my eyes—those "eyes of a man," like the Navigator, Harlin Fox, had preached about, in college—leapt into action, penetrating the sheer fabric of her blouse.

I forced my gaze away, cheeks burning. Why couldn't I dam these desires?

Several weeks later, on a Friday, I stayed in my classroom a little longer than usual, getting ready for next Monday's lesson. When I reached my car, I noticed a small envelope with a real flower placed under the wiper.

I grabbed the note, and before even getting into the car I ripped it open. A pink card with perfect handwriting inside:

Teacher,

Thank you for teach me English. You are best teacher in the world. I like you.

Valentina

Her perfume wafted out of the envelope and into my nostrils. I had the urge to flee.

I tossed the card and envelope onto the front passenger seat. As I drove, Valentina's perfume circled around my head.

At home, I placed the note next to my bed and inhaled its aroma several times during the night. I pressed it to my face repeatedly, even into Saturday. Why couldn't I put it aside? I had no answer. Like sacred incense, the fragrance transported me to an unknown realm. Or was this realm already known? Perhaps it brought back feelings of someone's Maja perfume.

That semester new students were enrolled regularly. I had trouble saying some of their names, much less remembering them. The Mandarin-speaking students coached me to say their names with a higher tone and a little flip-up for the first syllable, then a downward tone for the last syllable. Yan Zhang. Pin Ahn. Of course, I didn't have any trouble saying Valentina Esperanza Daiquiri Zamorro.

One morning, I noticed several new faces in the classroom. Men! I had to ask one of them to help me find ten extra chairs to place around the periphery of the room. The regular students had already dutifully taken out their books, and they busily reviewed the previous day's lesson as I began to call out the names on the roll sheet.

A blond shock of hair draped over a book near the back of the room. Valentina was already bent down over her book, markers spread out in front of her, taking notes and highlighting today's vocabulary words. I liked students who were diligent.

I began to call out the names. "Ching Chen."

"Here, Tih-cher," a squeaky little voice said as a small hand raised itself over the edge of the grammar book in front of Ching's face.

About halfway through the list, I called out, "Sae Kow." I reminded myself to inflect UP and then DOWN: *Sigh Cow.*

No response.

I looked over the classroom, searching for a raised hand. I wondered why all the heads of the Asian students were bent down, their books hiding their faces. "Sae Kow," I repeated, more loudly.

All the textbooks jiggled up and down slightly, faces still hidden. I felt confused.

One more time I said, "Sae Kow."

The jiggling and juggling of the textbooks increased, and I could hear muffled giggling. These were adults, not children. Why would they be giggling?

A hand raised up. "Miss. Eh... eh... no, no." The voice sounded insistent.

"Are you Sae Kow? I carefully inflected my voice the way the Mandarin-speaking students had instructed me.

"No, Miss," she said. "No say more."

Perplexed, I shook my head.

Suddenly, one of my Chinese students ran to the front of the room, cupped her mouth with both hands, stood on her tippy toes to reach up to my ear, and loudly whispered for all to hear, "Teacher say 'dog shit.'"

The class exploded into nervous laughter. Apparently, essential words such as *dog shit* had been learned the previous semester, before I became their teacher. I too laughed.

I concluded that Sae Kow was absent that day. It turned out that she was from Thailand, anyway. Not China.

Valentina's head bobbed up and down over her folded arms, her shoulders heaving with laughter.

CHAPTER 23

MUSIC AND ROSES

During the next few weeks I found more notes on my car. Sometimes I slipped a note to Valentina in the classroom, too, though I made sure the messages I wrote were professional and always had to do with learning English.

One day after class, she paused to speak with me as the other students were leaving and asked, *"¿Usted quiere escuchar esta música bonita?"* (Do you want to listen to this beautiful music?) She handed me a cassette tape.

"Thank you," I said awkwardly.

That evening, the sound of alluring Cuban love songs filled my living room. Why would a student share such romantic music with her teacher?

⌒ℓℓ⌒

Some disasters, such as a tornado or monsoon, can be predicted with enough lead time for people to take shelter. Other natural disasters, such as a tsunami, might come suddenly, with no warning, wiping out an entire coastline.

Faint voices tried to warn me about this Cuban young lady, seventeen years younger than me, but I couldn't hear them. Was I hearing but not listening? Would I survive the disaster that was about to strike?

⌒ℓℓ⌒

I knew just what to do: pray for Valentina's salvation. I was a minister of the gospel of Jesus Christ, no matter where I worked, so I would invite Valentina to attend a service with my old congregation. Valentina would hear the Bible's message, accept Jesus as her personal Savior, and become my Christian sister. My lustful thoughts and feelings would be brought under the control of the Holy Spirit. I envisioned my arms raised high, fists pumping a victory chant. Problem solved.

After class one afternoon, I said with confidence in my voice, "Valentina, I'd like to invite you to church with me."

"*Gracias*, I'd love to join you," she responded with a smile. "Can I bring some friends?"

"Sure!" I was caught off guard. I'd assumed it would take some convincing, but she'd bitten the bait right away. Maybe she was interested in Jesus after all.

～◦ఴ◦～

That Sunday before the morning service, we met in the parking lot of Pastor Quesada's church. I breathed a sigh of relief that she actually had brought a couple of friends along. I hadn't been able to sleep well the previous night, wondering how I'd feel sitting with her in church. Why was I so nervous? I hoped that she wouldn't mention those perfumed cards she kept giving me.

Valentina stepped toward me and nodded to her friends. "*Hola, Señorita Smith. Le presento a mis amigos, Amelia, Felipe y Renzo.*" (Hello, Miss Smith. I'd like to introduce my friends, Amelia, Felipe, and Renzo.) "Renzo and I graduated from the same university in Havana a couple years ago, but we never met until recently."

As I shook hands with them, I breathed easier. My thoughts had a way of racing ahead of me when I was near Valentina. *Surely Renzo must be her boyfriend*, I thought. *She looks so pretty today with her loose, light green dress with matching shoes. Could she have put light streaks in her already-blonde hair? I wonder if...*

It took me a moment to collect my meandering thoughts just to focus on going into the door of the church.

Once inside I could relax more easily. The church service was quite similar to the style of worship that I'd used when I'd been a pastor. Hearing the same choruses and listening to Pastor Quesada preach brought back many fond memories. After the service ended, I happily greeted Eduardo, Michell, and a few others who had been my parishioners at Pasadena Covenant. I certainly hoped that they'd never heard any gossip about me. Especially about Bela.

The church service over, Valentina suggested that we all go to El Condor Mexican Restaurant in Old Town Pasadena. Her three friends, plus Eduardo, Michell, and a few more people from Pastor Quesada's church decided to join us. I was relieved that I would have a buffer of several more people around. My nerves were getting a bit frayed because evil, sexy-type thoughts kept popping into my head. I silently sent up an impatient prayer: *Oh God, why do I always have to spend so much energy tamping this down? Fix this already!*

∽⁀ℓℓ⁀�i

Lunch at El Condor included good food, laughter, stories and more laughter. All in Spanish, of course. I just loved Valentina's Cuban accent and her spicy Cuban vocabulary. When we sat down at the tables we were all mixed in with the church people and I noticed that Valentina was sitting between Eduardo and Amelia, not next to Renzo.

As Valentina finished telling a funny story to the crowd, she said, "Amelia and Renzo got married last year and they're already expecting." A cheer rose from the happy group. "And Felipe is going back to New York City next week to start his grad program at NYU."

My mind shifted into overdrive. *Oh my God. Neither guy is her boyfriend. Well, at least it seems that Eduardo enjoys sitting next to her.*

By the end of the lunch, several people in the crowd were talking about starting up a little Bible study at a home. "Where should we meet?" asked Michell. "My apartment is too small."

Valentina leaned across the table, her light brown eyes drilling into mine. "My house is small too. How about in Miss Smith's house?"

I started. Was she volunteering my little apartment for a Bible study?

The group applauded and briefly chanted, "Miss Smith, Miss Smith, *estudio bíblico, estudio bíblico*."

I felt cornered but at the same time honored that this group respected me enough that they would volunteer my home for this. I couldn't refuse.

Before two weeks had passed after our lunch at El Condor, a group of eight had started coming to my place for Bible study. We sang, read Scripture, and prayed. I told them of my back injury in Mexico and my knee disease. Concerned, they prayed for me. Friendships bloomed. I wondered if it was okay for me to be friends with students. I told myself it was fine. They were all adults. Besides, I was doing the Lord's work, wasn't I?

The following Saturday, a deliveryman came to my home with two-dozen red roses in a fancy green-glass vase. "From Valentina," the little card read. Never having received red roses before, I stared at them with dumfounded wonder, then took the huge bouquet and placed it on my carved leather-topped coffee table in the middle of my living room. Why would a student send me roses? I just didn't get it.

The next day, my parents came to visit me. I ushered them inside with gentle hugs.

"My ESL job is turning out well," I said nervously. For some reason my heart felt like a yacht pitching up and down in the waves. They hadn't even sat down yet.

Covering my nervousness with humor, I told them the Sae Kow/dog shit story. "It's a challenge to work with so many Asian students without knowing their languages," I finished, chuckling, and finally invited them to sit down.

They acted as if they hadn't even listened to the story. My father quietly perched on the edge of the sofa, staring at the big bouquet. My mother stood by it, her fingers stroking several velvet petals.

"Where did these come from? Surely you didn't get these roses for our visit today." Her voice sounded flat.

I had gone to wash up a few cups in the kitchen sink. Without turning around, I said, "One of my ESL students sent them to me."

"A student? Why would he send you red roses?" she asked, bending to inhale their delicious scent.

"Just somebody in the class. She's in my little Bible study too." *Please don't ask me anything more*, I prayed silently into the soapy dishwater.

"She?" Her voice was level. "Sharon, when someone sends red roses it means that they love you."

"I don't know what you're talking about, Mom." I busied myself in the kitchen, wiping down the already-clean counters, keeping my back turned to my parents. The temperature in the kitchen rose by 10 degrees. Streams of perspiration coursed down my neck and between my breasts. I pushed back my glasses, which had slid down my sweaty face.

My mother said no more. I knew she knew too much already. *Can Valentina really be sending me a message of love?* I wondered. I decided that I'd have to talk sternly with her soon to clear up this uncomfortable misunderstanding.

"When you come up to Santa Barbara again next month, let's go to Dan and Kelly's Vineyard Bible study at their house," my mother suggested.

"Sounds good, Mom." I was glad we weren't talking about those roses anymore.

⌒⨆⌒

Several weeks later, I drove to Santa Barbara. My legs were still swollen, but I felt okay to drive.

After dinner on Friday evening, as my mother and I prepared to leave for Dan and Kelly's home Bible study, I called out, "Dad, you coming too?"

He was still eating ice cream in the kitchen and hadn't gotten ready at all.

"Not this time," he said. "The repetitive songs drive me nuts."

My mother and I went without him, and arrived just as the repetitive songs began.

I had grown to love those songs and enjoyed singing the Spanish translations in my Bible study at home. I'd play the guitar accompaniment, and Valentina often jazzed it up with tambourine or maracas, giving the songs a Cuban beat. I thought she was quite talented with those rhythms.

"Welcome!" Dan greeted us with a too-tight hug.

We joined in the singing. I raised my hands up and closed my eyes for the first ten minutes or so, and then spotted my mother sitting in a chair across the room. She was smart; my legs were swelling up again and I needed to sit down too.

After a while the singing concluded and Dan took control of the meeting.

"We have a new sister here who needs deliverance," Dan announced to the dozen or so people still standing. I looked around to see who he might be talking about. He caught my eye and motioned for me to stand in the middle of the group.

Were they going to pray for my knees? *Oh, good*, I thought.

I stood and let them place their hands on my shoulders and head. Their hands felt like the soft paws of a cat kneading my shoulders. As they prayed softly, some enunciating that strange language, I did my best to absorb their prayers and let myself dissolve into God's Spirit. Oh, how I yearned for healing. This prayerful experience was quite unlike the heavy hands and yelling at the Anaheim Vineyard.

As I breathed in the love and prayers of these wonderful people I heard a man begin yelling, "The cross of Jesus is a hoax! I hate you!"

I was perplexed that no one made him stop, so I opened my eyes, but all I could see were shoes. And the carpet. My face was on the floor, and the blasphemous words were spewing from my own mouth! My body shook as if I were having an epileptic seizure. How could this be happening again?

After a while, the convulsions ceased and the people calmly returned to their seats in the crowded living room. No questions asked.

When it was time to go home, we said our good-byes. My mother and I got into the car in silence.

Flushed with embarrassment about what had happened, I could only manage, "Mom?"

Her voice was firm but not unkind. "Remember when Jesus healed a man with an evil spirit and cast it out of him? I guess that's what happened to you."

She made no further comment. Not even after we arrived home.

Sharon Wulfensmith

CHAPTER 24

THE HOLY KISS

I couldn't wait to share my good news with my little Latino Bible study group at home. The next time we met, with animated drama, I told the group about my experience, as if I were relating the most exciting adventure of the latest Star Wars movie.

"And then I heard a man's voice yelling, but that voice was coming out of my own mouth."

The group members gasped.

"And my mother even thought that an evil spirit had been cast out of me." I made sure that I referred to the so-called demons of my back and leg pain and not to the slithering locks of Medusa that relentlessly tormented my brain and body.

After my impromptu synopsis of *Sharon's Demonic Voices Episode*, we carried on normally with our meeting: we read Psalm 100 aloud, about King David's praises and music, had good discussion and questions, sang many rhythmic Vineyard praise songs with guitar, and ended with prayer time.

With a hug and peck on the cheek, each member of the group said their farewell—*"Que Dios te bendiga, buenas noches."* (May God bless you, good night.) Then they all headed out the door. Except one.

Valentina stood inside with her back against the closed door. I walked toward her, reaching for the door handle. She took a step toward me as I extended my arms out for a quick, Latino-like good-bye hug and peck on the cheek. Instead, she reached up and, hands caressing my face, guided our lips together.

She kissed me tenderly once. Then she thrust her flicking tongue deep into my mouth. A volcanic intensity erupted between us.

I too thrust into her, drinking her in, devouring her. Our passionate agony transporting me to...

"No!" I cried out. "Get away from me!" I placed the flat of my hands squarely on her shoulders and shoved her back against the closed door. "This is evil!" I quoted what Jesus had said to Peter, the disciple: "Get behind me, Satan!"

Valentina's eyes widened, her face a mask of pain.

"I am a bad person. Leave my house!" I pled like a whining child.

"*¡Tú ni sabes quien eres!*" (You don't even know who you are!) Her words slapped my face. "Sit down! Now!" she commanded.

My body folded down onto the sofa, my head sagging into my hands, as I sobbed.

Still standing by the door, her voice now gentle, she asked, "*¿Ni sabes que eres una lesbiana?*" (You don't even know that you are a lesbian?)

I would not trade my eternal destiny for a frivolous moment of passion. I would sin no more. Still weeping into my hands, mucous running down over my lips, I repeated, "No. No. No."

Valentina quietly seated herself on the sofa, not too near me. She offered me a wad of tissues.

I blew my nose and then, gasping for breath, said, "I am not a... a..." I couldn't even say the "L" word.

"I need to tell you something, Miss . . . uh . . ." Valentina said gently.

I nodded for her to go ahead, but kept my eyes on the floor. "The very first day I arrived tardy to your ESL class I knew you were a lesbian. The way you leaned on the wall crossing your booted feet. The way you walked. Your dowdy clothing. Your short, unruly hair. I wanted to get to know you, but you hid behind your professional behavior. I left you notes, shared my music cassettes with you, even sent you red roses. After many months of trying to get your attention, I couldn't resist any longer." She extended her hand to mine and clasped it. "I don't have to call you Miss Smith anymore, because the other day I withdrew from your ESL class. I have fallen in love with you, Sharon."

My eyes, blazing slits, shot daggers into her. Jerking my hand away, I stood, jammed Valentina's Bible and notebook into her hand, opened my front door and demanded, "Don't ever come to my house again."

It didn't occur to me that I had done exactly the same thing to Bela.

Wordlessly, Valentina made her exit.

I closed the door and sank to the floor, wailing like someone whose child had just been murdered.

Hadn't a demon been cast out of me at the Vineyard Bible study? Why hadn't I been healed? Had God forsaken me? That's what Jesus said as he died on the cross.

That night I kissed Valentina again and again in my dreams.

⟨✽⟩

My mind was so engulfed in the passions raging inside of me that it never once occurred to me that there might be some conflict of interest in the fact that Valentina had been, until recently, my student. Apparently she was a step ahead of the game, however, because she transferred out of my class before pulling me in for that first kiss.

⟨✽⟩

A couple of days later, I called all of the Latino Bible study participants and told them that something had come up and that I was not able to continue our group any longer. Then I called Dan Sims to ask for help.

"I have been struggling with a personal issue for a long time and want to ask you and Kelly to pray for me," I told him. "Not in a group setting. I know an evil spirit came out of me recently at your home Bible study, but it wasn't enough. There are more evil spirits living inside of me." I recalled the Bible story in the Gospel of Mark, Chapter 5, about the man they called Legion, who was possessed by many demons.

Dan's warm voice was unction for my wounds. "Sounds like you need prayer for deliverance. Can you come to our home next Saturday morning?" he asked. "Kelly and I will fast twenty-four hours, and we ask that you do the same. The praying will be long and intense, so wear comfortable clothing. We'll be praying for you this week."

I was glad that Dan didn't ask me what types of evil spirits I might have. I couldn't even accurately name them for myself, let alone for someone else.

"Thanks," I said. "I'll take all the prayers you can lift up. I'm at the end of my rope these days." As I hung up the phone I felt a surge of hope that this would finally be a significant turning point for me.

⌀

The following Friday I packed my car with a few things to be ready to leave for Santa Barbara at dawn on Saturday morning. As I was getting ready for bed that evening, my doorbell rang. I could see Valentina's face through the peephole of the door.

I wrenched it open. *"¿Y ahora qué?"* (What now?) The words snapped like a rubber band.

"Can I come in?" Her eyes implored me to respond with friendship and not fury. As if on autopilot, my gut leaped with sexual desire. Damn!

She took a small step forward, yet remained in the doorway. "Please. I'd like to speak with you."

"You have five minutes. I am busy." I sounded like a tough football coach. She stepped inside, but left the door open behind her.

I didn't invite her to sit down. I told her that I was sorry about what had happened and promised it would never happen again. Then I told her about the prayer time slated with Dan and Kelly for the next morning.

Valentina's eyebrows raised two inches. "Exorcism?" Her voice raised in volume and pitch.

"I need it. A demon lives inside of me."

She drew in a deep breath and then blew out the air a long, slow stream. Her delicious breath almost toppled me to the floor.

"You just don't get it, Sharon, do you? You are a lesbian!" She looked at the floor and shook her head.

"No. I am not... uh, that! I am a Christian." I spat out the words through clenched teeth.

Taking another deep breath, Valentina said, "Let's make an agreement. You go have your... um... exorcism, as you insist, tomorrow morning. After you have left I will come to your apartment in the afternoon and wait for you. When you get back home, I'll be here, and you can let me know how it went. We'll go from there. Agreed?" She folded her arms over her chest and waited for my answer. "Of course, I'll need a key."

I felt like a skunk caught in a trap. What was the way out? I didn't know. Or was I afraid to know?

I turned and got a spare key from a hook on the coat rack. "Agreed," I said icily. "Here it is." I dangled it off my extended pinky finger even as an inner voice told me I was being a fool.

She lifted her gaze to mine and smiled ever so slightly. "See you tomorrow afternoon."

After her curvaceous silhouette disappeared into the darkness, I closed the door, locked it, and placed the safety chain into its slot, as if I were locking out something mysterious and dangerous, seeking to pounce upon me in the night.

I told myself that when I returned home the following afternoon I would be finally cleansed, healed and stronger than ever. I would finally be able to be a friend, and nothing more, to Valentina. A Christian sister. Nothing more.

My regrets of what had happened to Bela flitted through my memory for an instant. The imprint of her Bell's palsy face of melted wax made my stomach lurch. Would my friendship with Valentina be different? I wanted to think so, but couldn't be sure.

~ ✎ ~

Early Saturday morning in Santa Barbara my trembling finger pressed Dan and Kelly's doorbell. Still sleepy but smiling, they invited me into their home. "Fasting?"

"Yup." My stomach was growling with the hordes of butterflies flitting around in there.

Their living room looked empty. I wondered why the furniture had been moved out into the dining area. Pillows were piled around a hardwood table, maybe too heavy to move. The carpet had been freshly vacuumed.

"Are you moving?" I asked, a little confused.

"No. Today you will need a large space so that you don't get hurt during our prayer time," Dan explained.

I couldn't imagine what he meant. Why would I need so much space? Was I going to be doing calisthenics today? Maybe sweat out the evil? I got the idea that this might be a hard run, but I had no idea that I was in for a marathon.

I sat on one of the pillows on the floor. I decided that I would trust the wisdom of my friends and trust our God to do his work in me.

Kelly began to sing, "Holy Spirit, come..."

Palms upward, I sat waiting for God to touch me. Four gentle hands rested on my head and shoulders as they began to pray. In less than a minute a foreign force thrust me off of the pillow and threw me down, and I began writhing and squirming across the floor in serpent-like movements. *This again*, I groaned inwardly. But then I reminded myself this was what I'd come here for. *Whatever it takes, I'm willing.*

"I hate the cross of Jesus Christ!" that otherworldly voice spoke, howling and screeching. "Don't torment me!" The disgusting demon was again using my larynx.

Somehow I didn't feel afraid. This was another illogical, bizarre experience, but this one seemed more intense than the others. Like a spider in a web on the ceiling, I observed everything from above. My hands clawed the carpet, my nails almost breaking. My body was eel-like, slithering its way around the entire living room area. Mucous ran from my nose into my mouth, mixing with the saliva that ran down my chin. My roiled stomach tried to retch and heave. Luckily, I had fasted. I had no control over the voice, which screamed louder and louder with a torrent of despicable words against the God I professed to love. My rational mind still functioned. *I'll probably have a sore throat again due to all the screaming.*

The whole ordeal lasted over an hour. Finally, the voice subsided. I sat up, but still on the floor. I panted to catch my breath as if I had just run a 50-K marathon. Bathed in sweat, I wiped my mouth and face on the inside of my T-shirt. I bowed my head, resting it on my swollen knees. I noticed that my knees felt pretty much the same. My back pain? About the same. What had transpired during this past hour of exorcism? I waited quietly. And waited some more.

I sensed someone close to me. It was Kelly. "Did you hear it?" she whispered in my ear.

"Hear what?" I whispered back, still staring at my shoes.

"God has given me a Word of Knowledge about you. Be still and listen."

Oh no. Hey God, did you tell Kelly about the same-sex attraction thing? I felt so ashamed. I willed my thumping heart to slow down, trying to listen to the voice of God.

After what seemed like five whole minutes I heard a gentle, but firm, audible voice inside my spirit. God's voice. "Sharon, I created you. You. Are. A. Lesbian."

The words were so very clear. My breath stopped.

Kelly still stood next to me. "Did you hear it?" she asked again.

"Yes, I did," I said, still keeping my gaze on the floor. I couldn't look at her face.

She waited a long time before finally saying, "I'm glad you heard God's message to you."

I was glad she didn't ask me exactly what the contents of that message were.

Dan helped me stand and motioned me toward the bathroom. They had left me a washcloth and towel. When I looked into the mirror, I saw a face that I didn't quite recognize.

I washed my sweaty body, changed into another T-shirt I'd brought, and felt like I floated out and across their vast living room. Dan and Kelly gave me quick hugs and said goodbye. I could hardly wait to get back to my apartment.

Driving all the way back to Pasadena that Saturday afternoon was wonderful. Was the sunshine unusually bright today? Were the few cloud formations fluffier than before? Was the ocean view along the Ventura coast clearer? I caught fleeting glimpses of Santa Cruz Island. Had I just been born again?

I felt like I arrived home in no time. I slowly turned the key in the lock with great care and opened the door inch by inch to peek inside. Would she be there?

She was. The most beautiful woman in the whole world was sitting on my sofa, looking gorgeous in her tight flowered top and black slacks, her fragrance better than all the Maja perfume in Barcelona. Am I dreaming?

"*¿Cómo te fue?*" (How did it go?) Her voice as gentle as a soft breeze.

"It went well," I said, looking past her at the wall. My heart was thrumming in anticipation of something that I'd never done before. At least not like this.

"*¿Qué te dijo Dios?*" (What did God tell you?) She asked this tentatively, as if her voice would break a charm. "Because if

God told you you're a sinner, I will leave and forever stay away. But if God told you you're a lesbian, then I want to make love to you. Here. Now."

I didn't waste time with words. I lunged at her, covering her with kisses. Clothes were quickly shed. Skin slid upon skin. This marked the first time I'd ever touched and been touched by a woman without feeling any guilt. It was an ethereal pleasure I'd never known was possible. On my sofa, on the dining room table, in the shower, and in my bedroom, my entire apartment became a sacred space for my body and soul's awakening.

Afterwards, I stood in my little bathroom to freshen up. "Why did it take me so long to find her?" I asked the glowing redheaded woman I beheld in the mirror,

My eyes filled with tears.

She nodded a knowing smile, and said, "Finding her has been a long, arduous journey, hasn't it? But you found her. I'm here."

Over the years, I had absorbed the notion that homo-sexuality and Christianity were incompatible. I suppose I'd heard of gay, lesbian, and bi people before, but my fear had pushed those concepts far from my scope. Christian and lesbian? I hadn't thought it was possible.

The tsunami had come with a devastating force—destroying my useless religious structures, lifting up the debris of my broken relationships and flawed interpretation of myself, and wiping all those detrimental beliefs clean off my coastline. After all these years, I was free to stop lugging around that heavy yellow suitcase.

Sharon Wulfensmith

CHAPTER 25

GAY CHURCH

E ven though I was forty-one years old by now, my sexual desire was insatiable as a sixteen-year-old's. Valentina and I managed to find ways and places to titillate each other in creative and exciting ways. The Pasadena Athletic Club swimming pool was a favorite, as well as the darkness of the women's sauna room there. I hadn't known before that, while driving a car, two people could...

One evening, Valentina came directly from her job to my apartment. After setting down her purse and keys on the dining room table, she grabbed me for a kiss and then said, "Sharon, Pastor Quesada called me today to invite us to a weekend retreat near Lake Arrowhead. It's only about an hour and a half away. Let's go!"

"Bien, mi cariño." (Good, my sweet one). I smiled and held her tight, thrilled at the chance to go camping with my special someone. I felt so happy to have Valentina in my life.

"Do you still have your little pup tent?" she asked. I had told her about my trip across the country with Montserrat. She squinted her eyes and said in a faux-jealous tone, "Are you absolutely sure, Sharon, that you and Miss Barcelona What's-Her-Name *did not* have sex in that little tent?"

"Nope. Never did. What a shame. Miss Evangelical Goody Two-Shoes was a goood girl." I danced away from her hand as she tried to playfully slap my butt.

⌒ℓℓ⌒

That weekend we joined about fifteen adults from Pastor Quesada's church. Arriving at our campsite at Lake Arrowhead, the church leaders set up two family-sized tents in one large camp spot. One for the men and one for the women.

I busied myself near the women's tent while setting up my pup tent. "Valentina and I can sleep here," I called out to one of the ladies. "You'll have more room in your tent without us."

"Sounds great," a voice called from behind the green nylon of the women's tent.

After songs, stories and s'mores, we all turned in for the night.

In my little tent, Valentina and I zipped our two sleeping bags together. In the comfort of the dark, our lips and bodies melded together. We tried to keep our voices contained within our nylon enclosure, but it proved quite challenging.

"Everything okay over there?" a voice called through the tent fabric after I cried out in pleasure a bit too loudly.

"A spider got in here," Valentina called back. "But we killed it."

Both of us buried our heads deep into our sleeping bag and giggled helplessly like two pre-teens.

Hiding in plain sight that weekend fueled our nighttime sexual enjoyment. I wondered whether any of the church members would catch on to what was really going on, but no one seemed to. Fortunately, she and I agreed to behave very discreetly while around others. Doing so actually added to our excitement for what we could do afterward in private.

In 1991, five years after the 1986 Immigration and Reform Control Act, ESL classes were still in high demand; immigrants continued to arrive in the United States in a steady stream, and the Pasadena City College campus could no longer accommodate the large numbers of adults who wanted to learn English.

Since I had maintained a positive relationship with the Covenant Church following my resignation, I asked if they could offer space for Adult Ed ESL that I continued teaching. To my surprise, the church agreed to host us for free. We began classes that February. A Satellite PCC Campus was born.

Still a pastor at heart, I obtained permission from the college to offer a five-minute optional devotional during the ESL class break time. My new Latino students responded positively to this, and soon, once again, a Bible study group was meeting at my apartment, this time led by Valentina and me together. She told me that she had accepted Christ as her personal Savior and so became my partner in ministry.

We were surprised by how many ESL students wanted to talk about spiritual things. We would often stay after class for an extra hour as people asked questions and requested that we pray for them. We encouraged them to attend Pastor Quesada's church or come with us to the Vineyard in Anaheim. Or both.

During those months, on many Sunday evenings Valentina and I took three or four ESL Bible study members with us to the Vineyard. One evening on the way out after the long service I glanced at the flyers on the Information Table and noticed a new edition of the Desert Stream Ministries tri-fold with Sedric O'Sullivan's photo on the front. Recently he had expanded his Ex-Gay ministry and had partnered with *Exodus*, the nation's largest *Pray the Gay Away* ministry.

How thankful I felt that I'd never joined O'Sullivan's group. I knew now that doing so would have been a huge mistake. My lesbian identity was who I was, and now that I had accepted that, I wasn't about to change it for anything.

It was time to say goodbye to the Vineyard and stop hiding my sexual orientation from others.

∽ℯℓℓ∽

That week Valentina and I discussed how we could respectfully come out to the people we knew and stop lying about our relationship. We agreed to start with Eduardo, the young man from Peru who had gotten his immigration papers a couple years back, and who clearly had a crush on Valentina.

We invited him out for coffee one evening.

"Eduardo," Valentina began, leaning over the table close to him. "We need to tell you something about Sharon and me.

We don't want to hurt your feelings, but..." Her eyes darted to mine for a split second.

Eduardo sat like a fence post, his eyes jumping back and forth between Valentina and me.

Not having come out to anyone before, and not having a clue as to what to say, my words stumbled out. "Eduardo, I have noticed that you have an attraction to Valentina, but that won't work out. She and I are lesbian lovers."

Valentina's lips pressed together.

Poor Eduardo! His brown face turned white, his eyes all but fell from their sockets, and he looked like he would need CPR. He had no words. He rushed outside.

"That didn't go too well, did it?" Valentina remarked, fixing a strand of her blonde hair back in place.

"I think we need to figure out how to do this better next time," I said, chuckling.

⁓⸜⸝⸝⸍⁓

A few days later, as we sat smushed together comfortably on the sofa in my apartment and I toyed with a gold crucifix around Valentina's neck, I asked, "Have you come out to your mother yet?"

"I think she might know already, but we don't talk about personal things like that." Valentina's fingers folded in, out, and over mine a hundred times as we talked. "Our family is Catholic, so you know what the church teaches." She twisted a strand of her hair. "Have you told your parents?"

"Not yet. I have no idea how they'd react. I'm scared to tell them." I leaned over into her shoulder and just enjoyed her warmth. I couldn't even imagine having this kind of conversation with my mom and dad. What would they say? Could they ever accept this?

⁓⸜⸝⸝⸍⁓

A few weeks after our last trip to the Anaheim Vineyard, I thumbed through the Yellow Pages and stumbled upon the Metropolitan Community Church of Los Angeles. It caught my attention right away. Perhaps I'd heard that name on the news or something. I later learned that since 1968, MCC had been an international leader for civil and human rights movements. It had been one of the first Christian churches to perform same-gender marriages and take action toward marriage equality in the USA. MCC had built bridges between Protestant denominations and Catholics for years. I thought that Valentina and I should give it a try.

The next week we attended worship services there for the first time. I couldn't believe it! We could be ourselves. A lesbian couple. The service began with a lot of singing, but not the same songs as the Vineyard. As the people around us sang, the old-fashioned choruses and hymns transported me back to my childhood.

⌒⊸ℓₑ⌐

My dad and I stood close to each other in the theater seats of the big KWHK radio station auditorium of Cleveland, Ohio. My two brothers, Kobe and Thomas flanked us, one on each side. We all loved to sing—at home together, at church, even in the car. Tonight was special because we were at Youth for Christ. I was proud I could read the musical notes in the chorus book that my father held for me to see. I was pretty small for eleven years old; I barely cleared my dad's waistline.

YFC was an evangelical ministry that targeted teens; my dad took us three kids to the Saturday evening event each month. I think I was the youngest kid there.

"Who wants to go to heaven?" boomed the voice of Florian Mannis, the Director. He was as big around as he was tall, and wore a grey suit with a blue bow tie on his fat neck. Everyone loved his smile, which split his face across the middle sideways. He stood on the platform of the huge auditorium and waved his hands, as if performing magic as a chord sounded from the organ. We lifted our voices and sang heartily: "Christ for me..." I sang loudly. *"Yes, it's Jesus Christ for me . . ."* I hoped the words I was singing were true.

After many more choruses and a message of salvation, Florian asked the crowd of several hundred, "Have you invited Jesus into your heart? Who wants to be saved from the fires of hell?"

I felt afraid.

At home, the Lord didn't seem to be answering my prayers anyway—not when I asked God to make me into a boy, or make me not a tomboy, or to help me get a good grade on my English test next week, or to make my brother Thomas not fight with me so much. Getting saved by praying at home just didn't seem to work, so I finally decided I'd have to embarrass myself and do it in front of all those people the next time we went to YFC.

That Saturday, somewhere during the fifteenth verse of "Just As I Am Without One Plea," my short wobbly legs carried me all the way down to the front where I knelt. A lady knelt next to me and told me to repeat some special words, concluding with, "Come into my heart, Lord Jesus. Amen."

After the service I was surrounded by shiny shoes and big bellies of men with shiny belt buckles, and women with pretty dresses. Florian gave me a big squishy hug. "You did it, Sharon! You are saved forever, and never will go to hell."

After that, I wasn't afraid anymore.

Sitting together with Valentina in the pew at the Metropolitan Community Church, singing those old traditional Christian choruses brought back those fond memories. Here in Los Angeles in 1991, seeing same-gender couples, young and old, holding hands and leaning in to each other during the worship service was totally new for me. I felt free. Free to be the lesbian that God had made me to be, and free to love the woman sitting next to me.

"Sharon, *¿Estás bien, mi amor?*" (Are you okay, my love?) Valentina gently rubbed her hand up and down my arm.

"Sí. These songs remind me of when I was a little girl, that's all. This church is unlike any I've ever been in." I grasped her hand and wiped away my tears with the other.

She leaned over to whisper in my ear. "It reminds me of the Catholic Church I grew up in. The priests with their clerical collars, their robes, and the Eucharist on the altar. I bet they'll let us partake of the bread and wine. It's been so long since I could do that. The Catholics have too many rules."

Rev. Nancy Wilson, the main pastor/priest, prayed for the sick and dying of the congregation that morning. She named a few names, indicating that we should pray for the men who had HIV. Then she began a longer list of names, praying for the souls of the departed who had died that week from AIDS.

My heart teetered with uncertainty. What had I gotten myself into? A community where this many people were dying? Prior to this Sunday, I had never paid much attention nor understood the epidemic of AIDS that was ravaging my city, my country, and my world.

Only a few years before, I had listened an announcement on National Public Radio about how many people were dying from AIDS, and the announcer had made some comment about gay men. Alone in the car, I had yelled to the inside of my windshield, "You filthy sinners. You get what you deserve!"

As soon as those words had escaped my lips I'd burned with regret that I, a Christian, would even think such a thing about another human being who was suffering terribly. And to think that I didn't even know that I myself was a part of the LGBTQ+ community.

Sitting in the MCCLA church that Sunday, I felt like my transformation into the genuine Christian I longed to become was just beginning.

Valentina and I continued to attend MCCLA's services for several months and eventually initiated a Spanish-speaking group with some of its members. Soon, about twenty Latino people were regularly attending. Here I was again, practicing ministry, but in such a different way than I had before.

At the end of the ESL school semester, Valentina and I disbanded our home Bible study group in order to focus our attention on the MCCLA Latino outreach. We didn't want to have the pressure of hiding from anyone anymore. I continued teaching Adult ESL for another couple of years.

One Sunday afternoon after I got home from MCCLA, my mother phoned me just to say hello.

"How was the Vineyard?" she asked.

I hadn't been to the Vineyard for quite a while. I cleared my throat. "Uh... Mom, I've been attending a different church lately." I hadn't told my parents about the big exorcism several months ago, or the message from God that I'd heard. I was not about to tell them about Valentina, either.

She peppered me with questions, but not unkindly; she seemed genuinely interested in the new church I was attending. I needed to talk about *safe* topics, so I told her about the church's location in Los Angeles, the songs, and the new little Latino group.

Finally, she asked, "What denomination is it?"

"It's an independent evangelical church. It doesn't have an official name yet," I lied. Then I said I had to go and we hung up.

Shame burned my cheeks. *Sharon, you cannot lie to your own mother*. My parents had raised me in an environment of trust, not lies. I needed to come clean with them.

⌒⊸⊱

Soon after that, someone at MCCLA told me about a group called PFLAG (Parents and Friends of Lesbians and Gays). I bought the book *Coming Out to Parents* and devoured it in a couple of days, then called the phone number inside.

Over the next few weeks I spent hours on the phone with a PFLAG volunteer, Sylvia. She encouraged me to write a coming out letter to my parents first, and hopefully talk with them later.

I labored for days on the letter, reading it to Sylvia over the phone. Finally, she told me to just mail it already, so I did.

May 12, 1991

Dear Dad and Mom,

I'm writing to give you a preview of what I'd like to talk about soon. This news will change our lives together,

*may be painful, but I hope it will bring us closer. (No,
I'm not sick or anything bad).*

*I'm writing to give you the chance to think first. I love
you both deeply and appreciate your love toward me. I
want to be honest with you about who I am. Several
times you have commented on how good I look, more
confident and happier than before.*

*God has helped me to understand why my relationships
with men friends never were successful and why I've
never married. I've been through pain and disappointment but now I feel free to be the real me. I want to be
honest with you. I am a woman who prefers the intimate
company and love with another woman. Not a man.*

*I have studied the Bible in a new way and now realize
that God has created me the way I am. I haven't chosen
this. I always felt different as a kid, but didn't know
what it was. I'm sorry I haven't told you this before. I
didn't have the courage.*

*I don't know how you will react to this information.
Take time to reflect on what I've said. This weekend I'll
drive to Santa Barbara so we can talk. My heart will be
pounding. I feel nervous already.*

*Dad. I love you. Mom. I love you.
You both are so special to me.*

God is our sustainer and guide.

*Lovingly,
Your daughter, Sharon*

A few days later the phone rang early in the morning. It was my
father. "We got your letter."

CHAPTER 26
COMING OUT

"Hi, Dad." I was sure that the drumming of my heart could be heard on the other end of the line.

"We waited a few days to let the news settle in, but we want to tell you something."

At least his voice didn't sound angry. My stomach clenched.

I heard my mom clear her throat, so I knew she was on the line.

Then my father's deep voice again: "We want to tell you that we thank God that you discovered who he made you to be."

I held in a big breath. My shaky voice squeaked out, "Dad? Mom? Is this really you?"

For the past couple of nights I hadn't slept well at all. I had prayed that my folks would respond well to my coming out letter, but my dreams were all a jumble of positive and negative reactions. Had my father really said what I'd just heard? Or was this just another dream? My fingers clutched the phone receiver but I couldn't say anything.

"Are you there, honey?" asked my mom. "We look forward to hearing your story this weekend. You don't have to be nervous. Just come. We love you."

I had only heard horror stories from my MCCLA friends. This reaction, so loving and understanding, was entirely unexpected.

While I waited for our weekend visit, my father's words echoed in my head: "*discovered* who God made you to be."

⌒◦◦⌒

That weekend, entering my parents' home, everything looked different. The paintings on the walls must have been new. Had Mom reupholstered the family room furniture? Changed the carpets? Painted the whole house? Or was it I who had changed?

I walked to the living room and dumped my backpack onto the pullout sofa. Standing there, I envisioned the night I had spent cuddled up next to Montserrat in 1978 before we both flew to Mexico, wishing that we could marry. In 1984, Joe had sat on that sofa, but my parents hadn't let him spend the night. Ethan also had been there the following year, but we had not slept together yet. Bela? No, she had never been invited to my parents' house. Would Valentina be welcomed here? I certainly hoped so.

⁓ℓℓ℈

We didn't talk about it that first night. My parents suggested that we wait until the next day—take the VW camper to Refugio Beach and spend the whole day there, talking. So, instead, we ate our usual chicken and rice for dinner and then watched one of my dad's slide shows about flowers. I was happy to postpone tackling the big item on the agenda a bit longer.

The next morning, as I packed some picnic things into the camper, I reminisced about the summer I'd borrowed this van—a few years earlier, before my knees had turned to hot sausages. A female friend from San Diego wanted to see the California coast, so we drove Highway 1 all the way to Monterey Bay and back. Each night we stayed in a camp spot and slept together, our hands wandering to intimate places and our tongues intertwining—but in the mornings we never spoke about it.

At the time, it never occurred to me that we were expressing our love like lesbians do. For a fleeting moment, I envisioned her form in that little camper bed, still feeling a pang of shame. *I must be such a slut*, I thought.

⁓ℓℓ℈

An hour later the VW van took my parents and me to Refugio Beach, just a twenty-minute ride north of Santa Barbara. *Refugio* is Spanish for "refuge." The beach's name was not lost on me.

As we three walked toward the water's edge, my dad started the conversation. "Know that we love you, regardless of what you say. We're listening."

My mom added, "We have all day long to talk and reflect. When your knees feel like they're going to give out we'll just sit on a rock a while to rest."

We walked along the rocky beach, skipped stones in the receding waves, watched a couple surfers ride the small swells, and got sand between our toes. I wasn't ready to talk yet.

"Look!" I pointed toward the water. "A pod of dolphins." Dolphins had always given me a sense of peace and wonder. "Could they be celebrating our conversation today?" I asked out loud.

After an hour or so we returned to the VW camper for refreshing drinks and turkey sandwiches in its little kitchenette. I sat next to my mother and across from my father and began to tell my stories.

"Remember when we lived in Berkeley and all the pre-schoolers were graduating up to the kindergarten Sunday school?" I asked. "The teacher tried to force me into a little pink graduation gown and I threw a fit."

"Oh yes, I remember," said my dad. "We could hear you at the back of the sanctuary shrieking at the top of your little lungs, and when the kids finally paraded across the stage we wondered why you were the only child without a gown."

"It's because I wanted blue, not pink." A tiny twinge of anger bobbed up for a moment as I recalled the scene. If my father had heard me screaming that day, why didn't he go to the back of the church to see what was going on? His intervention at that moment could have changed a lot of things for me.

My mind shifted to another memory. "Do you know why I had that vicious fight with Mary Ellen when I was about thirteen?"

My mom shook her head and her sky-blue eyes locked onto mine, the same color. "I just recall that you disliked her intensely and always played with her two younger sisters."

"One summer afternoon she made fun of me by calling me Flatty and forced me to take off my shirt to show all the other girls my flat chest with no breasts. They all laughed and called me a boy." I couldn't, even at this moment, reveal to my parents my childhood desire to actually become a boy. "Those girls made me feel ashamed of my body."

My mom took my hand. "I remember that, Sharon." Her eyes welled with tears. "You came home crying so hard, tried to explain what had happened, and I just couldn't understand why you felt so hurt. I'm terribly sorry I missed that..." She trailed off.

"Mom..." My tight throat choked off my words. I rubbed the back of her neck. The swishing sound of the surf washed away any lingering resentment.

My dad leaned over the little table towards me. "Even when you were a young teen, sometimes I had to chase you around the house to cooperate long enough for me to take your picture in a dress." He chuckled. "If you hadn't flung it off already."

I continued sharing with my parents why I had hated dresses—how I'd felt different from the other girls and hated being called a tomboy.

Together, we shared tears and laughter as my stories tumbled out for over an hour.

Then my mom reached over to get a package of Oreos and set them on the table.

"Now it's our turn to tell some stories, isn't it?" she said. "Just before your senior year in high school you were keen on going to that very conservative church camp, weren't you? We didn't approve of that kind of church teaching, but we let you go anyway because you insisted."

"Yes, you know how our family always cherished music of the great classical masters, in addition to big band, and jazz," my dad said. "That Holiness/Pentecostal group almost made you lose all that."

Feeling a flush of embarrassment, I said, "Oh golly, I do remember."

⌒⊶⊷⊸

I went to a Holiness Camp Meeting for a week at Camp Sychar, near a rural Ohio town, the summer before my senior year in high school. Some friends from a Methodist youth group had invited me, and I looked forward to being surrounded by lush forests and rivers, away from the bustling city of East Cleveland.

My heart's deepest desire then was to love God and follow in Jesus's steps. After a fire-and-brimstone sermon I knelt at the front, seeking prayer for who-knows-what.

The preacher's trembling hands pressed on my scalp, making my whole head and neck vibrate. "Deliver this young saint from the clutches of Satan! Cleanse her mind of the evils of worldly lusts! Bubba phlele Jeheezus..." The glossolalia continued for a few minutes.

I too trembled. With fear. What if God told him about the backrubs with that girl Brenda in the camp cabin? Or our sensuous kiss? I hoped that God wouldn't rat on me.

Pausing, the preacher spoke to me in plain English. "Is there something I should know about you?"

I froze and lowered my eyes. I refused to tell him my sexy-feeling stuff. I thought it'd be safer to talk about my music. I looked up. "I'm one of the top clarinetists in the high school orchestra and play lead alto saxophone in our jazz band."

The preacher's shouting pierced my eardrums. "Jazz music is barbaric and immoral! It's the devil's music!" His hands again trembled like palsy as he placed them on my shoulders and continued ranting, "Jeheezus..."

When he finished praying, his gaze drilled a hole into my face. "Are you going to follow the Holy Spirit this evening and renounce this evil music?"

I could hear my heartbeat whooshing. I dropped my head to avoid his stare. "Yes, Reverend, I want to obey God in all that

I do." I swallowed, but there was nothing to swallow. My mouth was dry as cotton.

⌐ℓℓ⌐

Sitting with my parents and remembering this story knocked the wind out of me. I sat rigid, twirling an uneaten Oreo on the table.

My mom piped up, "When you came home after that horrific camp and told us how you wanted to quit playing what you called 'sinful music,' I remember telling you, 'That's. Total. Nonsense! You will do nothing of the kind. You have a God-given musical talent and you have worked hard. We are proud of you and that's that.'" She clucked her tongue several times and exhaled loudly.

I leaned back on the little VW seat cushion and looked up at the tan canvas ceiling of the pop-up camper. "Yeah. I was so glad later that I didn't give up music. I had such fun playing lead alto sax in the Shaw High Rhythm Teens my senior year." I was glad we could talk about the music part of this story.

My mom snatched the twirling Oreo and popped it into her mouth, then said, "You practiced that alto saxophone like you were in love with it. Your friend Molly McNeill would come over to our house and the two of you would play big band music. She was talented on the piano, and you'd picked up quite a skill on that alto sax. I would sit in the living room and listen. Those tunes reminded me of the days I used to dance swing before I met your father."

"I remember Molly," commented my dad.

I nodded. "I have some very fond memories of her."

⌐ℓℓ⌐

"Hey Sharon! Get over here!" Molly McNeill was my best friend in the Shaw High music department. "Help me hoist this dang sousaphone up over my head!"

"Can't you do it yourself? You're the one who decided to carry around that monster in the marching band." I laughed out loud.

"Help me!" She cried, crumpling under its weight. "It's gonna swallow me whole."

"Oh, for goodness' sake!" I exclaimed (sounding very much like my mother). I ran to her side.

The serpentine brass coils were wrapped around her slight frame. I grunted as I lifted it and placed it properly onto her little shoulder. "You look like a tiny ant carrying a house. At least you aren't playing piano in the band."

"Verrry funny." Molly scowled at me and marched out the door.

I liked Molly. I loved how she talked, but especially how she walked—how she moved her body, taking big strides, like a guy. It never occurred to me to question why I noticed these traits in particular. I enjoyed talking with her and playing music with her. She never ignited in me those sexy kinds of feelings I felt with some girls. We were simply friends.

In the VW camper, my mom began clearing the paper plates and sandwich crumbs from our meal. The sunlight was still dancing on the ripples of the ocean.

"I remember how once you got an idea in your head, there was nothing and nobody that could change your mind. We would try to convince you otherwise, but sometimes..." She inhaled through her teeth.

My father interrupted. "Sharon, you could be so very stubborn in those days. These hours here talking with you make us so glad to have you back."

"Have me back? Was I gone?" I asked, bewildered.

My father leaned forward and looked me square in the eyes across the little table. "For the past few decades, we've felt you drifting farther and farther away from reality."

My mom added, "The Baptist high school youth group. The Holiness Camp. The Christian college, Taylor. The worst one was the Navigators. It was almost like a cult!" She sat down across from me. "When you graduated from Kent State University you were twenty-two years old. Not a child anymore. We helped you buy your first Toyota, then that summer you went to that special Navigator 'training camp' in Indianapolis."

"Yeah, I remember I called to tell you that they wanted to take away my car keys," I said.

"Oh, Sharon." My mother shook her head. "You tried to explain to us their silly system of men being the leaders, and women being obedient to them without question. They told you that only men could drive cars." She trailed off, making a tsking noise.

"They wouldn't let me drive my own new car for the whole summer." I felt flushed with anger just remembering this.

"You were brainwashed," said my dad. "We were afraid for you for a very long time. For all those years you hid from yourself by choosing those hyper-conservative Christian groups that told you exactly how to live your life."

Unshed tears stung my eyes. I stared at nothing in particular. *You hid from yourself,* Dad had said. I'd never had thought of it this way. My parents were speaking the truth.

"Hiding in a closet of conservative evangelical Christianity," my mom said. She moved to the seat next to me and started scratching my back, gently and slowly, up and down. It felt soothing and reminded me of her back-scratching when she'd put me to bed when I was little. Quietly, my father slid over to where I was sitting and sat on my other side.

I sat still for a while. "Hiding. Closet. That really sums it up, doesn't it?" I murmured. Lowering my head down onto the little kitchen table, I began to weep. Tears of gratitude for these parents of mine who loved me. Tears of shame for the people I'd hurt along the way. Tears of loss, for the wasted years of my life hiding in that damned closet.

We three sat on the little bench and scrunched together, Dad on one side, Mom on the other, and all three of us wept, our arms wrapped around each other, rocking back and forth gently. It was a sacred moment in a sacred space.

When we finally broke out of our family embrace, the dancing sun had changed into an orange ball about to slip behind the undulating, watery horizon. My mother started putting away the kitchen things and my father readied the seats for driving again.

"Mom, Dad . . . words can't adequately express the love I have for both of you. Today has been such a gift. Thank you." I stood up, then sat down again. "Hey. One more thing. How did the two of you end up being so open-minded about this whole gay thing? Being evangelical church folk and all."

My father stopped what he was doing, and said, "I have a story to tell you. Remember Phoebe?" The three of us sat down again.

"Of course," I smiled, remembering my tenth-grade catechism teacher at our church in East Cleveland.

Tipping my chair way back, hanging on to the edge of the table in the small classroom at Calvary Lutheran Church, I raised one hand to ask, "Why were the disciples all boys? Didn't any girls follow Jesus?"

The other dozen kids groaned, wanting the lesson to be over already.

I slammed the feet of my chair back onto the floor. "C'mon you guys, I wanna know the answer."

A few more groans floated through the room.

Phoebe, our catechism teacher, studied the patterns on the cracked yellow ceiling of the Sunday school room. "I don't really know, except to say that there are twelve names of men that were disciples. Since crowds of people followed Jesus there were undoubtedly women and children among them, but..."

"It's not fair that the women weren't chosen," I complained, interrupting. "And why can't girls grow up to be pastors?" I'd learned this fact eight years earlier, after telling Pastor Secrist I wanted to be a pastor, just like him, when I grew up. His response was, "Only boys can be pastors. Maybe you could teach Sunday school one day."

I wanted to kick him in the shins.

I looked at Phoebe expectantly as she continued with her explanation. "Even I can't be a pastor. A girl can grow up and marry a pastor, though." She nervously ran her fingers through her curly brown hair. "I'm going to..." She broke off.

"But you're not really answering my question." By now my voice was a whine.

Back in the VW, with the cool, salty breeze chilling our bare arms, my father said, "We were very proud of you when you became a pastor. In fact, we are very glad that in many churches today there are women pastors. Phoebe would have made a wonderful pastor, but that wasn't permitted back then. She felt close to your mother and me, and brought her fiancé, a Lutheran pastor, to dinner at our house in East Cleveland one day."

"Oh yes, I remember that time, but I can't remember his name." I leaned in toward my dad. He could tell stories and make you feel like you were right there in the room.

"Rob Keelor."

I smiled and nodded.

"After you finished your catechism class they got married and moved to New Jersey. I made business trips there from time to time. They always invited me to stay with them."

"I sort of remember. And then something happened, and later they divorced. Right?" The chain of events was still a little foggy in my mind because it had been so many years ago.

My dad nodded. "On one occasion when I arrived, Phoebe was crying and Rob was trying to comfort her. They shared with me what was wrong and asked me to keep it a secret. I haven't told anyone for almost thirty years. But here goes." My dad glanced at my mom, who nodded for him to go on. "On their wedding night,

Rob told Phoebe that he was gay, and that he had married her to try to un-gay himself. It was a disaster. They never consummated their marriage, even after two years. It was impossible for him to function with a woman. Understand?"

"Yes, but..." I knit my eyebrows together. "Why are you telling me this story right now?"

My dad said, "Because Rob was a man of God. That day I told him, 'When I first met you I saw the Holy Spirit in you. As I look at you right now I still see the Holy Spirit in you.' What else could I tell him? That's what I saw."

My eyes widened. "And that was before any kind of gay movement in society. Wow, Dad."

My mom reached over and slowly ran her hand down my back. "Rob showed us that being gay is just the way that some people are created by God. Just like you. We see the Holy Spirit in you too, Sharon. More than ever before."

I closed my eyes, absorbing the beauty of their words. We three sat for a while in silence.

Then my dad said, "It's almost dark; we should get going."

My mother stood. "Let's fold up the table.

I spoke with urgency. "But there's another *one more thing* I want to share. I'm in love. With a beautiful woman." I couldn't believe I was actually announcing this to my own parents. I wasn't seventeen; I was forty-one!

"Oh." My father sighed. "It's late, so how about tomorrow we hear about this... um..."

"Lover, Dad. The word is lover."

Sharon Wulfensmith

CHAPTER 27

LIVING MY TRUTH

The next morning over pancakes and eggs at my parents' house, we continued our conversation.

My words tumbled out. "I met this student in my ESL class at Pasadena City College. She's an adult, of course, and she's from Cuba—she's sort of younger than me—her name's Valentina and we're lovers now." My face heated up. I looked back and forth between my mom and dad.

My mom smacked her palm loudly on the table. "Ha! So that's where the bouquet of a million red roses came from! I thought something was cooking, but you had your mouth clamped shut so I just waited." Her eyes probed my face.

I studied a hangnail on my thumb. "Yeah. When I got those red roses from Valentina I was clueless as to what it all meant. But now we are a... a couple." Talking with my parents about having a lover was new territory for me. I knew they were supportive, but for some reason I felt I had to be careful not to reveal too much. I didn't want to tell them about the exorcism I'd arranged with Dan and Kelly. Most of all, I wasn't about to tell them about making love for hours on end with Valentina.

I looked up to meet my mother's eyes. "Actually, I'm still learning about this gay thing. Valentina and I found a gay church, the Metropolitan Community Church of LA." Talking about the church put me on more comfortable ground for conversation.

My dad added, "So that's the so-called new church you mentioned on the phone recently, saying that it didn't have a real name yet. I think we've heard about that church in the news recently."

I squinched up my face and nodded. "I was scared to tell you what was really going on."

Clearing up the breakfast dishes, my mother said, "Now that the cat's out of the bag you know you don't have to be scared, honey. At any rate, we'd love to drive down your way sometime soon and see what MCCLA is like."

My father stood up from the table. "When are you going to bring this lucky lady, er... lover home so we can meet her?"

Even though I was shredding a couple of cuticles, telling my parents about a real relationship with a woman gave me a buzzing giddy feeling. Like the feeling you get when you buy a brand new car. Maybe I was finally growing up.

"I'll see if the two of us can come up soon," I told them.

Making this small plan with both of my parents felt like a grand stride, and it gave me more confidence.

A few weeks later I took Valentina to Santa Barbara. On the two-hour drive we talked a lot about our families. I remarked, "I still can't believe how encouraging my folks have been since I came out to them."

Valentina cleared her throat. "I wish my mother would be positive like yours is. I think my mom knows, but I've heard her say mean things about gay people," she commented. "I think my father would be okay with it, but I haven't seen him in years."

"Give your mom time. Maybe she'll come around." I tried to sound encouraging. "Let's just enjoy the day with my folks. They're looking forward to meeting you."

"I hope they'll understand my English," Valentina said. "I've been working hard to improve. At least I have a very good teacher!" She gave my hand a squeeze and giggled.

She had learned enough English to converse easily, but her words still had a thick Cuban accent to them.

We arrived to Santa Barbara in the evening just in time for dinner. After introductions we enjoyed my mom's roast beef with potatoes and veggies.

"Thanks for good meal," Valentina said. "I like."

My mother responded with a smile and brought in some ice cream for dessert. My parents easily chatted for a while, covering topics from politics to hairstyles. We all discovered that laughter was an international language that we could fall back on.

Later, Valentina gave my mother a chance to practice her Spanish, which she'd learned back in 1978 when I first met Montserrat. My mother had told me then, "I'm only sixty-three. If you can learn Spanish, so can I." And so she had. I still liked to brag about her Spanish abilities to my Latino friends; it made me happy to see her use it with Valentina now.

I was sorry that Valentina had to get back home that night to go to work in the morning; it meant we wouldn't have the chance to sleep together on that pull-out sofa. Its cushions held so many secrets.

As we were leaving, Valentina hugged my mom and said, "Your Spanish better than my English. I hope you be proud."

Seeing my lover interact with my mother and father gave me deep joy. I remembered how my parents had embraced Miriam, my brother Thomas's fiancé, so many years ago. It had taken me over twenty years to bring home the person I hoped to marry someday, but now here we were. Like a happy family. I wondered if Thomas would be welcoming when he met Valentina.

On our way back to Pasadena, Valentina said, "I really like your parents. They make me feel welcome in their home. I wish I could introduce you to my mother and older sister, but I don't see that happening anytime soon. They're just too Catholic."

~ ❧ ~

A month or so later, when I was visiting Santa Barbara alone, my mother and I decided to visit Arroyo Burro Beach, only a few minutes' drive from my parents' house. My knees had improved enough that I was able to walk with her a ways down on the hard-packed sand to our favorite spot.

We sat on a big boulder, waves crashing closely. We didn't mind the intermittent chilly spray. Perched above my mom on the rock, I said, "Mom, Valentina and I are sexually intimate. You know that, right?" I fidgeted with a few black mussel shells clinging to the rock where I sat, making sure I didn't pull them off, like I would my cuticles. "Is it true that we are sinning?"

My mother's head spun around to stare at me. "Sinning? Sharon, you're forty-one now," she said matter-of-factly. "You spent decades of your life trying to be good, trying not to do what you thought was wrong, and you never even had the chance to have a sexual fling. That's what teenagers do. That's what people in their twenties do! You missed all that. So take time to enjoy every passionate moment with Valentina. You're making up for lost time!"

My mom said that? I almost tumbled down off our big rock. Her words shocked me so much I wouldn't have even felt the frigid water if I had.

⌒⟶⟵⌒

My parents' acceptance of me gave me the confidence to move forward with my life as a Christian lesbian. Like a debut of my real self. Nonetheless, I still struggled with the old, traditional values I'd embraced over the years. It would take me a while to fully unfurl my new wings of freedom.

⌒⟶⟵⌒

Another day, while riding in the car alone with my mom, I said, "Valentina and I can't get married legally, so when we have relations it's fornication, isn't it?" My old theological trappings were still crunching up against my new life experiences.

"Fornication? For heaven's sake, Sharon!" said my mom, speaking a little too loudly into the steering wheel. "Don't you dare call my daughter-in-law a fornicator!"

"But Mom, how is she your daughter-in-law if..."

"The law is a ass, said Mr. Bumble!" My mother laughed; this was a line she liked to quote from *Oliver Twist*. "The two of you are married in your hearts. Isn't that enough?"

I was again stunned.

"And," she added, "If things don't work out between the two of you, you will be a better person in the end, and one day find a woman to spend your life with, get married and settle down. Maybe even have children. You'd make such a good mom."

Golly, how much good stuff can come from the lips of this woman called Mother? I wondered. Her words washed over me like healing hot springs. My mother was one of those people who could cut to the chase and say things just right.

It would take many more conversations like these, though, to peel away the many layers of guilt and shame that had become such a part of my emotional flesh.

Since I had come out to my parents, I decided it was time for me to come out to the rest of my family. I'd start with my siblings, talking with each one face to face over the next couple of months— beginning with my older sister, Marci.

On a sunny Saturday afternoon, Marci and I took a picnic basket to Hendry's Beach in Santa Barbara.

"I'd like to tell you something personal today," I told her as I spread a big striped towel under our orange beach umbrella.

We sat and watched the surf for a while; Marci waited patiently.

"I've struggled all my life to figure this out," I eventually said, "but I've finally realized that I'm lesbian."

Her eyes got big as ping pong balls and her smile lit up the sky. "You? My little sister?" She began to giggle. "A lesbian? And you're the Christian!" (She was proud not to call herself Christian as I had defined it.) She leaned over and pounded the sand with her fists and howled with laughter.

I felt a little tense at first, but then I began to laugh too.

"No wonder you never brought any good men home to meet the family," she said. "I do remember that Mexican guy though."

"Oh yeah, Joe Dido." I winced.

"He seemed like a creep," she said.

"He was."

"So who are you in love with now? A woman? Do tell!" Her words sing-songed with the sound of the waves.

Marci and I spent the afternoon telling stories of love and conquests, like two teenagers. It was fun. She gave me the confidence I needed to tell my three brothers.

Next, I went to have dinner with my younger brother, Greg, who was an active member of the Methodist church in Santa Barbara my parents attended. He listened to my story, his blue eyes crinkled at the corners, and when I finished he said, "Why did you take so long to tell me? I love you just the same. I'm wondering about..." and he asked many questions to better understand.

That evening while Greg and I talked, I felt such warmth. I could relax and be my genuine self around him. With nine years between us, he and I had grown up with a feeling of friendship, not rivalry. That day, he and I became closer than we already were.

A few weeks later, I flew to Portland, Oregon to come out personally to my brother, Kobe, eight years older than me. He responded by saying, "As soon as I saw you get off that plane and walk toward me, I knew something wonderful had happened to you. You look so relaxed and happy."

Kobe and I had also grown up without any sibling rivalry. He and his wife had many questions about how I had met Valentina and how my friends at home were responding to my coming-out story. Being genuine with Kobe and his wife drew us closer, just as it had with Greg.

Then there was Thomas. Growing up, we'd had a tumultuous relationship. Many times I had felt pushed aside by him, powerless and inferior in his presence. I wasn't eager to divulge my personal story to him. I decided to wait. A long while.

As I contemplated how I'd come out to Thomas, a painful memory from our childhood surfaced.

At age twelve, I went to Camp Mowana for a week. I loved being with kids my own age, but I especially relished time away from Thomas—Tommy at the time.

On the last day of camp, I spied my parents' car pull into the parking lot. They were there to pick me up. Tommy bolted from the car, his red hair flying, running as fast as he could, with my mother running behind. *Are they having a race?* I wondered.

Reaching me first, panting, Tommy proclaimed, "Hi Sharon! Archie flew away!" He grinned from ear to ear.

Archie was my beloved yellow parakeet. "Nooo!" I wailed, sprinting to my mother's waiting embrace. "What happened?"

Before my mother could answer, Tommy's haughty voice announced, "His cage was out on the back porch. Someone didn't close his little door all the way. He got out. That's that." Laughing, he danced a little jig.

I cried more loudly. "Who did that? Why didn't you take care of my parakeet while I was at camp?"

My mother stroked my matted hair and knelt down to my level. "Archie flew back and perched on the outside of the cage. He knew where he lived. I went out and he gently climbed onto my finger and I guided him back into his home. He's fine now."

I wrenched free from my mother's arm and swung a fist at Tommy. He dodged.

"Sissy! Crying over a dumb little bird!" He scampered out of my reach.

Growing up with a bully for a brother didn't exactly pump me up with much moxie. Thomas knocked the wind out of me, literally and figuratively, time and time again as we were growing up.

Once, when I was about nineteen, I tried to share my hurt feelings with him while we were both home on a break from college. I was glad we had enrolled in different schools. For two whole semesters I had been free from hearing put-downs like:

You got a C-minus in that class? Last year I got an A.

Why are you wearing your hair like that?

Why are you dressed in those clothes?

You're going to a small Christian college? I go to UC Berkeley.

Each time I heard those comments, my self-esteem cracked a bit more, like broken glaze on a ceramic pot.

During this particular home visit I had garnered enough courage to confront him, and invited him to talk with me about this. I wanted to clear the air.

"Can we have a little conversation? Let's go upstairs to Mom's sewing room." I could feel my stomach tightening with too much insecurity inside. I told him some of the phrases that I was just plain tired of hearing. "Why do you always say things to hurt me?" I asked him.

Thomas's response shouldn't have surprised me. "You know I love you. But you are just too sensitive. You take things the wrong way. You need to toughen up."

Recalling incidents like this did nothing to bolster my courage to tell this brother my coming out story.

Now I finally knew why I had always felt different. But I still had a lot of trouble explaining it to others—mostly because I was just plain afraid to do so.

CHAPTER 28

FEAR

Attempting to be fueled by faith and not by fear, I decided to come out to more relatives and friends before telling Thomas.

Next up was Aunt Elaine in New York City. She was my mother's best friend and my favorite aunt in the whole world; because of her I loved my middle name, Elaine.

I dialed the long-distance number. Would she be able to feel my phone receiver shaking as I held it? We chatted a little, I stalled, and then finally I blurted out, "I'm a woman who is attracted to other women. Not to men." Those words felt strange spilling from my lips to my Aunt Elaine. "I have a girlfriend." Using the "L" word was still challenging for me.

Her light laugh abated my fears. "Honey dear, I always thought that you were different. And you're so courageous. Congratulations! I'll be in California for Christmas. I'd love to meet the woman who loves you."

After that uplifting conversation, I wrote a letter to Dan and Kelly Sims from the Vineyard.

Dan's response was full of Bible verses condemning my *homosexual lifestyle*. An arrow pierced my heart. I couldn't help but wonder what message from God Kelly had heard at the conclusion of my exorcism. I was happy that she hadn't told me anything then. Unfortunately, though, I never did have an opportunity to have another conversation with the Simses face to face, because, as I soon learned, Kelly had just died of cancer. That news stung me like a burning ember; I would never forget Kelly's kindness when I confided in her about Joe and Ethan.

I wrote to my college friend, Sarah Szabo, to explain why I had experienced those feelings toward her when we were at Kent State, and reminded her of the conversation we'd had at the top of the stairway at the library. Surely, after twenty years of exchanging letters, she would understand now. But no—at her evangelical church in South Carolina, she had learned that the Bible condemned what she believed to be the sinful homosexual lifestyle, and she wrote back telling me I needed to repent of my sins, or hell would await me. After that, she and I ceased exchanging letters and our friendship faded like a sad fog.

I thought of Xavier, my boyfriend from Fuller Seminary whom I never had kissed, next. He would listen to my story, wouldn't he? I called him.

"Xavier, I haven't seen you in forever. Come over for dinner. I'd like to show you my apartment in Pasadena."

"Thanks." I could feel his smile beam through the telephone cord as he agreed to come over that Friday.

<hr />

After a pleasant dinner, Xavier stood to admire some framed photos I had on my living room wall. He flashed his chocolate Salvadoran smile. "This must be a picture of you and your parents. I remember meeting them a few years back. My gosh, you sure do resemble your father."

"That's what people tell me." I felt proud to resemble the man I admired so much.

"And who's that lady you're sitting with in this picture?" He pointed to a recent photo of Valentina and me, taken on my last birthday.

I puffed out a breath through tight lips. "Let's go talk out on the back patio." *Here we go*, I thought, my heart thrumming like a hummingbird's wings.

We sat down on a couple of lawn chairs next to the garden and sipped cool lemonade. I told him a too-long story from tomboy to exorcism, and concluded with, "And God told me that he had created me like I am. A lesbian."

Xavier's face had gone from initial interest, to horror. His lips trembled and opened and closed without a sound. He coughed, then stood and spat out, "Satan has claimed your soul. This is not from God, Sharon!" Eyes brimming with tears, trembling fingers finding his car keys, voice pleading, he shouted, "Repent of your sinful lifestyle, or you will burn in hell forever!" Then he found his way out through the flowers and ferns and vanished from my life.

I sat alone for a while, studying the beauty of my rose garden. I felt stunned by his vehement reaction to my vulnerability. Would my other friends be so hurtful?

After a few days, I was able to gather enough confidence again to share my truth with more people. I called Jude and Finja, and asked if I could visit them.

"It'd be wonderful to see you," Jude said. "Don't forget that it was you who introduced the two of us." His words bounced with joy. "Come and see our new baby."

"Baby? Congratulations! I can't wait to see you guys." I was pleased that we had stayed in touch.

The couple now lived in a small house in downtown Los Angeles doing ministry among homeless people. As I drove through Los Angeles, my heart twinged with a note of doubt. *What if they have a problem with my news?* I quickly dismissed these thoughts. Surely nothing could ruin this friendship.

After lunch in their bright yellow kitchen, I told them my long story. They both listened without expression.

Finja began first. "You actually heard God tell you that he created you a lesbian from the get-go? Tell us more about—"

Jude leapt to his feet, almost knocking over his chair. "Sharon. That was the devil's voice! Not God's! You have been deceived. Two women or two men are not designed to have sex. Their bodies don't even fit together. Sex is for procreation!" Each word came at me like a battery of bullets.

I glanced back at Finja, hoping for a slight sign of encouragement. She sat in silence, staring straight ahead.

I felt like a naughty child that had had just gotten a spanking. Tears burning my eyes, I retreated to the garden behind their house and sat on a bench in the sunshine to catch my breath, Jude's angry words pounding at my soul.

A few minutes later Finja quietly appeared, sitting next to me. "I don't agree with the conclusions you've come to, but I'd like to know more. I hope we still can remain friends. I'm so sorry that Jude was harsh with you." We chatted a short while longer, and then I left through the garden without going back inside the house as hot tears streamed down my face.

Determined to stay the course of what I felt I had to do, I began in earnest to write letters, make phone calls, or arrange personal visits with my most cherished long-term friends. By now, I knew that others' reactions might be quite painful. But for me, the gain was worth the cost.

I sent a letter to my friend Bethany from Fuller. She had finished her doctorate and was living in Kenya, ministering with tribal peoples using her expertise in ethnomusicology. Her response, via postcard, was encouraging. *If God doesn't reject you, neither can I. Sharon, I sense the sincerity and struggle of your pilgrimage. You are making me deal with the issues I have always wanted to set aside. May you grow in the richness of God's love.*

Her words were like healing salve on a wound. I would save her postcard and occasionally read it to remind myself that not all my friends had tossed me aside.

Since our time at Kent State University I had continued corresponding with Harlin Fox, the guy from the Navigators who'd preached the *Eyes of Man* sermon. He and his wife had become Navigator missionaries in Croatia. One day I was surprised to get a phone call from him.

"We're in the United States on furlough, and next week I'm going to be in Pasadena to visit my son at Cal Tech," he told me. "I'd like to connect with you. I understand you've got some good news to share."

For years I'd corresponded with many of my Navigator friends. I hadn't divulged the exact truth about my so-called good news. I was afraid that if I actually wrote that I'd fallen in love with a woman, much less used the "L" word, all of them would surely reject me on the spot. So, I sort of skirted the issue and figured I'd tell them more details in another letter the following year. Later on, I would realize that this strategy was bound to backfire in my face.

When he got into town, Harlin suggested that we share a picnic lunch at a park that Sunday afternoon. In my mind, I rehearsed what I would say, knowing that he knew the Bible pretty well. I decided I'd make my arguments strong. Surely he'd be able to respect my point of view. Wouldn't he?

Arriving at the park, we sat at a picnic table in the shadow of big pine trees. I explained my story, telling him how I'd reacted to his sermon when we were both college students. I shared how confused and angry I had become at that time, not knowing how, or with whom to talk about my same sex attraction. I finished up my story with the exorcism experience saying, "... and God's voice told me that he had created me a lesbian."

Harlin's eyebrows lifted clean off his forehead.

The cool breeze at the park seemed to abruptly stop and the trees parted, letting the blazing sun scorch my face.

Harlin stared at me and stopped chewing the bite of food he'd just taken. "I thought your good news was that you had met the husband God had chosen for you." He hastily gathered up his picnic food, stood up and brushed off his hands. "I am deeply disappointed that you have listened to the voice of the Enemy and have been led astray." He quoted several Bible passages that, to him, clearly indicated the sin of homosexuality. "I'd better be going now."

I had developed a close friendship with Michell Zurreva, the Latina woman who'd stood first in line four years earlier, when we started the ESL classes. I'd decided that I would not hide anything from her about my sexual orientation; though I was quite fearful that I would lose her friendship, I decided I had to take the risk.

"Let's go grab some food at El Paso Restaurant," I suggested one Sunday afternoon. "I'm bursting with news I want to share with you."

We sat across from each other in a booth munching chicken tacos. My stomach was in knots and I didn't feel very hungry at the moment. "You know that Cuban woman, Valentina?" I tried to explain our relationship, but was fumbling for words.

"Yes," she replied. "I've seen the two of you together a lot. Why do you mention her?"

I told her the story of my feelings for women, and how I'd struggled for so long. I concluded by saying, "I realize that God made me a lesbian, and now Valentina and I are lovers." I hadn't intended for my story to be so abrupt, but it'd come out that way.

Michell sat quietly for what seemed like a long time. Finally, she said, "I think I understand, Sharon. But I just hope that you and I can still be friends, and that Valentina won't come between us."

I reached out to clasp Michell's hand in relief. "Yes, you and I will stay friends forever, won't we?"

She smiled. "I hope so."

I was still unable to bring myself to come right out and tell certain people that I was in love with a woman. What would I tell Montserrat?

Afraid of telling her the whole truth, I wrote a letter saying that I'd met a Cuban, we were in love, and we hoped to marry some day.

Right away, I received a pretty card emblazoned with "Congratulations," signed by Montserrat and her husband. Backpedaling, I had to write again right away to apologize and reveal that the Cuban was a female. I felt ashamed of myself and sure that I'd lose this friendship as well. I was pleased and surprised to receive this response:

> *My Dear Friend Sharon,*
>
> *Thank you for telling me the truth about your friend, Valentina, but I was under the impression that you were dating a Cuban man. I have very happy memories of our trip across the States. I wonder if we ever would have had that lovely trip if you hadn't loved me so. I remember a couple of conversations we had on that difficult topic. It makes me sad. But because I consider you my friend I wish very much that I could say I understand that you want to marry a woman.* [She must have forgotten that, twelve years before, she had lamented that she and I couldn't marry.] *From what I have been taught about the Bible, such relationships are not God's plan. But I would like to hear your point of view.*
>
> *Love always, your friend, Montserrat.*

I was grateful that she did not shut the door on me. We would continue writing for several decades more. Our friendship would endure.

⌒ⲗⲗⲟ

It took me another year to garner enough courage to come out to Thomas. I asked my parents for advice and decided to share my story with him in person when he came to California the next time. My mother assured me that he would be patient and understanding.

By this time I had already studied many theological books on the subject of being gay and Christian. I was surrounded by a community of gay, lesbian, and bisexual Christian friends. For over a year, Valentina and I had been active in the Metropolitan

Community Church as well as in Latino community outreach. Our lifestyle was full, busy, and rewarding. I had finally come home to myself.

My mother called to tell me that Thomas had arrived in Santa Barbara. I drove up the next day but lacked the happy anticipation of my usual visits there.

For about eighteen months, Valentina had been included as part of our family and part of normal conversation. After arriving to my parents' house, however, I had to choose my vocabulary carefully with Thomas, making sure not to mention anything about my personal life. Hardly a relaxing afternoon at all.

After dinner, I took a big breath and said, "Thomas, I would like to share some things with you. Maybe we could go to the lounge area near the pool to talk."

"Sure." He gave me a quizzical look. "What do you want to talk about?"

"You'll see." I could feel the tightness rising from my legs up to my neck. I willed myself toward de-escalating, but didn't think I was doing a very good job. Knots had invaded my body, and I hoped that my two vocal cords and uvula weren't braided together.

He and I walked in the cool evening air toward the pool and found a secluded little area in the lounge with comfortable sitting chairs. I folded my hands on my lap to keep them from shaking. I had come out to everyone else in the family by now; I hoped that no one had spilled the beans to Thomas, and I prayed for a positive outcome today.

I figured I'd start at the beginning, when we were both young. "You probably remember how, as a girl, I hated wearing dresses, and acted like a tomboy..."

He smiled. "Yes, I remember when—"

"Please hear me out today and don't interrupt. Okay?" I hoped my voice sounded calmer than I actually felt.

I must have droned on for a full hour, recounting how I struggled as a child and a young adult to be like the other girls, but always felt different. I told him how I'd been bullied by the girls on our block. I told him about the Navigators and how my Bible study leader had shut me up for twenty years when I confessed to her that I was attracted to the other gals in the group. I told him how I had prayed for many years that God would heal me of these homosexual proclivities, but that my feelings persisted nonetheless.

During the whole time I was talking, Thomas appeared to be sinking lower and lower into the armchair, like a melting wax figurine. His eyes looked droopy, as if I were putting him to sleep.

I wrapped up my story by telling him about the exorcism experience at Dan and Kelly's house. At the end I said, "When I listened intently to the voice of God, I heard him say that he'd created me to be a lesbian. I was surprised, but also very relieved to capture this truth."

Thomas didn't move. Then, as if emerging from a chrysalis, he stretched his arms, unfolded his legs to stand, took a deep breath, looked into my eyes, and declared, "Sharon. You are Wrong. Wrong! WRONG!"

Those three words, like a pounding jackhammer, dislodged some of the foundation underneath me.

I stood up, wanting to run away as far as I could from his damning voice. But my feet felt nailed to the floor.

He stepped toward me, opened his arms, and said, "I love you."

Foolishly, I allowed him to embrace me. Crush me. Crush my spirit. Crush my sense of victory for having come through that dark tunnel of hiding, lying, struggling to be the free woman I thought I had finally become. The familiar pattern of power that he'd held over my head as we grew up momentarily took control. It was like he'd found a loose thread and tugged, unraveling everything I'd struggled to piece together. As we hugged, my dignity fell to the floor in tatters.

Perhaps desperate for something positive, a quick slide show of some of our better moments flashed behind my eyelids. The time we ran into each other in the middle of nowhere during my road trip with Montserrat and we shared a picnic lunch by the side of the road. The times I visited him in Germany, and we were able to set aside our childish bickering and competition and enjoy one another's company.

Yet here we were today. How could hearing this new information about me so easily erase all those good years that we had worked so hard to develop? I felt that during this past hour, with one damning poke of a huge DELETE button, all the progress we had made during the past decade or more had been obliterated. Gone.

His wife Miriam would tell me the next day, "If you have a girlfriend, like a lover, you may never bring her into our home."

I had liked Miriam up until this moment, but now I never wanted to visit their home again. I kept them in my life after that only because I wanted to see my niece and nephews.

⌒ₑₗₑ₂

A few days after my disastrous conversation with Thomas, I discussed things with my mother, and she helped me sew together the straggly strands of my self-esteem, though I still felt like there were a few ragged places left after we were done. Luckily, I had done my homework diligently over the previous six months, studying the Scriptures in context, seeing new interpretations of old stories, and discovering that ultimately, the Bible was not my enemy.

Thomas himself wasn't my enemy either, of course. Traditional evangelical teaching, ignorance, and fear—those were the enemy.

I had finally come out of the closet to my most challenging nemesis: Thomas. It would later dawn on me that *he* was the one still in a closet—a closet of traditional church teaching. In that closet hung old theological suit coats with tattered collars and shrunken sleeves and the worn-out shoes worn by those who needed to walk the same path with the same companions on the same journey, with unwavering obedience to the God of Same, for all their lives.

Fear of *Different* can be mighty powerful.

⌒ₑₗₑ₂

In a letter to me, dated March 1995 Thomas wrote,

> *As I listened to your story, I thought of all the times, as children, I was despicable to you, and realized I had done you damage. My sins have consequences, and they contributed to your identity struggle and played a role in your sexual orientation. No one is born a homosexual. They become that way. Please forgive me for the effect that my sins have had on you.*

I answered,

> *You and I have had a history of conflict, I agree. In your letter I hear you saying that you had power over me to make me into a lesbian. Thomas, you do not have that power at all. I cannot forgive you for influencing me or causing me to be a homosexual. Actually, if I were to believe that you somehow caused my homosexuality, I would extend to you my deepest gratitude, because I love living a life that is finally true to my being. I am not ashamed of who I am nor of how I live. It is apparent that your beliefs about me make it impossible for you to accept who I am.*

I think that Thomas believed he loved me. He certainly didn't hate me. I would wager to guess that he was simply scared shitless of what might happen to his faith paradigm if he accepted his sister as a Christian lesbian. Created by God. Just like that.

The opposite of love is not hate. It is fear.

If traditional Christians could only open their hearts to the inexplicable, profound, *inclusive* love of God, their fear would dissipate. Maybe then they would finally discover a God whose love could, like the perfume of sweet-smelling holy incense, permeate all the world.

As for me—fear can cause you to make some stupid mistakes, but I get first prize for making some pretty big bloopers along the way as I came out to more friends and family members. Bit by bit, I learned how to tell my story more effectively—still truthfully, but with more finesse and more conviction than I started out with.

Nonetheless, some people were quick to un-friend me even after hearing the more polished version of my story—and Facebook hadn't even been invented yet.

CHAPTER 29

CATHERINE

For the two years I was with Valentina, I had to admit that I did a pretty damn good job of making up for lost time, like my mother had advised me. I'm convinced we had some of the hottest sex in the world—best accomplished with those Cuban love songs playing in the cassette player. Somewhere along the way, though, things broke down between us. Valentina had changed my life in remarkable ways, but after some disagreements, I guess she decided to move on and change another woman's life.

We amicably broke up in the fall of 1992. I would remain forever indebted to her for being the tsunami I needed to wipe away my useless religious paradigms, discover my God-given sexual orientation, and dive headfirst into this wonderful *gay lifestyle.*

Hoping to find more gay and lesbian friends, I went to Gay Pride Christopher Street West in June 1993. Having spent most of my life as a straight-laced Christian girl, I wasn't accustomed to being surrounded by so many overt sexual expressions. My eyes popped their sockets seeing Dykes on Bikes in their leathers, voluptuous breasts flopping, and men walking around in thongs, their scantily clad dicks bopping freely. I wandered through the fair, astonished by the booths of jewelry, paintings, clothing, leatherwork, and more. I stopped and chatted with people at booths that offered information on sex education, health, counseling, healing, outreach to young people, and a few church groups that welcomed LGBTQ+ folks. In no time, my little backpack was stuffed with folders, flyers, candy, and lots of wonder.

After a while I saw a booth with two words on a large sign: *Evangelical and Gay.* My heart skipped a beat. *Evangelicals Concerned Western Region,* the subtitle read. The Metropolitan Community Church was gay and Christian, to be sure, but this group was specifically evangelical and gay.

I lingered in front of their table. "Help yourself to some information," a normally dressed (according to my standards) young man smiled at me. "I'm Justin. This is Keith." My hand was smashed in their firm handshakes. Justin was a well-built young man with a short beard and big smile. "We're not a church. Your eyes tell me that you've never seen a group like this before."

I chuckled. "Yep. That's the truth." He had read my face pretty well. "I'd love to know more."

Curly blond hair bouncing over his eyes, Keith told me about the Bible studies the group had established in the Orange County area and how ECWR was starting up groups in the San Gabriel area as well.

"I live in Pasadena," I said. "Anything close to me?"

"We've got a new group in Glendale," said Justin. "That's close to you. You'd be welcome to join us this Tuesday." He wrote the address on a card and held it out for me.

I took the card and tucked it into my pocket. "Thanks. I'll be there." A warm glow filled my chest. I hoped I'd meet local people who had similar church backgrounds and had faced struggles similar to mine. Perhaps even meet a new lover.

⌒ℒℯ ⌐,

The following Tuesday, I drove to Glendale—and promptly got lost. The address I was looking for must have literally fallen through a torn fold in my old, tattered AAA map. After floundering for twenty minutes, however, I managed find the house. Must have been one of those small modern-day miracles of God.

The meeting had already begun. As I stepped inside, the front door closed a little too hard. Oops. I looked around the room, blushing—and was shocked to see about twenty-five men jammed in the space, sitting on sofas and dining room chairs and on the floor, heads buried in their Bibles. Several men wore crisp slacks and dress shirts. They must have just come from work. Others wore shorts, T-shirts, and flip-flops.

When the door banged the men looked up, their eyes and smiles drawing me in a warm welcome. Justin flashed me a big grin. They shared names around the circle, and I managed to grasp on to a few. *They can't all be gay, studying their Bibles like this*, I thought. *They look like a bunch of Navigator men.*

A piano sounded from the den off to the side. "Let's sing 'How Great Thou Art,'" someone said.

I felt like I was hearing the voices of angels.

Tears rolled down my cheeks. My constricted throat couldn't make a sound, though the song was one of my favorites. I remembered singing it with Thomas the time we went to hear Billy Graham, the great evangelist, preach at the Cleveland Indians baseball stadium in 1962. Thomas was fourteen, I twelve, and we had taken a public bus by ourselves to get there. George Beverly Shea, the soloist for the Billy Graham Crusades, became well known for how he sang *How Great Thou Art.*

That evening at the Evangelicals Concerned Bible study, the life-giving oxygen of those powerful lyrics inundated my heart and pumped their energy through my body. As the men sang, my spirit reached out to God as I prayed the words of the song:

> *Oh God, I wonder how awesome you are*
> *You have made the worlds and the stars*
> *I feel your power*
> *There is not just one way to see you*
> *But infinite ways of connecting with you*
> *My soul sings!*

During the evening I learned most of the men's names. Deep voices prayed aloud. Jay prayed for his friend Daniel, whose partner, Jonathan, was losing his battle with AIDS. Eric prayed for another friend with AIDS. Richard prayed about his job. Henry prayed that he wouldn't feel so lonely. And on and on they went. Just talking to

God as if he were their closest confidant. I didn't see any women. Just men.

Yet I felt like I had really come home.

That night, I resolved that I would never allow anyone—family member, friend, or church—to steal away the love relationship I had with my Creator. Somehow, this group touched a deep place inside of me. Deeper than the MCCLA church had. Probably it was because this group felt more familiar. Evangelical.

When I drove home after that memorable evening, my inner spirit reassured me that I was finally living a wonderful life. Mine!

～ℓℓ～

For the next several months, I continued to attend the men's EC Bible study.

"Don't any women ever come to this group?" I finally asked one evening.

"Some have come and gone, but I guess we men are so fierce that we scare the women away," Samuel said, laughing.

He was one of the guys that had a quick sense of humor and liked to pretend to flirt with me. I would flirt back by making some lewd comment and we'd all laugh. Quickly, I grew to love these gay brothers of mine.

Samuel suggested, "Why don't you start up a women's group? You could advertise in the LN."

I cocked my head to one side. "What's the LN?" I was entering a whole new world.

Samuel explained that the *Lesbian News*, started in 1975, was the longest-running lesbian publication in the US and had articles about lesbian art, music, history, literature, film, and more. "You ought to place an ad for a women's group. Gals will start calling you." His mischievous eyes sparkled. "You could find a new babe!"

I pinched his muscular arm as he tried to scoot away.

～ℓℓ～

The next day I got a coffee in Old Town Pasadena and stopped by Barnes and Noble Bookstore. I picked up a copy of the *LN* and scanned the ads, looking to see what was already there. One caught my eye: *Christian Lesbian Bible Study*, South Pasadena. Somebody had beaten me to the punch!

I called the number, and the following week I went to Giselle's house in anticipation of meeting some Christian lesbians.

I was the only one who arrived at the agreed-upon hour.

"The others will be here shortly," Giselle explained, her voice sounding hollow in her sparsely furnished apartment living room. "I'll make some tea and we can get acquainted."

I perched on the edge of her only chair. She sat cross-legged on the floor near me. She told me about her life, discovering that she was homosexual, but a Christian.

Why had she said, "*But* a Christian?"

"Let's get started with the Bible study, even though you're the only one here," she suggested. She scooted closer to me so I could see her open Bible. She easily found what are known within the gay community as the "Clobber Passages" (for more on this, see Appendix A), the few biblical references that purportedly condemn homosexual behavior. Red warning lights flashed in my brain. I knew that these passages were commonly used as a sledgehammer against gays, especially gay Christians.

Giselle explained, "Here in Romans Chapter 1 Paul the Apostle says, 'Their women exchanged natural sexual relations for unnatural ones. In the same way the men also abandoned natural relations with women and were inflamed with lust for one another. Men committed shameful acts with other men, and received in themselves the due penalty for their error.' You see, Sharon,? God calls lesbian relationships unnatural. In fact, God has used AIDS to strike gay men dead because of their sin. The Bible clearly states that if you have sexual relations with someone of your same gender—"

"Giselle. Stop!" I stood up. "The Bible clearly teaches that? It's clear to me that you have not studied the cultural context of Scripture. It's also clear to me that by running an ad in the LN

Magazine, you are trying to attract lesbians to make them Ex-Gays. You're like a Venus flytrap!"

I walked out of her sticky trap, slamming the door behind me.

Once home, my fury gave me the energy to fly into action. I phoned the *LN Magazine* to place my own ad: *Christian Bible Study for Lesbians. Come with your questions.*

Within a week I received phone calls from lesbian teachers, office workers, musicians, college students, and other women who wanted to reconcile their Christian faith and sexual orientation.

A group of women began to meet at my home: The Women's Evangelicals Concerned Bible Study. I used materials published by ECWR that explained how to use historical and cultural context to more accurately interpret the Clobber Passages and how to engage homophobic Christians in a way that could, hopefully, open dialogue. I was pleased to be a Bible teacher again, leading people to a greater truth for themselves.

In the women's group each week we passed around a list for names and phone numbers to stay in touch better. We started small, but soon grew to about a dozen women, sometimes taking turns hostessing the group.

I continued meeting on Tuesdays with the EC men. When I told them about the women's group they were very supportive. Every couple of months we'd have a BBQ or a pool party with the women and men together. I also participated in EC conferences of hundreds of gay evangelicals from several California counties—a thrilling experience.

One evening in November 1993, the women's group met at my home. I was delighted that so many women had shown up that there weren't even enough places to sit. We passed around the sign-up sheet to make sure that we got contact info for everyone. The new gals copied down my name and phone number to stay in touch.

The next day, a woman called me. "This is Catherine Wulf. I met you last night at the EC women's group."

I had to think a minute. There were several new women... Which one was she? My heart raced. "Hi... uh..." My words came out like a pulsating lawn sprinkler—*pfft, pfft, pfft.* I asked her how she liked the group, where she went to grad school, and on and on. I couldn't picture her in my mind.

A hesitant voice said, "I'd like to go out to dinner with you."

"I see. Well, I have..."

The lawn sprinkler continued to sputter out the things I had to do that day and the next. She repeated her invitation to dinner. I chewed on a torn fingernail. I'd broken up with Valentina thirteen months ago. Was I ready for a date with a new woman?

Finally, I said, "Dinner would be nice. Sure. Let's meet before the Bible study at Linda's house next Thursday." We made arrangements to meet at Pasadena's Soup Plantation—quite the opposite of a calm, quiet, romantic venue, but I wasn't exactly well-versed on how to date.

During dinner Catherine and I talked nonstop about our lives, families, church life, and love of camping. She had recently completed an M.A. in Marriage and Family Therapy and worked evenings in private practice. She worked days at the same Barnes and Noble where I'd picked up my first copy of the Lesbian News.

I shared with her my journey of self-discovery and coming out of the closet. I was surprised when she told me she was a survivor of Love In Action, an aggressive Christian Ex-Gay Ministry founded in 1973 that touted Conversion Therapy. (The memoir and movie entitled *Boy Erased* would, years later, show just how tragically deceptive that group was.) Obviously, and lucky for me, their tactics hadn't worked on Catherine.

During our conversation, an electric current ran between us. She and I were both evangelicals. We both had master's degrees. We both liked chocolate. We both had the same middle name: Elaine. We talked for over two hours, leaning toward each other across the small dinner table to hear each other in the noisy restaurant. She looked strong and was tall, a contrast to my wiry, skinny frame. Her personality was deep as a slow-moving stream, while mine was like crazy, cascading water tripping over rocks. I still used Maja perfume, but she used the woodsy-fresh fragrance, Diptyque Philosykos. We had so much in common, yet we were quite different.

Eventually, I glanced at my watch. "Oh my gosh!" I exclaimed. "The women's EC Bible Study in La Crescenta starts at seven; it's already seven twenty!"

"Linda's house is twenty minutes away," said Catherine, grabbing her purse and jacket.

"Let's go," I said, gathering up our trays and spilling a cup of water onto the floor. We hustled out to our cars.

⌒ᴥₔ

As soon as we burst in through the door of Linda's home, just before 8:00 p.m., the already-gathered, waiting women burst into laughter.

"Just look at the two of you! All red in the face. Where have you been?" Linda said, giggling.

"And no guitar!" Denise laughed. "You're our song leader, Sharon! Got your mind on something else?"

"Guitar? I think I forgot it in my car!" I declared, a little out of breath. But we'd arrived, hadn't we?

All the women smiled and laughed. What a joy to have the freedom to show the glow of nascent love with no shame. We had caught a wave and were proudly surfing atop its crest.

Less than a week later, I would begin spending nights at Catherine's apartment, sometimes calling in sick to my new job at Pasadena High School. "I hab a bab code," I'd tell the receptionist at the front desk as I pinched my nose. Catherine, pressed against my body in her bed, would stifle her giggles. We'd continue to enjoy our lovemaking up through lunchtime.

A few weeks later I invited her to join me for Thanksgiving dinner at my parents' house.

⌒ᴥₔ

I was almost forty-four years old and was bringing home another female lover to introduce to my parents. During dinner, my mother and father showed their usual friendly manner and expressed genuine interest in getting to know Catherine. I felt anxious; a slight shadow of embarrassment hovered above my forehead like a moth. I waved it away with a swoop of my hand before it could settle. I wasn't aware as to why I felt uneasy. Perhaps I was playing an old *should-have* memory, telling myself that by this age I should have been able to figure out my life already.

After dinner, when Catherine stepped out of the room for a moment, I hissed, "Mom! Mom! What do you think?" I sounded like a little kid.

"What a mature, lovely woman. A deep thinker, and seems so sensitive to others," said my mother. "She's a keeper, Sharon."

"But we only met a few weeks ago. How can you say she's a keeper already?"

My mother retreated to the sofa. As I sat down next to her, she smoothed out a few wrinkles on her apron, and I noticed, as always, those blue-river veins on her hands. Such comforting hands. She smiled.

"Don't forget that your father and I met on a blind date. And he asked me to marry him three weeks later. Add three more weeks: our wedding day."

My mind was whirring like a little gyroscope.

Just then my dad walked into the living room. "Sharon, it feels like the time is right for you to settle down, don't you think?" He sat down next to my mom.

My mom gazed at one of her own flower paintings hanging on the wall. "We've been married almost fifty years now." I could imagine her in her long white gown, flanked by her bridesmaids. Her voice sounded like velvet. "When you know, you know. And I think you know. Don't you?" My parents exchanged glances.

Blue butterflies flitted around my head, in through my eyes, and down into my stomach. I sucked in a breath. "I get it. Yes, I think we know." I grabbed my mom's hand and whispered, "But I'm scared."

Catherine walked in at that moment; seeing her, my body filled with a profound love.

"Want to take a walk on the beach?" she asked.

"Sure, let's go." I threw a quick wink to my mom over my shoulder as Catherine and I headed out the door.

Nine months later, in August of 1994, Catherine and I celebrated our Holy Union in a small Episcopal church near Glendale. Pastor Nancy Wilson of the Metropolitan Community Church of Los Angeles officiated. We'd donned necklaces and earrings of white carved shells, white calf-length lacy dresses, and colorful high-topped Keds. I'd even coifed my hair, painted my nails, and wore make-up! Our ushers were Justin, Samuel, Eric, and Richard, friends from Evangelicals Concerned. Each of them wore a tight white T-shirt emblazoned with the words, NOBODY KNOWS I'M A LESBIAN. We thought that was hilarious.

Catherine and had I planned the whole affair, agreeing that neither of us needed to be given away. We also came up with a unique idea for our ceremony: In the small sanctuary, we arranged one hundred chairs so that the aisles formed the shape of the letter "Y." The stem of the "Y" was at the front of the church, and the two branches of the "Y" reached out to the two rear corners of the sanctuary. From those two back corners, Catherine in one and I in the other, we would begin walking alone, then meet at the middle of the "Y," join hands, and proceed together toward the altar at the front.

My mother, father, brother Greg, sister Marci, Aunt Carla, Aunt Elaine and Uncle Al had arrived early to help us set everything up. Thomas was not made aware of the event at all. No one from Catherine's family even knew about the wedding either; her parents believed that being gay was a sin. It was devastating that their misled beliefs had robbed her of their support on this momentous day.

Two o'clock came faster than we'd imagined on that hot afternoon. We waited for our one hundred guests, most of them from our EC group, to be seated, anxious to begin the ceremony. We were already boiling in those dresses and Keds.

I was ready in my corner near the main door. Rather than cross over all the people already seated in the back rows, Catherine headed out of the church to walk around the building and re-enter at the back corner opposite me.

Expecting Catherine to appear momentarily, I waited at my back corner of the sanctuary, holding the bouquet of flowers my mother had made from her garden. Sweat poured down my face and dripped onto my hand, where the flowers began to shake uncontrollably in their own seismic spasms. I was glad that my father, our photographer, had taken a zillion photos of us prior to the ceremony. Any photos he took of that bouquet now would have been a blurry mess.

The organ played softly as a few more people came in and sat down, filling the church to capacity. I glanced over at Catherine's corner . . . but where was she? The organist nodded to me, asking for the cue to begin the traditional wedding march, but I shook my head and shrugged my shoulders. She continued to play her soft, bland background music. By now, people in the congregation were turning around and looking at me, gesturing that I should start down the aisle. *Where is Catherine?*

Samuel, the stud usher in his NOBODY KNOWS I'M A LESBIAN T-shirt, rushed all the way down the aisle, paused, looked around, trotted to the wooden door in the other back corner, opened it, thrust his head in, slammed the door, rushed up the aisle again, and ran past me out of the church. More people turned around to look at me. My flowers vibrated in my hands. *Where is Catherine?*

Minutes later, Samuel reentered the church — without Catherine. As I was trying to make eye contact with him, however, she suddenly appeared at my side, flushed and perspiring, and almost bowled me over as she began clumsily climbing across the legs of the people seated in the back row. "Excuse me, excuse me, excuse me," she whispered as she clambered along making her way toward her corner. Finally, she went through the wooden door on the other side and banged it closed.

What's going on? Why doesn't she come out? My flower petals threatened to dislocate themselves from their stems.

Catherine did not reappear for a full five minutes, during which time a woman arrived late, pressed past me, and looked for an available seat. She clambered over the same legs of the same back row, murmuring, "Perdóname, perdón, perdón." Valentina!

The organist glanced at me. I shrugged again. At that moment, the wooden door on the far side opened and a beautiful bride emerged, eyes darting to and fro, her face glistening with perspiration.

I nodded to the organist. She began the wedding march. Catherine and I walked forward. As we met in the middle and joined our hands, she quietly hissed, without moving her lips, "Stare straight ahead. Don't you dare start laughing."

I obeyed. But felt totally confused by what had transpired in the last ten minutes.

We arrived at the altar just in time. We said the vows we had composed, and were pronounced *Holy Unioned* by Pastor Nancy. Gay marriage wouldn't be recognized in California for another fourteen years.

⁓

At the reception, our three-tiered carrot-cake wedding cake sloped to one side in the 103-degree afternoon, almost toppling the two naked, rainbow-haired little trolls perched upon the creamy icing.

Dying of curiosity, I demanded, "Catherine, what in the world happened to you out there?"

Before she could answer, Samuel giggled. "You thought she was going to stand you up, huh?" Everyone laughed.

She laughed too. "You all won't believe this, but, when I went around the building to get to the other side, there was a locked gate in a chain-link fence about ten feet high. I figured that I'd just climb up, swing my legs over, jump down, and go into the door on my side of the church. Trouble is, I had on this stupid wedding dress, and when I got to the top of that fence, one of the metal barbs got caught in the lace on the front. I couldn't get it untangled. I was stuck up there, yelling for help, but didn't want to attract the attention of the people inside. Finally, Samuel came looking for me and helped me get down. I ran in, almost toppling Sharon, who must have been worried sick, and climbed over the people's legs and shut myself in that little vestibule to catch my breath."

The crowd roared with laughter.

"I see it this way," continued Catherine. "I finally got off the fence, came out of the closet, and married Sharon."

I beamed at everyone. "This is the happiest day of my life."

Sometimes we have to wait a long time to discover the happy.

Sharon Wulfensmith

CHAPTER 30

OUT AT WORK

Two months prior to meeting Catherine at that EC women's group I had signed a teaching contract at Pasadena High School (PHS). As if I weren't stressed enough already, I had lied during my interview, telling the administrator that I had no significant health problems and that I had experience teaching high school. Did one semester of student teaching over twenty years ago count? I made sure I didn't ask that question. I desperately needed full-time work to get health insurance and cover my basic expenses. Pasadena City College Adult Ed had been only part time, with no benefits.

When I was initially hired at PHS, I hadn't known that on top of working full time in a public school I'd have to complete a California Teaching Credential program at a nearby college plus pass the BCLAD (Bilingual, Cross-Cultural, Language and Academic Development) exam to qualify to work with Spanish-speaking students. This high school ESL-teacher job was overwhelming even before I began, but I knew it was my best shot at getting a job with a decent salary.

I learned quickly how to navigate the large campus on my super-sized knees. Arrive early so no one will see my difficulty walking, and haul myself upstairs to my second-floor classroom. Don't go downstairs until after school. Find a few good confidants to back me up.

It was 1993 and I had a new job and a new love, but I was afraid to share my personal good news with colleagues. That first year I kept a low profile.

After our wedding in 1994, Catherine and I legally combined our last names. She had been Wulf. I had been Smith. Hence, Wulfensmith. We wore wedding rings but could not be a legally married couple. I tried to guard my secret at the school—refraining from talking about my home life, dancing around gendered pronouns, and such—but I knew I couldn't sustain that for very long. I decided I could trust a few teachers and administrators at PHS, but shouldn't come out to the students. At that time there were no employment protections for gay or lesbian teachers in California. It sapped my energy to cloak myself in secrecy at work, but I certainly didn't want to risk getting fired.

In the spring of 1995, Pasadena Unified School District's Board of Education planned to discuss health insurance benefits. I chose not to hide any longer. I realized that if I made a presentation to the Board, I would be outing myself to many teachers and administrators—a big risk. But it was worth it. I prepared a petition to ask that Catherine be considered my spouse so that we could get family coverage for health insurance.

That May, I stood in front of the crowd gathered in the Board Room, grasping the sides of the tiny podium so my hands wouldn't shake, and said, "I spend an extra $400 per month just to insure my life partner." My voice was steady. "Please give us family benefits. A *couple* makes a family."

"Take a seat, Miss Smith," said the moderator (some people still refused to use my correct last name, which was infuriating). "This topic is tabled for this month. Next?"

I would make many more petitions to the Board in the years to come; each time, they would deny that petition. Not until July of 1999, when California would finally legalize domestic partnerships, would they change their policy.

On this day in 1995, I withered back down into my chair, deflated.

I don't know if she was actually approved to be the next speaker, but a tall woman, clad in black head to toe, rushed to stand behind the little podium. I wondered why she carried a big, floppy Bible. The woman shrieked, "Did you hear that skinny girl?" She pointed a crooked finger at me and shook it. "Family insurance? God only recognizes heterosexuals, n-n-not hom-m-mo... sick-shuls." She had a noticeable stutter.

I sighed and took a long, cool drink from my water bottle. *Here we go again.* I was sure I'd seen her here before.

"The Baah-bul says..." She fumbled to find a particular page, couldn't, and proceeded to flap the Bible above her head instead, yelling, "Forni . . . forni . . . for*ni*ficators are going to hell! They don't need health insurance!"

Upon hearing her mispronunciation, *for-ni-fi-cators*, a guffaw escaped my lips, my mouthful of water spewing out.

The moderator's voice boomed, "Ma'am! You need to leave right now. Get out! You!"

I smiled, gloating that the moderator would be throwing out that horrid witch.

"You!" he yelled again. But he was pointing at me, not at that woman.

My stomach dropped. I hastily grabbed my things and rushed from the meeting, followed by Deena, a colleague from school.

Once we were outside the board room she pointed at me and said, "Fornificator!"

My embarrassment vanished. We both dissolved into giggles as we scampered down the hallway like two mischievous girls.

I liked Deena. Her crazy sense of humor gave me a lighter perspective.

<hr>

The following year, Catherine and I bought a 1920s Craftsman home in Monrovia and planned an Open House celebration. The invitation had both our names, and stated that we hoped to have children some day. I was glad that the people at the Board meeting hadn't outed me to the staff at Pasadena High. Among my PHS friends, I carefully selected who would receive an invite, especially avoiding Miss Petty, an English teacher that I didn't particularly like.

One afternoon after school she corralled me in the hallway. "I heard you had invitations to something. Don't I get one?" Her nasal voice was like the whine of a metal gate.

"Uhh... I have one left." I plopped the small pink envelope into her waiting hand.

Opening it, she scanned it then raised her eyes to look at me without speaking. Swiveling around, her high heels click-clacked away down the hall.

I was sorry already.

I had a special office next to my classroom at school because I was now the department chair, and responsible for monitoring data for the immigrant students taking ESL. The day after Miss Petty had gotten my invitation, I noticed that quite a few students were in my office area during lunchtime, chatting with Mrs. Gomez, the receptionist. I was too busy to pay much attention to the hubbub.

After the students left for the day, Mrs. Gomez called me over to her desk. "Did you give one of these invitations to Miss Petty?" She held up the invitation I'd given to her.

"Yeah. Why?" Dread filled the cavity that was supposed to hold my next breath.

"The students told me that in her classroom this morning she talked about the evils of homosexuality, and the tragedy of gay adoption. She implied that maybe one of the teachers here was a homosexual, and then mentioned your name. After class, all the students rushed in here to ask me if you were a lesbian. I had to tell them that you were." Her head dropped forward, her long black hair covering her face. "I am so, so sorry."

My blood boiled up from my legs and out of my steaming head. "Mrs. Gomez, thank you for being honest with the students. You have done nothing wrong. I'll have a talk with Miss Petty right now."

I stormed into her classroom. She was sitting at her desk, grading papers.

"What have you done?" I yelled.

Calmly, she pulled the small envelope from her drawer and held it up between thumb and forefinger as if it were a smelly sock. "This invitation shows a woman's name. Not a man's. I thought you were a married woman. Not a homosexual. And children? I can't believe that you would even think of such a thing." She let the envelope drop. Her fingers fluttered to straighten out her pile of papers.

My lips tight, my breath shallow, I seethed, "I *am* a married woman. You outed me to the students! How could you...?"

"Tsk tsk." She shook her head and sighed. "Please understand, Sharon. I am a *Chrissstian*," she said as she carefully folded her pink manicured nails in front of her ample bosom. "I must tell the truth of God wherever I am, even if it is uncomfortable for others to hear." Her eyelids fluttered momentarily as her eyes brimmed with tears. "This is my Christian duty. The Bible says—"

I inhaled through clenched teeth and shouted, "I don't care what you think your Bible says! You've done something terribly unethical!" I exhaled what was left of my breath and stormed out of her classroom.

That evening at home, I discussed the day's events with Catherine. Wisely, she advised me to talk with the school principal so that everything would be out in the open. Mr. Luna wore his religion on his sleeve at PHS and we all knew that he was an evangelical Christian of the conservative Nazarene denomination. I felt it was a "damned if I do and damned if I don't" situation, but knew I must talk with him anyway. Soon.

After arriving at the school earlier than usual the next day, I gently tapped on Mr. Luna's office door.

He opened it wide and leaned close to give me a quick hug. "What brings you here so early, Sharon? Take a seat." His wide smile in his brown face had always been a welcome light for me. Would that be snuffed out in the next two minutes?

I explained to him what had happened the day before, and concluded, saying, "I thought you should know everything that happened. I am angry with Miss Petty, and I'm scared about what could happen with the students and their parents if they know about me." I exhaled all my air, slumped in the chair and studied my lap.

"You're a highly respected teacher, Sharon," Mr. Luna said.

I looked up at him.

"I suggest that you seize the teachable moment and find a way to engage the students on this topic. Go ahead and come out openly to all your classes and welcome their discussions about homosexuality."

I almost fainted to the floor; was he really saying all this?

His voice got louder. "If any student or parent has a problem here, send them to my office and I'll teach them something about tolerance!" He smacked his hand on his desk. "And I'll deal with Miss Petty. Okay?"

I gawked at him, my heart thudding with excitement. "Mr. Luna, I haven't got the words to say how much I appreciate this."

We shook hands and I went to my classroom.

That day, the students were unusually quiet in class. I was too.

~elez

After school that afternoon, I prepared a story to read aloud to my students the following day. I covered an empty Kleenex box with a sign that said, QUESTIONS, and placed it on the front table. I was ready.

The next day, I began by saying, "I understand that many of you have some questions about families and love and relationships. I have prepared a little story to read today. Afterwards, please put your questions into the box here." I hoped I appeared calm, even though I could hear my own thumping heart. "Here we go."

CHOICES

Many years ago a little girl grew up knowing she was different but had not chosen to be different. Kids, and even some family members, called her a tomboy. Her friends made fun of her and called her ugly names. As a teenager she felt even more uncomfortable. No boys wanted to date her. As an adult she unexpectedly fell in love with another woman and realized that she was a lesbian. But she hadn't chosen that sexual orientation. Later, she fell in love with another woman and they chose to be life partners. Together they are choosing to adopt a child. She chose to become a teacher at Pasadena High School. Today, she chose to stand in front of you to read her personal story.

I smiled uneasily as I set the paper down on my desk. They sat in frozen silence for a bit and I froze too, unsure of how to proceed— until they burst into applause. I sagged with relief as they began tearing paper into little slips to write questions on, chatting and smiling at each other.

The questions they stuffed into the box were remarkable:

How old were you when you realized you were gay?

What did your parents say when you came out?

Are you religious?

How do gays adopt?

Are there other gay teachers at school? Why don't they talk about it?

Why did Miss Petty talk about you behind your back?

I did have to toss out a couple of them, however:

How do lesbians "do it?"

Is Mr. Luna gay? (Wow. That one made me wonder.)

I felt so proud of myself. I had broken my chains of deceit and denial.

My openness and honesty empowered me to forge ahead in the years to come, to educate and advocate whenever the opportunity arose. My LGBTQ+ students would be empowered to come out to parents, priests, pastors, and peers. I would become the Pasadena High School staff advisor of the Gay Lesbian Bi Straight Alliance Club for many years.

Miss Petty would resign.

CHAPTER 31
OUT AT CHURCH

In 1996, after taking a hiatus away from church for a couple of years, I felt drawn to become involved in a church again. Because Catherine and I were both from evangelical backgrounds and enjoyed Evangelicals Concerned so much, I suggested that we give my old church, Pasadena Covenant, a try together.

First, I wanted to share this decision with my parents. I phoned them to explain.

"I just hope you'll feel welcome in your old church," my father said.

"I would think that your *true* friends there would be interested in hearing your coming-out story," my mother cut in.

I told them the *fornificator* story and we all laughed. "I want to give this church a try again, and not hide," I said.

"Just be careful, dear," my father cautioned. "Sometimes church folk can be pretty mean-spirited. You know the stories we've all heard."

I twisted the coils of the phone receiver cord around my fingers. "I know. I feel so fortunate that both of you love me just the way I am. I'll let you know how things work out. I love you. Bye."

My first Sunday back at Pasadena Covenant Church felt strange, like a kid returning to school after a long absence. I went alone to scope things out. Pastor Howard had left, and new faces and families crowded the foyer after the service.

"Hello, Sharon," a familiar voice called to me.

"Carl Goodwin! So you're the new senior pastor now. Great!" I beamed at him as we shook hands. He and I had worked closely together from 1984 to 1989.

"So Wulfensmith is your new last name," he said, smiling. "Why don't you come by my office sometime soon so we catch up. I'd love to hear what you've been doing the past few years."

Carl and I met in his office a few weeks later. I told him about Evangelicals Concerned and my Holy Union with Catherine. "We'd like to come to this church, and when we have children, raise them with an evangelical foundation." I tried to ignore the tense feeling in my face while I spoke.

Carl rubbed his chin. "Children? Wonderful. I, myself, respect you. But I have to admit that there's no way that I can fully comprehend the struggle that you must have had with being gay and Christian. Is it okay if I ask you something?"

"Sure. Go ahead." I wondered what he could be thinking. And why was my eye twitching so annoyingly just now? I poked at it nervously.

He fidgeted with a paperweight on his desk. "A few years ago I remember that you took a leave of absence from our pastoral team for a while. At the time I wouldn't have ever asked you what that involved."

My stomach lurched. *No! Please don't ask me about Bela.*

"I have to admit that it came to my mind that you might have gotten involved with another woman."

Now it was my turn to fidget. I tore at an old hangnail. It began to bleed, so I stuck it into my mouth and looked at the floor, burning with shame. *Calm yourself, Sharon. Breathe.* I grabbed a Kleenex and pressed it on my bloody finger.

He had walked to the window and was looking out. "I'm sorry I brought that up. I want you to know that I am glad to see you again, and admire you for walking a difficult journey. It seems like you're doing well now, with your partner and all." He came back to sit across from me again. "You need to know that I cannot speak for this entire congregation. There may be people here who don't understand you, or who flat-out disagree with you calling yourself Christian and gay." He looked me in the eye. "Are you sure you want to re-engage here at this church?"

"Of course," I answered with no hesitation, overwhelmed with relief that he wasn't asking about Bela.

"Just so you are warned," he continued, "The Evangelical Covenant denomination has not, and may never, endorse gay marriage."

I looked directly at Carl. "Catherine and I would like to try anyway. We'll just be ourselves. No hiding. And I'd like to sing in the Morning Song Choir too."

"Good." Carl moved towards his desk and straightened out a few papers. I couldn't help but wonder if he felt nervous too. "We'll see how things turn out. If anything gets, you know, stirred up, I'll let you know."

The following Sunday Catherine and I went to the church together. During Meet-and-Greet time, a woman I knew from before, Becky, came over.

"Great to see you again, Sharon. Do I see a wedding ring on your finger? Where's the lucky man?" She peered past Catherine.

"*She's* right here," I said, emphasizing the pronoun. "This is Catherine, my life partner."

Becky reached over, took Catherine's hand, and practically dislocated her shoulder with her vigorous shaking. "Welcome!"

Catherine forced a smile back at Becky. Several other members came over to chat after that.

On our drive home, Catherine remarked, "You seem to know a lot of people. Don't forget, I'm an introvert, and it's not so easy for me to . . ."

Sharon Wulfensmith

"We'll be fine. You'll make new friends." I waved my hand dismissively.

"You can go ahead and attend," she said. "I'll wait. I don't want to get into a situation where we'll both get hurt."

"I just wish you'd come with me, that's all," I said, discouraged.

But she wouldn't be swayed.

⁓

When the next Sunday's service ended I was quick to exit, anxious to get home to Catherine. But then a friend caught my eye.

"Hello, Inez!" I was happy to see her.

Inez was now married and I could see her big baby bump. I only had butterflies. No bump.

"Let's have coffee soon," she said, tucking Baby #1 into her stroller. "I'd like to hear what you've been up to. Life changes so fast, doesn't it?"

"Yep," I replied. I was curious as to how she'd react when I told her about the changes in my life. Would we remain friends? *Of course we will*, I told myself.

Just as Inez disappeared, a woman named Carrie caught up with me out on the sidewalk. "Welcome back." She gave me a quick hug. She grasped my shoulders and held me at arm's length. Even her freckles smiled. "Been a long time!" She glanced down at my hand. "Oh! A wedding ring? Where did you meet the lucky guy?"

Taking a step back and taking a deep breath, I answered, "I met *her* at a Bible study."

"Herrr?" She dragged out the word.

"I married a woman. Not a man." My voice was more like a squeak.

Her mouth curved into a small "o" shape. Her high-pitched words pierced my flesh. "Don't you know the Bible? In Romans Chapter 1 it says that God gave them up to their sinful lusts. 'Gave

252

them up' means that God has given up on you. Homosexuality is sin. An abomination!" She wagged her crooked finger into my face, then whirled around and marched away.

I gazed down at the empty sidewalk. *Maybe this is going to be harder than I thought.*

⸺

Was I home at this church? I asked myself that question many times. I just hoped and prayed that everything would work out positively. I missed Catherine and wanted her to come with me to services, but respected her decision to stay away.

As the year progressed, the thread that had tied me to my evangelical roots began to unravel. During choir practice prayer time one evening, one of my fellow singers, Kurt, said, "I feel an evil presence among us."

His wife Thelma added, "Our church needs cleansing."

My eyebrows knit together. I could only conclude that they were talking about me.

At the end of the evening, Kurt pulled me aside as we were about to exit and hissed, "We hear that you're living a homosexual lifestyle. Don't you know that's sin?"

As his wife hastily brushed past me in the doorway, my eyes welled with tears.

Natalie, a fellow alto, walked to my side and put her arm around my shoulder. "Sharon, you need to know that people are talking about you. We know that there are gays and lesbians who attend this church, but they don't talk about it like you do. They stay quiet." Her index finger lightly touched her lips.

"Natalie," I said, trying to keep my voice level. "I hid for most of my life. I will not hide here."

Head held high, I retreated to my car. I had to sit out in the parking lot for a few minutes before leaving; the drumming of my heart was so loud, I felt it would shake the fenders off of the car.

Several weeks had passed since I'd run into Inez on the sidewalk. Finally, we managed to grab a chance to talk: we agreed to have lunch at El Prado, a restaurant a couple blocks up from the church.

"So this is your second baby?" I smiled over our burrito lunch.

"I love being a mom." She gently circled her hands over the curve of her baby-belly. "What have you been doing for the past few years?"

"I've had a tough time because of the knee disease. It's a bit better, but I still don't know what it is."

"I remember how you struggled." Her voice was kind.

I reminisced about the friendship we'd had during our time on the pastoral staff. As we chatted, I wondered if she had heard any rumors about my so-called lifestyle. I went ahead and took the risk to share my story, concluding, "... and I married Catherine Wulf... and we're planning to adopt a child."

When I got to this part—our desire to adopt children—I noticed that Inez had shredded her napkin into a thousand little pieces and was scooting them around on the tabletop.

"I did hear rumors about you," she said, "but I didn't want to believe it."

"Why?" Butterflies were fighting for space inside my tummy.

"Aren't you embarrassed?" she spat out her words. "Marrying a man would be normal. Not a woman! Besides, why do you have to talk about it so much?"

I let out a long breath. "I talk about Catherine because I love her, just like you love your husband."

Inez just stared at me; then she stood up and walked out, leaving behind two things: a half-eaten burrito and our friendship.

Had I stuck my head into a beehive by returning to my old church? Would I get stung all over? Maybe Catherine had been right after all.

And after fighting so hard for what I thought was the right thing to do.

CHAPTER 32

LIMITED WELCOME

I could hear his breathing in the phone receiver. "I need to let you know that things are stirring up around here," Carl Goodwin told me.

"What's happening?" I braced myself.

"I warned you that people might have differing opinions about you being gay and out." Carl spat his words out rapid-fire. "A Morning Song member told the choir director that you shouldn't be singing because that's leading worship, and since you're living a homosexual lifestyle and don't seem concerned to get help for your condition, you shouldn't be allowed to do that. And that's not all..."

I steadied my voice to interrupt. "Carl. I am a lesbian Christian. I'm not going to lie or hide."

He coughed. "Listen! My phone is ringing off the hook. People are asking me why you're at this church and why you're in a leadership capacity."

My voice was firm, and I hoped not too loud. "I'm not a member of the pastoral staff anymore. I have been discreet. Some people accept me. Others send me to hell." I was talking on the phone in the hallway at home, and I knew that Catherine could hear me from her La-Z-Boy in the living room. I was glad that she wasn't the kind of person to say, *I told you so.*

"I'm sorry that some people have been mean to you," Carl said, his deep voice a bit too loud. "I don't know why it's coming to a head right now. Perhaps it's because the media is making us all more aware of homosexuality. Especially since Ellen DeGeneres came out publicly." He was quiet for a moment, then continued more calmly, "Sharon, I'm letting you know ahead of time that I'm going to take a treacherous step this Sunday. I hope that what I'm going to do will help the situation."

"What are you planning to do?" My thoughts tripped over each other.

"This Sunday my sermon is entitled, *Since You Asked About Ellen.*"

"Geez!"

"I'm not going to preach about homosexuality, per se, but about self-righteousness versus mercy and non-judgmental acceptance of people who are different than the so-called norm."

Astounded and relieved, I said, "I look forward to that!"

The next Sunday—May 4, 1997—Carl paced back and forth in the front of the sanctuary rather than standing in the pulpit as he preached for about twenty minutes about acceptance.

"The parables in Luke Chapter 18 teach us that we need to be humble and merciful to all people. Even to people like Ellen. Today's sermon is not about being gay or straight. To love and respect others doesn't mean that we agree with them, but that we are merciful, as Jesus was."

Carl explained that our life decisions encompass how we respond to the world around us, and said that no one really chooses his or her identity—that God is the one who makes that choice. He concluded by saying, "Each one of us has a choice this morning. Think about someone you might know who is different than you are. Perhaps someone with whom you do not agree on some issue. Ask yourself, *How can I be loving and merciful to him or her?*"

While he paused, my mind raced and I could hear the thumping of my heartbeat in my eardrums.

"Would anyone like to share some thoughts?" Carl extended both hands out, palms up.

My head swiveled left and right as I scanned the people near me in the front row. I couldn't believe that he was actually inviting people to respond aloud to his message.

A woman stood. "My husband threw our son out of the house because he said he was gay. What should I do?"

A young man spoke up. "Can a person be gay and Christian at the same time?"

Carl answered each question gently, focusing on the theme of love and mercy. Then he waited for another question. After a long silence, he prompted, "If your heart is pounding wildly, it just may be a prompting from God."

Surely he could hear my drumming heart from where he stood. I turned around to face everyone as I rose to my feet. I drew in a deep breath, my voice ringing out clearly to say, "I thank God that he made me a lesbian. It is a gift."

I heard an audible gasp from people around me.

I sat, trembling from head to toe. I did it!

A deafening silence followed. Mercifully, Rowan began to play the next hymn, "Just As I Am, Without One Plea." I remembered these words from my childhood. I told my inner self, *Yes, I am who I am, just as I am.*

As the prayers were said and the bread and wine were blessed in preparation for Holy Communion, about a dozen people walked out.

When I went forward a few minutes later to receive Christ's body and blood, my hands were shaking so much that I spilled some of the juice from the tiny cup. Could I be unworthy to drink Christ's blood? My mind swirled with conflict.

A week after the Ellen sermon, I got a call from Carl.

"I'm drowning in phone calls and messages," he told me. Some were positive, he said, asking him for advice and telling him about friends and family who were gay, but other were demanding that Carl, unfit for pastoring, resign immediately. "I promise to keep you in the loop," he whispered.

After that phone call, a bubble of encouragement bloomed in me regarding staying at the church—but it popped all too soon. Only a few days later, a friend tipped me off that a secret forum had convened to discuss the issue. People were threatening to split the church.

What was happening? Wasn't Carl supposed to be informing me of what was going on?

The next day, Carl called me again. His voice was quick and urgent. "Are you free this afternoon? The pastoral staff wants to talk with you in the church office."

Luckily, I had the day off, so I drove to the church, hands shaking on my steering wheel.

My feet dragged up the stairway to the church office. Upon entering, I saw that a group had already gathered. No, I wasn't late. No one greeted me.

I sat down in the one vacant chair and felt every eye in the room bore a hole into my forehead. My friend, Inez. Or was she now my ex-friend? Rowan, my beloved choir director. The co-pastor, Alex, who had told me I'd end up in bed with Ethan. Agatha, the chairman of the Church Board. And Carl, of course.

Was I the subject of an inquisition?

Agatha sat tall in her chair, her wavy, long brown hair cascading to her shoulders. "Sharon, the church has reached a consensus about you."

So, they voted about me? Gee, I didn't realize I was nominated for anything. My private sarcasm tasted good.

Agatha spoke as if addressing a formal audience in an assembly hall. "The entire church met together last Thursday evening. You were not invited, of course. After deliberation, we voted, and the agreement is as follows." She straightened her shoulders, then carefully perched a pair of silver reading glasses on her narrow nose. She eyed me over the glasses. "You must immediately step down from any leadership role whatsoever here, because you are living in sin with another woman. Our denomination cannot allow leaders to engage in this type of unholy lifestyle. It will stain our church."

My thoughts screamed inside my head. *How could they?*

Adjusting her little lenses, she focused on a typed page in front of her and read the damning words.

> "*Sharon Wulfensmith is no longer a member of the Morning Song choir. She may not lead any Bible studies or discussion groups at the church. She may not pray aloud in gatherings or lead worship by singing or playing her guitar. She is welcome to partake of Holy Communion. However, she may not assist in serving it in any way.*"

Agatha continued reading a few more rules, but I had stopped listening already.

This indictment felt even worse than Sue yelling at me over twenty years earlier to shut up about my same-sex attraction. What a travesty that the Pasadena Covenant Church would impose on me these rigid restrictions just because I was finally telling the truth about myself. I could taste the bile rising in my throat.

Carl took the helm. "Sharon, we ask you to receive these instructions with humility, as we are not asking you to leave this church. We want you to continue fellowshipping with us. We are a Christian family. One family together is our motto. Therefore, we are extending to you what we will call a... a..."

Agatha's voice filled the void. "A limited welcome." She removed her reading spectacles. Her thin lips stretched into a tight smile.

Those two words hit me like a speeding garbage truck. I raised my voice. "Limited welcome?" I shot back at them. "What an oxymoron!" *Morons*, I thought. "I understand now." I couldn't help myself; my words took on a mocking tone. "Gays must stay hidden! And lie!"

I huffed out a breath. It had taken me a lifetime to discover who I was. Finally, I knew. The leaders of this church wanted me to revert back to the person I had been when they first came to know me, but I had already abandoned that person.

"You don't even *want* to know who gay people are, do you?" I demanded.

Carl spoke softly. "You have been remarkably respectful in your participation here. You must feel hurt by all this."

"I do feel very hurt," I said. And then—since I knew how to preach, didn't I?—I spat out an impromptu mini-sermon, quoting from Jesus's teaching of the Judgment Day using the familiar parable of the sheep and the goats from Matthew 25. I concluded by saying, "The Bible that I read shows a Jesus who welcomed all who came to him. He broke the Jewish rules of his day and the religious leaders pushed him away. I can't imagine that you'd even recognize Jesus, much less welcome him if he dared enter this church!" I bolted up from my chair. "God have mercy on all of you!"

I fled the office and marched down the stairs, angry and defeated. Once inside the safety of my little Toyota, the dam holding back my tears finally burst.

Somehow during the past couple of years I had built up my hopes and mustered enough confidence to forge ahead to live in integrity instead of falsehood. But I had entrusted all of this into the wrong hands. For heaven's sake, what was I thinking... to go back to that evangelical church? Carl had warned me, hadn't he?

Catherine had seen behind the curtain right away. I hadn't because I couldn't. I had kicked and screamed against what would not, could not, and would never change in the Evangelical Covenant denomination.

⁓

Even though I wouldn't return to the church, I wasn't done yet. True to my assertive, impetuous character, I wrote a letter. The church logo—*One Family Together*—now incensed me. I tore it into pieces, pasted them roughly together, and used it as my own letterhead, writing the words, *One Broken Family* on top of it.

My letter was direct, angry and sad. I included several biblical quotations about how Jesus welcomed the marginalized. I mailed it to each of the 260 members of the congregation to respond to the *limited welcome with limited participation* they had extended to me.

Many people responded.

A letter from Rowan, the choir director, read:

I feel discouraged. Maybe I could have done things differently. I didn't agree with any of the people who said that I must ask you to leave Morning Song. But choir members warned me that folks would leave the church and never return. I wish you could share your wonderful gifts with us, but I think you wanted us to endorse your point of view about homosexuality, and we can't do that. It seems that there are no winners here. Only losers. You must have felt more hurt than anyone. I am grateful for the time you were with us, for your songs and prayers and participation.

A letter from Holly, a psychologist, read:

You have been trapped into a web of deception. Homosexuality is not a God-given, inborn, unchangeable quality like race. This lifestyle is fraught with danger, suicide, drug use, HIV, depression and despair. Studies show that gays have sex with up to 500 or more partners! Their focus is only on the pleasure of sex because gays cannot procreate. Gays should not adopt children either. This kind of parenting has a crippling effect on the child's development and identity. You do not have a gift from God. You are disobedient. Don't trade your place in heaven for a passing tragic philosophy. I am not intolerant; I am just telling you the truth.

Ouch! I thought. Such ignorance, even from a person who had studied psychology.

The most surprising letter came from my beloved Fuller Seminary professor, Dr. Daemon Fanger, who had changed my view of the Bible by teaching Contextual Theology. Starting with the address "Dear Sharon Smith" (not Wulfensmith), he wrote:

> *I remember you from my classes, and don't know if you were struggling with lesbianism at that time. I'm so sorry you have chosen to defy God, live in homosexuality, and embrace a delusion. I'm sure you have fought many battles to overcome your homosexual propensities. I'm so sorry you have given up. But now you are out of the church and out of the Kingdom of God. Unless you repent you are no longer welcome here. We exclude those who choose to be cursed by Satan.*

> *God has His rules. Do you want our church to abandon God's standards? You are so entrenched in your position that you are immune to Scripture. You, Sharon, who, at one time, won others to Christ, will have no part in heaven yourself. You are playing a game that you will lose for eternity. You have chosen a sad life and a sadder future. God says He has given up on you. But I haven't given up on you. I would be glad to meet with you if you're willing to confess that homosexuality is a sin. I love you and pray that you will return to God.*

It was evident to me that Dr. Fanger had lost his way. His letter included specific Bible passages, sorely taken out of context, that condemned the marginalized. Poor Jesus! What would Dr. Fanger have done if he had come face to face with that rabble-rouser of the first century?

I had maintained close friendships with the guys at Evangelicals Concerned and talked to them on a regular basis. One Saturday I met one of them, Henry, for coffee to give him an update on the final chapter of my church saga.

We sat across from each other in a small cafe. After I finished telling my story, I said, "Thanks for listening to me, Henry. By the way, where do you attend church, since you've been out of the closet for quite some time now?"

He didn't respond right away, so I studied his face. He seemed to be thinking how to answer.

He dropped his eyes to stare at the swirls in his coffee. "I'm sticking with my regular evangelical church, Life Baptist in South Pasadena. I love the music, and I've been in the choir for twenty years. It's my home." He fiddled with the sugar packets on the table. I had to wonder if the "Venus Fly Trap" woman was from his church.

I made an effort to keep my voice calm. "With all due respect, I have to ask you why in the world you would stay at a mainline evangelical church for twenty years if they don't welcome and affirm you as a gay man."

He didn't lift his eyes. "They welcome me, just so long as I stay relatively quiet about the gay thing. My pastor knows. A few friends know."

I squinted, trying to focus on his words. "Henry, if you fell in love with another man and wanted to marry, would your church respect your love and honor your commitment?" I leaned across the table to find his eyes again. He glanced up at me. I beheld the eyes of a bereft child.

"Of course not. But I'll always be single, so I don't have to worry about that. There are other gays at my church, but we just don't talk about it." He found another sugar packet, ripped it open, poured, stirred, and stared into the lukewarm brown liquid in his cup.

This brief conversation hurt my heart. Henry seemed to me to be a man who had never quite found his way. He had been married, had one child, then divorced. Had he ever really experienced true love?

In conversations with several other Evangelicals Concerned friends over the ensuing months, I discovered that most had left their evangelical churches. They were active in the United Church of Christ (UCC), or at All Saints Episcopal of Pasadena, a progressive, liberal congregation, or they had left church altogether. How sad, I thought, that evangelical churches had lost so many members from their ranks.

As for me, I had triumphantly flung myself out of that damning evangelical closet and into a life of authenticity and joy.

CHAPTER 33

HOME AT LAST

At home, I dumped out the pile of Pasadena Covenant Church letters onto our dining room table—at least fifty in all.

"What do you think about all my fan mail, honey?" I called out.

Catherine walked into the dining room and sifted through the messy pile. "I don't want to say *I told you so*, but I have to admit, those words do come to mind."

In a theatrical tone I began to read aloud some of the juiciest letters, punctuating phrases like "demon possession" and "cursed by Satan." Lifting a thick letter in a large envelope, I began to laugh uncontrollably. "It just hit me! Dr. Fanger's first name is Daemon! And Fanger means *catcher* in German. He's a demon catcher!"

Catherine shook her head. "You're so silly, Sharon." She moved toward the family room. "Come in here with me. Why don't you just take a break from church for a while?"

"Sounds good for now," I admitted, following her.

"It's Sunday today." She held out her arms. "Come sit with me here on the sofa and let's watch today's bicycle marathon in Los Angeles."

I sighed. "It's nice to be home with you, sweetie." We snuggled together and enjoyed our Sunday without church.

"I wish I could ride in that marathon," I said after we'd been watching for a while.

"I think you've just finished a marathon. Time to catch your breath now." Catherine had a way with words, like my mother did. She paused and then said, "Can I ask you something? One of those letters said that homosexuals sometimes have five hundred different sexual partners. How many did you have before me?"

I jabbed her arm. "You have to answer first, since you asked first."

Catherine scratched her head in thought. "Let's see. I had just one . . . or was it two? Maybe three...? And you?" Her pretty blue eyes met mine, sparkling with amusement.

"Let's see . . . one, oh yeah, three, no... fourteen, twenty-five... and... hmmm... I think you are number four hundred ninety-nine! I've gotta find one more to meet the quota!"

Laughing, she threw a pillow at me and tried to tickle my ribs. I grabbed her leg and tipped her over onto the floor. We ended up in one another's arms, right where we wanted to be. After all those years, I had finally found my way home.

EPILOGUE

My past is inscribed with many chapters of physical, emotional, and spiritual pain. When I finally embraced my true self, instead of lamenting the lost years of my history that could never be changed, I chose to redeem it and embrace it, forging new pathways of healing and redemption. The journey of truth and authenticity became my freedom.

I am deeply grateful for the people who accompanied me along the way. Montserrat taught me how to fall in love for the first time. Valentina taught me how to act on it. Catherine taught me how to build upon that love. Thomas taught me how to choose my own truth and not bow to someone else's. My parents loved me unconditionally, just like God does.

Catherine Wulfensmith and I adopted two children, Micah and Luke. (I would later become guardian for three more.) We lived as life partners and mothers for fourteen years. My fast-paced, crazy-cascading-water personality and her deep, slow-moving-stream personality caused us to experience more differences than we were able to handle, and we ultimately divorced—but we have amicably maintained our roles as moms to both of our kids.

My parents, Stanford and Bernell Smith, passed away in their mid-nineties.

I enjoy emails, regular calls, and visits with my siblings, Marci, Kobe, Thomas, and Greg.

Montserrat Gregori and I continue to stay in touch. She lives with her husband in Barcelona.

Michell Zurreva and I still see each other regularly and enjoy our friendship.

Jude and Finja are missionaries in South America, working and living with poor people. After twenty-seven years of not communicating, they surprised me with a visit in 2019, but the wounds still remained.

Molly McNeill still lives in Cleveland. We talk by phone quite often and reminisce about our high school days together.

Carl Goodwin now attends All Saints Episcopal Church. We greet each other occasionally.

There have been countless others who have walked with me for a spell or crossed my path, and I am grateful even for those who tried to get me to go in the wrong direction. I learned something valuable from each and every one.

Time itself carves additional chapters into my life story day by day. I'm not done living yet. I am confident to live as an out Christian lesbian, undaunted by those who are still unable to understand. I have no need to defend myself. I am free, and I find comfort knowing that God made me just the way I am.

May the footprints I leave behind guide the steps of those who follow, until those footprints are washed away by the waves of eternity.

APPENDIX A
THE CLOBBER PASSAGES

The Clobber Passages are the verses in the Bible that anti-gay Christians use to clobber gay folks on the head. They usually start by saying, "The Bible says . . ." or "The Bible clearly teaches that . . ." and then go on to quote the few biblical passages that purportedly condemn homosexual behavior—using them entirely out of context—to condemn LGBTQ+ persons.

Studying contextual theology on my own after coming out to myself facilitated one of the most significant paradigm shifts I've experienced in my life. I was grateful then for some of my classes at Fuller Seminary, which had taught me how to use the tools of cultural context to more accurately interpret the meaning of the Bible passages most often used to condemn gay people. The books that I found most helpful in reframing and empowering my thinking were the ones I found way down on the second-floor basement archives of the Fuller Seminary Library (I had to wonder if they had been hidden down there for some reason):

Christianity, Social Tolerance and Homosexuality, by John Boswell, 1980

Is the Homosexual My Neighbor? Another Christian View, by Scanzoni and Mollenkott, 1978

Coming Out to Parents: A Two-Way Survival Guide for Lesbians and Gay Men and Their Parents, by Mary V. Borhek, 1985

Stranger at the Gate: To Be Gay and Christian in America, by Mel White, 1994

(Mel White was the pastor of the Pasadena Covenant Church right before Pastor Graydon [actually John Bray], who hired me in

1984. White left the ministry after reconciling his faith and his own sexual orientation. He and his husband have grown old together for over forty years and counting.)

THE MOST COMMON CLOBBER PASSAGES

First, there is the well-known story of Sodom and Gomorrah, from Genesis 19:1-38. These two cities were located near the Dead Sea. Most likely, we have all heard the word *sodomy*, coined after the city of Sodom. The biblical passage tells a story of angelic men who arrive at Lot's house. Lot is Abraham's nephew. Rather than being welcomed as guests, as is the custom of the time, they are not.

Inhospitality was a terrible offense back then. In Matthew 10:14-15, Jesus refers to the sins of Sodom and Gomorrah as *inhospitality*. Jesus never uses the term *sodomy* to refer to homosexuality. In fact, Jesus never speaks of homosexuality in any way. Unfortunately, church dogma has egregiously misinterpreted the Genesis story so much that *sodomy* has become a synonym for *homosexuality*. Thus, the church teaches that God destroyed a whole nation because of homosexuality. This misinterpretation fuels the church's inability to include LGBTQ+ people into full fellowship in their places of worship.

This historical biblical story is used to condemn homosexual people, and is often employed to defend the position that "God hates fags" and will send them straight to hell. The Westboro Baptist Church of Topeka, Kansas, is known for using this despicable language—proudly. Sadly, LGBTQ+ people are the recipients of this vitriolic, ignorant interpretation and often pay for it with their very lives, despite the fact that the story of Sodom and Gomorrah has nothing at all to do with consensual, loving relationships between members of the same sex.

In addition, it is interesting to note that according this story, God's wrath is appeased when Sodom offers his own two virgin daughters to be raped by the men who visited his house. I find it impossible to conceive of a loving God whose anger would be appeased by such a heinous act. One might think that traditional Christians suffer from selective amnesia regarding *those* particular verses within the same story. I doubt that a true Christian father of any stripe would openly offer his virgin daughter to be raped by a stranger who's appeared at his door.

The second of the Clobber Passages, Leviticus 20:13 states, "If a man lies with a male as with a woman, both of them have committed an abomination; they shall be put to death, their blood is upon them" (RSV); "If a man has sexual relations with a man as one does with a woman, both of them have done what is detestable. They are to be put to death; their blood will be on their own heads" (NIV). This verse is part of what is called the Holiness Code, which was written for the Jewish people approximately five hundred years before Christ. These were laws regarding procreation, designed to help them multiply so as not to die out as a race. Thus, if after a sexual encounter the "seed"—the sperm of the man—was either wasted on the ground or deposited into the "wrong receptacle," the Holiness Code called for that man to be put to death. A man's sperm was to be planted, like a flower seed, into a woman. Women, meanwhile, were considered useful in that their vaginas led to the uterus, like a flowerpot, where the seed could be planted and grow into a baby.

I wonder if Christian men who claim to believe in a literal interpretation of the Bible fear for their very lives each and every day when their little seeds get wasted.

The Holiness Code contains hundreds of other laws, most of which are not followed today. Laws concerning health included prohibitions of eating pork and shellfish, where to defecate, how to wash hands, and how a man's female "property" was considered filthy during menstruation. Women were relegated to a tent away from the general populace so as not to contaminate anyone with their unclean issue during their menstrual cycle. Husbands were not allowed to have sexual relations with the bleeding wife. Quite possibly, they had a few other wives to choose from to satisfy their desires—a tidy way to compensate for their "sacrifice."

The third Clobber Passage, I Corinthians 6:9, states, "wrongdoers will not inherit the kingdom of God . . . neither the sexually immoral . . . nor men who have sex with men will inherit the kingdom of God" (NIV). Another translation adds "nor sexual perverts" to the list (RSV). Yet another includes "nor effeminate"

(KJV). Finally, another explicitly says, "or practice homosexuality" (NLT).

It appears that the Bible translators have wrestled over which English vocabulary to use to translate this particular passage, written by the Apostle Paul to the church at Corinth during the first century AD. The Ancient Greek words that Paul used to write his epistle, *paiderastía/pedophilia,* were clear to the recipients of his communication. In its cultural context, it seems that Paul was admonishing the church regarding conduct between a man and his boy slave. (Roman soldiers could purchase boy slaves for their pleasure, similar to sex trafficking today).

Today, sex trafficking is a crime under federal and international law. It is a modern-day form of slavery. Any rational person, Christian or not, knows (or should know) that any form of slavery is wrong. I would assert that many translators of the Bible have grossly misinterpreted what Paul's intended message was. I believe that traditional, conservative and evangelical Christians who use this Scripture passage today to condemn consensual sexual behavior by LGBTQ+ persons are not only incorrect but also devalue our lives and personhood in using it out of context.

The fourth Clobber Passage—and the most commonly cited New Testament Bible excerpt used to condemn same-sex relationship—is Romans 1:26-27: "God gave them over to shameful lusts. Even their women exchanged natural sexual relations for unnatural ones. In the same way the men also abandoned natural relations with women and were inflamed with lust for one another. Men committed shameful acts with other men, and received in themselves the due penalty for their error" (NIV).

During the 1990s especially, the words "receiving in their own persons the due penalty for their error" were misinterpreted to mean that God was punishing gay men by giving them HIV and AIDS. "It serves them right!" many religious people proclaimed. This horrid belief directly contributed to thousands of deaths, due to laws enacted to withhold funding from, prohibit care for, and instill fear in those who were suffering from a dreadful disease.

This passage from Romans seems to state quite clearly that lesbian and gay relations are sinful. Or does it? We need to take a look at it within its cultural context.

Paul the Apostle wrote a letter to the church at Rome because the people at that time and place were practicing human trafficking, cult prostitution, and sexual exhibitionism. Paul was actually addressing the issue of slavery, which was legal under Roman law at that time. In ancient Rome, the law punished the rape of a slave only if it "damaged the goods" and the client (of either sex) wasn't useful anymore. Paul was trying to teach the Roman Christians to worship God and not engage in behavior, such as prostitution, that used human beings as objects. This kind of first-century Roman behavior really does not have much in common with today's LGBTQ+ community members, who simply want the freedom to express their desires and safely love the individuals of their choosing—to live in peace.

The fifth and final Clobber Passage I'll discuss here comes from Paul's letter to Timothy, a leader in the first-century church in the city of Ephesus, also under Roman rule. Paul taught that the law of God was to instruct and correct disobedient sinners, "the murderers . . . immoral persons, sodomites, kidnapers, liars, perjurers . . ." (I Timothy 1:9, 10, RSV). Verse 10 alone speaks of "the sexually immoral, for those practicing homosexuality, for slave traders" (NIV).

Taking into account what I have already explained above, it seems evident that the word sodomite has been misunderstood and mistranslated. To make matters worse, the word *sodomite* has been replaced by the word *homosexual* in many other more modern translations. Notwithstanding, other translations use the words *no self-control*, or *perverted*, or *trafficking of the bodies of others*. At any rate, it is a travesty that the words from Sacred Scripture are used by traditional, conservative, or evangelical Christians to re-vile, condemn, legislate against, and even justify the murder of LGBTQ+ persons in today's societies worldwide. In my opinion, this is the real perversion.

Finally, it might be interesting to note that the English word *homosexual* didn't even exist until about a hundred years ago. It is a compound word. *Homo*, meaning same, comes from Greek. *Sexual*, from Latin, means, well, sexual. The RSV (Revised Standard Version) Bible, which I've quoted from extensively above, inserted the word *homosexual* into its texts in 1946 for the first time, compiling two Greek words, *arsenokoites* and *malakos*. *Arsen* means male. *Koite* means bed. *Male + bed* was a euphemism meaning a place to have sexual relations. *Malakos* means squishy (i.e., weak), or effeminate. In ancient Roman culture, much like today, men who were perceived as effeminate were ridiculed, hated, and frequently murdered.

Many Biblical scholars who strive to interpret these New Testament passages in their proper context have maintained that, for all intents and purposes, the word *homosexual* is an inaccurate rendering of those two Greek words.

In the narrative of my memoir I mentioned a group called Desert Stream. Desert Stream/Living Waters Ministries was founded in 1980 by Andrew Comiskey, a graduate of Fuller Theological Seminary and later a staff member with the Vineyard Church in West Los Angeles. At first, Desert Stream operated under the ex-gay organization, Exodus International, established in 1976, which became one of the largest organizations claiming to "cure" homosexuals. By 2013 Exodus shut down, its leaders confessing to being involved in their own hidden gay relationships, and finally apologizing to the LGBTQ+ communities that they had egregiously harmed. Notwithstanding, Desert Stream continues to this day as an ex-gay ministry, claiming that homosexuality can be overcome. Comiskey considers himself an American political activist and ex-gay leader, "helping" LGBTQ+ people be healed from their brokenness.

It deeply saddens me that I, as well as countless other LGBTQ+ people, have been, and continue to be, made the victims of such abhorrent interpretations of the Holy Bible, a book meant to share stories of God's love and of Jesus, who showed us a better way to live. May God have mercy upon us all.

KJV: King James Version of 1611

RSV: Revised Standard Version of 1952

NIV: New International Version of 1973

NLT: New Living Translation of 1996

In traditional evangelical churches, these translations are still commonly used.

APPENDIX B
MY KNEES

Eosinophilia-Myalgia syndrome is an incurable neurological condition linked to a toxin found in specific batches of an L-tryptophan health aide (used as an alternative to sleeping pills) manufactured by a Japanese company in 1989. Thousands of people were affected by this epidemic.

Unaware that the FDA had pulled that product from shelves, I continued taking my supply of pills from Trader Joe's for several months after they had been recalled, because my back pain was interrupting my sleep. Even after the initial swelling of my knees, I kept taking the pills, unaware that I was poisoning myself. All of my doctors misdiagnosed me for several years.

The toxin causing EMS manifests itself suddenly, with acute, irreversible muscle atrophy, fatigue, pain, and cognitive loss. Fortunately for me, it only affected my knees and right hand and elbow. In a number of victims, the muscle atrophy affected their diaphragm, lungs, or heart. Others were affected in the muscles of the larynx or hands. Initially, thirty people died. Speakers, vocalists, musicians, athletes, and more lost their professions, as well as their dreams, to this damaging toxin.

Even though I suffered greatly (and missed out on the Trader Joe's class-action lawsuit that ensued), I consider myself one of the lucky ones. I survived, and the symptoms eventually faded, albeit not entirely. Perhaps I will use my wheelchair after my hundredth birthday.

APPENDIX C
RESOURCES

All Saints Church Pasadena: www.allsaints-pas.org

At All Saints Church Pasadena, their mission is to make God's love tangible through spirituality, community, and peace and justice. Jesus's central message of compassion and respect for all people undergirds all that they undertake. All Saints is an LGBTQ+ welcoming and affirming congregation.

Metropolitan Community Churches: www.mccchurch.org

Metropolitan Community Churches are part of the Body of Christ, people on a journey who affirm all types of gender and sexuality, embracing diversity and building community through God's radically inclusive love for everyone. The Rev. Nancy Wilson is a moderator of the MCC and the author of *Outing the Bible: Queer Folks, God, Jesus, and the Christian Scriptures.*

Mel White: www.soulforce.org

Rev. White began Soulforce twenty years ago. It is an LGBTQI organization that works to sabotage Christian Supremacy and end the political and religious oppression of all marginalized people through research and informed strategy, political and theological education, and spiritual and community healing.

Colby Martin: www.colbymartinonline.com

Colby Martin is the author of *UNclobber: Rethinking Our Misuse of the Bible on Homosexuality.* He is a co-pastor of Sojourn Grace Collective, a progressive church in San Diego, and an author, teacher, blogger, and straight guy who believes that God's love can embrace us all. His new book, *The Shift: Surviving and Thriving after* Moving from Conservative to Progressive Christianity came out in April 2020.

Garrard Conley: www.garrardconley.com/boy-erased

Garrard Conley, author of *Boy Erased,* also a major motion picture. After being outed, Conley was forced to attend an evangelical conversion therapy program (Love in Action) to "cure" him. Surviving a tortuous journey, he was able to break away and find the strength to embrace his true self as a gay man.

Rachel Held Evans: www.rachelheldevans.com

Rachel Held Evans, a straight Christian from Tennessee, was a best-selling author, theologian, speaker, and advocate for the LGBTQ+ community and beyond. Her books, especially *Faith Unraveled,* offer a challenging, raw, and refreshing interpretation of Scripture. She passed away in 2019.

Connie Tuttle: www.connietuttle.com

Connie Tuttle is a lesbian, feminist, single mom and mystic. Also she's a pastor, teacher, and unconventional theologian, and the author of *A Gracious Heresy: The Queer Calling of an Unlikely Prophet.*

Amber Cantorna: www.ambercantorna.com

Amber Cantorna is a national speaker and educator, and the author of *Refocusing My Family: Coming Out, Being Cast Out, and Discovering the True Love of God.* The daughter of an executive leader for the ultra-conservative Focus on the Family, her view of Scripture focuses on finding the liberating love of God.

Jeff Chu: www.byjeffchu.com

Jeff Chu, award-winning journalist and author of *Does Jesus Really Love Me?* interviewed scores of Christian leaders, from the "God Hates Fags" church to the Episcopal church, and presents a well-researched, political, emotional, and spiritual message of a God who is big enough to love us all.

Jo Ivester: www.joivester.com

Jo Ivester is an author and speaker, focusing on LGBTQ & civil rights advocacy. Her most recent book, *Once a Girl, Always a Boy* is her son's journey from childhood through coming out as transgender and eventually emerging as an advocate for the transgender community.

Austen Hartke: www.austenhartke.com

Austen Hartke is an Old Testament/Hebrew Bible scholar and the author of *Transforming: The Bible and the Lives of Transgender Christians*. As a transgender man of faith, he teaches, preaches, and is a respected leader dedicated to spiritual care and faith formation for LGBTQ+ Christians.

Kathy Baldock: www.canyonwalkerconnections.com

Kathy Baldock is a straight conservative evangelical, committed to repairing the damage/breach between the church and the LGBTQ+ community through education, encouragement, and engagement. Kathy is a speaker and the author of *Walking the Bridgeless Canyon*.

Judith Favor: www.judithfavor.com

Judith Favor, grounded in Quaker tradition and contemplative practice, is a retired minister, teacher, and speaker. She is a spiritual guide at Pilgrim Place, a retirement community in Claremont, California, where she resides with her husband. In her novel, *The Beacons of Larkin Street*, her strong and humorous voice slices through church structure to expose the conflicts between clergy and laity. See her website for her many other spiritual books.

NAMI: www.nami.org

NAMI, National Alliance on Mental Illness, the nation's largest grassroots mental health organization, is dedicated to building better lives for families and friends of the millions of Americans affected by mental illness.

Friends of Project 10: www.friendsofproject10.org

Friends of Project 10, founded in 1984, was dedicated to providing educational support services to LGBTQ+ youth who attended public school campuses. Its founder, Dr. Virginia Uribe, fought against pervasive and legal discrimination to protect all students' rights to respect and dignity, whether gay, lesbian, or straight. Project 10 officially closed its doors in 2019, after Dr. Uribe's passing, and now encourages high schoolers to seek help through many of its sister organizations.

GLSEN: www.glsen.org

GLSEN, Gay Lesbian Straight Educator Network, is a United States-based education organization working to end discrimination, harassment, and bullying based on sexual orientation, gender identity, and gender expression in K–12 schools.

PFLAG: www.pflag.org

PFLAG, Parents and Friends of Lesbians and Gays, was founded in 1973 after the simple act of a mother publicly supporting her gay son. PFLAG is the nation's largest family and ally organization. Uniting LGBTQ+ people with families, friends, and allies, PFLAG is committed to advancing equality through its mission of support, education, and advocacy.

Hillcrest Retirement Community: www.livingathillcrest.org

Hillcrest Retirement Community, established in 1947 in La Verne, California, offers senior residents a vibrant living environment in addition to maintaining control over their future health care needs and services.

ABOUT THE AUTHOR

Sharon Wulfensmith has been an active member of All Saints Episcopal Church, Pasadena, since 1997. She is in one of the adult choirs, and enjoys singing the great masters of classical music, as well as jazz. Her church affirms all LGBTQ+ people and constantly challenges all to participate in the arc that bends toward justice.

She retired in 2015 after twenty-five years of teaching ESL and English at Pasadena City College, and Pasadena High School. She regularly substitute teaches at two high schools near her home. She talks with teenagers about her memoir and the various challenges of life.

Sharon earned her Bachelor of Music Education degree from Kent State University, Kent, Ohio, in 1972, and a Master's in Cross-Cultural Studies at Fuller Seminary in 1984. Presently she is a volunteer teacher with the National Alliance on Mental Illness, supporting and educating families who have a loved one living with mental illness. She lives in a retirement community in La Verne, California, and enjoys walking, bicycling, camping, and being a mommy to her red toy poodle.

Finding Her is Sharon's debut memoir.